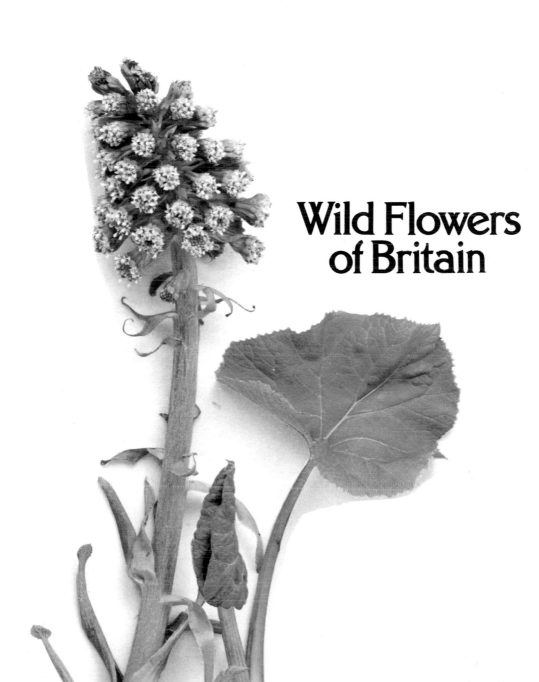

# Wild Flowers
## of Britain

In memory of
Philip Swann Phillips

# ROGER PHILLIPS

assisted by Sheila Grant  edited by Tom Wellsted

# Wild Flowers of Britain

**A Pan Original**

ACKNOWLEDGEMENTS I am indebted to many people for their help and cooperation in making this book possible and I would particularly like to thank the following:

Martyn Rix, for patiently reading the text and checking identification, David Bale, Eileen Cox, Linda & Adrian Christie, Lesley Clegg, Nicola Foy, Kathleen Gordon, John Grace, Elsie Grant, Susannah Hall, Ted Leyshon, Isobel La Croix, John Mason, Vivien Meek, Roger Mellors, Elsie Phillips, Philip Rheinberg, Duncan Thomas, Mark Smith, Rosalind Smith, Pearl Small, Beverley Stokes, Lucy Su, John White, Hector Willis

I am also grateful to the following organisations:
The Royal Botanic Gardens, Kew
Royal Horticultural Society at Wisley
Forestry Commission at Westonbirt Arboretum
Nature Conservancy Council at Edinburgh and Huntingdon
British Museum (Natural History)
University of Cambridge Botanic Garden
University of Bristol Botanic Garden

ADDITIONAL PHOTOGRAPHS I would like to thank the following for allowing me to use their photographs:
M. A. Atherden, 26(f), 71(f); Joan M. Cooper, 70(e); W. Elfyn Hughes, 111(a); J. A. Etough, 50(d), 51(e), 71(e), 89(a), 89(f), 110(a), 111(f), 156(d), 156(e), 157(b), 157(d), 157(e); P. H. Hazle, 70(c), 70(d), 71(d), 110(b), 137(a), 156(f); A. Huxley, 26(e), 50(e), 51(b), 51(c), 88(e), 88(f), 89(c), 156(a); Arthur Lang, 70(f), 110(f); Peter Lawson, 111(e); J. L. Mason, 27(e), 50(b), 71(b), 89(d), 89(e), 136(a), 136(f), 157(a); G. R. Miller, 88(b); D. A. Robertson, 88(a), 110(d); Martyn Rix, 136(e); Joan Small, 26(a), 26(d), 27(a), 27(b), 27(c), 27(d), 27(f), 50(a), 50(c), 50(f), 51(a), 51(f), 70(b), 71(a), 88(c), 89(b), 110(c), 110(e), 111(c), 111(d), 136(b), 136(c), 136(d), 137(b), 137(c), 137(e), 156(b), 157(f); Mark Smith, 26(b), 26(c), 51(d), 111(b), 137(d); Mary Stevens, 70(a), 71(c), 137(f), 156(c), 157(c); Duncan Thomas, 88(d)

First published 1977 by Pan Books Ltd,
Cavaye Place, London SW10 9PG
8th printing 1980
Text © Roger Phillips 1977
Illustrations © Roger Phillips 1977
ISBN 0 330 25183X
Printed and bound in Great Britain by
Cripplegate Printing Co Ltd, Edenbridge, Kent

# Contents

# Introduction

Seven years ago when my son Sam was five I felt that growing up in London he was missing the dirt and damp of the countryside. So, we started a Sunday routine of going to the country, rain or shine, summer or winter, and cooking a picnic lunch over an open fire. At first this was a toughening up process, a sort of personal 'outward bound' course, but now it has become a popular ritual—last week nine children joined us.

Going out as I have done for seven years, I have watched the land change and the plants grow and die through the seasons. I began to wonder and question the identity of plants that I found in the marshy wilderness around the canal near Denham and I consulted flower books that came to hand. But my lack of understanding of the formal methods of cataloguing plants, family by family, left me in a position of not knowing where to begin my search. Having no idea of either the name or family group of a plant, I had

to resort to searching the pages of illustrations one by one; and even so I frequently failed to make a positive identification.

I am a photographer and all my background and training has been in the visual rather than the academic. I have tried to make a book in which the visual is paramount. I have tried to make the book I needed seven years ago.

The prime object of this book is to create a system of visual identification that may be tackled by anyone, however slight or unacademic their knowledge. To this end, I have approached wild flowers in four ways.

Firstly, I have put the plants in chronological flowering order, rather than in family order, since placing flowers by their botanical family is only ideal if the reader can decide to which family any specimen he finds belongs. I have attempted to photograph each flower during its correct flowering time. When the flowering time is short – say, one or two months – this is straightforward but when, as quite often happens, a plant flowers for as long as six months, I have placed it near the beginning of the relevant period. Where possible, plants of the same habitat and flowering time have been grouped together.

Secondly, I have used photographs. When searching books myself to identify plants, I was continually amazed at the lack of photography used in plant books. Britain has a fine tradition of botanical drawing, but I feel that for the newcomer to the plant world, a photograph gives a better instant 'feel' of a specimen. People have criticized this approach, saying that drawings can show an average specimen and bring out the salient identifying characteristics. True, but I maintain that the strength of this argument is its weakness. My specimens are not idealized versions but normal ones in the typical condition that you might find them.

Thirdly, I have used a large format for the book. The disadvantage of this is that the book cannot be carried in the pocket (a small consideration in the day of the motor car) but this drawback is far outweighed by the advantage of being able to allocate a much greater space to the illustration of each specimen.

Fourthly, to facilitate identification for the reader, I have described the habitat and distribution of each plant.

# How to use the book

The flowers are arranged in calendar order, beginning on page 12 with the first plants to flower, and by turning the pages through the book you pass through the year. Plants which look similar and could be confused are cross-referenced so that they are easy to find. In addition, I have included more than one photograph of many plants so that they can be seen at various stages in their chronological development. Thus, plants which bear fruit will be illustrated twice. Another advantage of this chronological approach is that it enables the reader to consult the book and quickly deduce which flowers may be found at any particular time of year. Below is a breakdown of how each part of the text was arrived at:

### English names
In the main, the English names I have used follow Clapham, Tutin and Warburg's *Flora of the British Isles*, but I have also consulted *An Englishman's Flora* by Geoffrey Grigson, and *The Wild Flowers of Britain and North Europe* by Richard and Alistair Fitter and Marjorie Blamey. The English name is always set in bold face.

### Botanical names
I have followed the *Flora Europaea* (published up to Compositae, Volume IV, at the time of writing) for botanical names. For those families not dealt with in *Flora Europaea*, I have followed *Flora of the British Isles* by Clapham, Tutin and Warburg.

The botanical name is written in italics. When a name has been changed, the older name, or synonym, is also included.

## The authority

The botanical name is followed by an initial, a group of initials or an abbreviated name, which refers to the botanist responsible for giving it that name. As you can imagine, over the years botanists in different countries 'discovered' flowers and named them. Sometimes much later, it was realized that the plant had already been 'discovered' in another country and given another name. The proper name is considered to be that first published for a particular plant.

## Family name

I have included the family name so that the reader can consult the family index at the back of the book to see which other genera and species are normally grouped with it.

## Status

This tells you whether the plant is an annual, biennial, perennial, a shrub or a tree. It also tells you whether it is considered to be a native British plant, a plant introduced at sometime to this country which has now naturalised, or a garden or agricultural plant which has escaped from cultivation and is now establishing itself in the wild.

## Incidence

This tells you whether the plant is very common, common, locally common, rare or very rare, and is followed by a description, as accurate as I can make it in the space alloted, of the habitat and distribution of the plant. For this information I have carefully analysed the *Atlas of British Flora* by Perring and Walters.

## Height

I have given what I consider to be the normal maximum height for each plant. However, under exceptionally good conditions, it could exceed this, though it is much more likely that your specimen will fall below the height I have quoted, due to unsuitable soil conditions or some incompatibility in the environment.

## Background

Here in the text, I have tried to give some historical, medical, magical or other special details about the plant. I have also indicated whether it is edible or poisonous.

## Flowering period

The months when you can normally expect to see the flowers are indicated. Plants in the Channel Islands or the extreme south of England can be expected to flower a week or so earlier. Those in the far north may flower as much as three weeks later.

## Cross reference

Finally, I have included at the end of each piece of text a cross reference where this is necessary. This enables the reader to turn straight to other plants of similar appearance for comparison or indicates that there is a second specimen, showing fruit or some other aspect of the plant. Members of the same genus are also indicated in many instances and where the group is large, the English generic name is used (e.g. see other Spurges), so the English index should be consulted.

## Specimens

Although, for the sake of furthering knowledge, I have picked specimens for most of the photographs, I would like to emphasize that I do not want to encourage you to 'take' specimens. If you pick the flower of a plant, the seeds will never form and distribute themselves as they otherwise would. Of course, certain plants can be picked quite happily if one uses commonsense. Garden weeds such as buttercups and speedwells can look terrific in small flower arrangements and no one will worry if you pick sorrel or dandelions to add to a salad.

The Conservation of Wild Creatures and Wild Plants Act 1975 protects the following plants:

| | |
|---|---|
| Alpine Gentian | Military Orchid |
| Alpine Sowthistle | Monkey Orchid |
| Alpine Woodsia | Oblong Woodsia |
| Blue Heath | Red Helleborine |
| Cheddar Pink | Snowdon Lily |
| Diapensia | Spiked Speedwell |
| Drooping Saxifrage | Spring Gentian |
| Ghost Orchid | Teesdale Sandwort |
| Killarney Fern | Tufted Saxifrage |
| Lady's Slipper | Wild Gladiolus |
| Mezereon | |

Except under license or under special circumstances, no one may uproot, pick or destroy any of the plants on this list. It is also now an offence for any unauthorized person to uproot any wild plant without reasonable excuse. An authorized person is the owner or occupier of the land, or someone who has his permission.

## The photographs

Scale: included in the majority of photographs is a hand-drawn circle 1 centimetre in diameter, from which to work out the relative height of specimens.

The large photographs have been taken on Whole Plate Daylight Ektachrome using a De Vere camera and a 210 mm lens. The intermediate size of photograph on the left hand pages was taken with the same camera using a 5″ × 4″ back and Daylight Ektachrome. The light source was flash. For those shot in my studio, I used Strobe Lighting and a Fish Fryer head; for those shot on location in temporary studios, I used two Metz 402 packs and a large reflector to soften the light. The single specimen photographs were taken in different ways; either on 5″ × 4″ as above and/or on a Hasselblad using Ektachrome Professional film. Those taken by other photographers were shot on $2\frac{1}{4}″ \times 2\frac{1}{4}″$ or 35 mm, using either flash or daylight.

## The indexes

I have given a complete Botanical and English index, listing all the names given in the book, including secondary names where appropriate. This book is not ordered by family, as are the majority of plant books, so I have included a family index, listing alphabetically the families illustrated in the book.

# Glossary

**Achene** A small, dry, single-seeded fruit, which does not split to release the seed.

**Aggregate** A group of closely related SPECIES or SUBSPECIES.

**Alternate** Referring to the leaves, means that they are arranged successively up to the stem, neither opposite to one another nor in WHORLS.

**Annual** A plant which completes its life cycle within one year.

**Anther** The part of the flower, on the STAMEN, which produces POLLEN.

**Berry** Fleshy fruit, usually containing many seeds.

**Biennial** A plant which completes its life cycle within two years, usually flowering in the second year.

**Bog** A wet acid-PEAT HABITAT.

**Bract** A small, modified leaf at the base of the flower stalk or sometimes beneath the flowerhead. Also refers to the parts of cones.

**Bulb** An underground organ made up of fleshy leaves surrounding the next year's flowerbud.

**Bulbils** Small, bulb like organs found at the base of leaves, or in place of flowers. Also sometimes found on roots.

**Calcareous** Chalky or limy.

**Calyx** The SEPALS as a whole.

**Capsule** A dry fruit which consists of more than one CARPEL and which splits to release the seeds.

**Carpel** A modified leaf, one or several of which make up the female parts of a plant.

**Catkin** A hanging spike of small, usually rather insignificant flowers.

**Compound** Made up of several similar parts. Often referred to leaves which are divided into several LEAFLETS.

**Corm** An underground storage organ formed by a swollen stem, lasting only one year and the next year's arising from the old one.

**Corolla** The PETALS as a whole.

**Coniferous** Cone-bearing.

**Cupule** A cup-shaped holder such as that holding an acorn.

**Deciduous** Sheds all its leaves annually.

**Dominant** The chief species in a plant community, e.g. pines in a pinewood.

**Dune** Low hill of wind-blown sand near the sea.

**Dune slack** Damp hollows between DUNES.

**Elliptical** Oval, slightly pointed at each end.

**Epicalyx** An additional ring of SEPAL-like organs outisde the true CALYX.

**Evergreen** A tree which retains its leaves throughout the year.

**Family** A group of plants more comprehensive than a GENUS.

**Fen** A wet, alkaline, or only slightly acid, PEAT HABITAT.

**Floret** Small flowers which form the parts of a compound head.

**Fruit** Ripe seeds and the structures surrounding them.

**Genus** A group of plants of closer affinity than those within a family. (Plural is genera.)

**Globular** Spherical.

**Habitat** The locality, or physical environment of a plant.

**Heath** A plant community, usually found on acid PEAT, dominated by low shrubs of the family Ericaceae.

**Herb** A non-woody flowering plant.

**Hybrid** A plant arising from the fertilization of one SPECIES by another.

**Insectivorous** Plants which obtain nutrients by digesting insects.

**Introduced** A plant which has been taken by man to an area where it did not previously grow.

**Involucre** A ring of BRACTS forming a CALYX-like structure around or below a condensed flowerhead.

**Keeled** A sharp edge like the keel of a boat. Usually refers to lower PETAL or petals which are keel-shaped.

**Lanceolate** Spear-shaped: two or three times as long as broad and tapering at the ends.

**Leaflets** The leaf-like parts of a COMPOUND leaf.

**Limestone** Calcium carbonate: soils formed on limestone are alkaline and rich in lime.

**Linear-lanceolate** As LANCEOLATE but with more or less parallel sides.

**Lobed** Referring to deeply toothed leaves, not divided into leaflets.

**Marsh** Plant community on wet, non-PEATY soils.

**Moraine** Debris left behind by glaciers.

**Native** Not introduced by man.

**Nectary** A glandular organ which secretes nectar, a sugary substance which attracts insects.

**Node** A point on the stem where one or more leaves arise.

**Nut** A hard, dry fruit.

**Nutlet** One-seed portion of a fruit that divides as it matures. The stone of a fleshy one.

**Opposite** Refers to leaves arising at the same level on the stem.

**Osier** Any willow whose branches are used in basket-making.

**Ovary** The basal parts of the CARPELS containing the OVULES which eventually become the seeds.

**Ovoid** Egg-shaped in outline.

**Ovule** The female part which on fertilization becomes the seed.

**Palmate** Having lobes or leaflets arising from the centre in a hand shape.

**Pappus** Downy hairs which occur on some fruits, notably those of Dandelions and Thistles, and which aid dispersal by wind.

**Parasite** A plant which obtains its nutrients from other plants.

**Peat** Soil composed of undecayed plant material, usually acid.

**Peduncle** The stalk of a flower or flowerhead.

**Perennial** A plant which lives for more than two years.

**Perianth** The CALYX and COROLLA together, especially when not clearly distinguishable.

**Petal** A COROLLA leaf, usually conspicuous and brightly coloured.

**Pinnate** Referring to a compound leaf having two rows of LEAFLETS on either side of a central axis.

**Pistil** The female part of a flower, composed of an OVARY, STIGMA and STYLE.

**Pod** The fruit, or its shell, of peas, beans and other members of the family Leguminosae. Also sometimes the fruit of some members of the family Cruciferae.

**Pollard** A tree, having the whole crown cut off, and left to send out new branches from the top of the stem.

**Pollen** The male reproductive cells or microspores produced by and discharged from the ANTHER of a seed plant.

**Procumbent** Lying down loosely along the ground.

**Prostrate** Lying closely along the ground.

**Rhizome** An underground organ formed from a swollen stem and which lasts for more than one year.

**Root-tuber** See TUBER.

**Runner** A form of creeping stem which roots at the end, forming a new plant which eventually becomes detached from the parent plant.

**Salt-marsh** The plant communities growing on inter-tidal mud on sheltered coasts and estuaries.

**Saprophyte** A plant which obtains nutrients from dead organic material.

**Scrub** A plant community dominated by SHRUBS.

**Sepal** A part of the CALYX, usually green and leaf-like, forming the outer ring of the PERIANTH.

**Sessile** Unstalked.

**Shrub** A woody plant, much branched and smaller than TREES. (Often taken as less than 13.5m (15ft).)

**Simple** Not COMPOUND.

**Species** A group of individual plants having common characteristics, which normally do not fertilize other species. Species are grouped within GENERA.

**Spur** A hollow projection from the base of a PERIANTH segment.

**Stamen** The male part of the flower, consisting of filament and ANTHER.

**Stigma** The surface of the female parts which is receptive to POLLEN grains; at the top of the STYLE.

**Stipule** A leaf-like appendage at the base of a leaf.

**Style** The section of the female parts which connects the OVARY with the STIGMA.

**Subshrub** A low, often creeping SHRUB.

**Subspecies** A division of SPECIES which are morphologically distinct from each other but which interbreed.

**Tendril** A coiling, threadlike organ forming part of a leaf or stem and used for climbing.

**Tree** A large plant with a single woody trunk, often taken as taller than 13.5m (15ft).

**Tuber** A swollen part of stem or root which lasts only one year, the next year's tuber not arising from those of previous years.

**Undershrub** See SUBSHRUB.

**Whorl** A ring of leaves or flowers, at one level, around a stem.

## Abbreviations used in the text
An asterisk * indicates those species which have text mentions but no photograph.

| | |
|---|---|
| Agg. Aggregate | Ssp. Subspecies |
| Sp. Species (singular) | Syn. Synonym |
| Spp. Species (plural) | × indicates a hybrid |

**(a) Winter Aconite** *Eranthis hyemalis* (L.) Salisb., family Ranunculaceae. An introduced perennial. Rare, naturalised from gardens and found in woods, mainly in southern England. Poisonous. Flowers Jan. to March. Photographed Feb. 10.

**(b) Snowdrop** *Galanthus nivalis* L., family Amaryllidaceae. A bulbous perennial probably native. A widely planted garden flower; uncommon, found naturalised in damp woods and by streams over most of England and Scotland. Height to 20cm. The flower of 'Hope'. Flowers Jan. to March. See 12(c), 20(n). Photographed Feb. 10.

**(e) Grey Poplar** *Populus canescens* (Ait.) Sm., family Salicaceae. Tree, probably native and frequently planted. Quite common in southern England; rare in Ireland and the north. Height to 30m. The bark is grey. Flowers Feb. to March. See others this page and Leaves. 160(l).

**(f) Aspen** *Populus tremula* L., family Salicaceae. Tree, native in woods and on poor soil. Common throughout the British Isles. Height to 20m. Christ's cross was made from its wood. Flowers March to April. See others this page and Leaves. 160(g).

**(g) Hybrid Black Poplar** *Populus* × *euramericana* (Dode) Guinier, family Salicaceae. This specimen represents the many hybrids which came from crosses between the true Black Poplar *P. nigra* and other species. They are commonly planted in towns, parks and on roadsides. See Leaves 160(h) and compare with 160(i).

**(h) White Poplar** *Populus alba* L., family Salicaceae. Tree, introduced. The backs of the leaves are covered with white hairs. Height to 25m. Flowers March. See others this page and Leaves 160(f).

**(i) Lombardy Poplar** *Populus nigra* var. *italica* Duroi, family Salicaceae. A much planted introduction. Flowers March. See Leaves 160(e).

**(j) Balsam Poplar** *Populus gileadensis* Rouleau, family Salicaceae. Tree, to 25m.; introduced. Very distinctive smell of balsam from the sticky leaves and buds. Flowers Feb. to March. See others above and Leaves 160(d).

**(k) Wych Elm** *Ulmus glabra* Huds., family Ulmaceae. A common native tree. Found all over the British Isles though much more common in the north than English Elm 12(l) and with larger leaves. Flowers Feb. to March. See below and 24(h), 158(h).

**(l) English Elm** *Ulmus procera* Salisb., family Ulmaceae. A common tree in England and Ireland; rare in Scotland. Height to 30m. Native in hedges and very common. Badly hit by Dutch Elm disease. Flowers Feb. to March. See above 24(i), 158(g).

**(m) Hazel** or **Cob-nut** *Corylus avellana* L., family Corylaceae. A common native shrub found all over the British Isles. Height to 6m. A magical plant; divining rods are made from it. Hazel was grown in oak woods and coppiced, the wood used for hurdles and wattle and daub buildings. Flowers Jan. to March. See Leaves 164(e).

**(n) Alder** *Alnus glutinosa* (L.) Gaertn., family Betulaceae. A very common native tree found all over the British Isles. To a height of 20m. Grows in wet places. Flowers Feb. to March. See Leaves 158(c).

**(o) Pussy Willow, Goat Willow** or **Great Sallow** *Salix caprea* L., family Salicaceae. A very common shrub found all over the British Isles; less common in Ireland. Height to 10m. Flowers March to April. The rest of the willows have leaves only illustrated. See 166(e)–(m).

**(c) Spring Snowflake** *Leucojum vernum* L., family Amaryllidacaeae. Possibly native; a bulbous perennial. Very rare in the wild but often cultivated. Found in damp woods on the Cornish peninsula, East Anglia, Cumbria and St Andrews. Height to 25cm. Flowers Feb. to April. See 12(b), 20(n). Photographed March 3.

**(d) Dog's Mercury** *Mercurialis perennis* L., family Euphorbiaceae. Perennial, native. Very common in England and Scotland except the far north; rare in Ireland. Grows in woods and shady places to a height of 40cm. Male and female flowers are on separate plants (male shown). Poisonous. Flowers Feb. to April. See Annual Dog's Mercury 116(d). Photographed March 3.

photograph taken 27 March ○ represents 1 centimetre

photograph taken 24 March

(**e**) **Groundsel** *Senecio vulgaris* L., family Compositae. An abundant annual weed of gardens and wasteplaces found all over the British Isles. Height to 40cm. A decoction of 40grm. of this plant boiled in one litre of water for 3 minutes and then allowed to diffuse for 10 minutes, is highly reputed for regularising menstruation. Flowers all year round. Compare with ragworts and 100(l), 152(h).

(**f**) **Red Deadnettle** *Lamium purpureum* L., family Labiatae. This is a very common annual weed of gardens and wasteplaces and found throughout the British Isles. Height to 40cm. Flowers March to Oct. See 14(g), 18(g), 50(a).
**Cut-leaved Deadnettle** *L. hybridum* Vill., is less common than Red Deadnettle and more slender with deeply cut leaves.

(**g**) **White Deadnettle** *Lamium album* L., family Labiatae. A perennial weed of hedgebanks and roadsides. Very common in the south; rare in north Scotland and southern Ireland. Height to 50cm. The young shoots may be eaten as spinach and also used to cure catarrh. Flowers March to Dec. For comparison see 14(f), 18(g), 50(a).

(**h**) **Petty Spurge** *Euphorbia peplus* L., family Euphorbiaceae. An annual garden weed. Very common in England and Wales, less common in Ireland and rather rare in Scotland. Height to 30cm. Poisonous. Flowers March to Nov. Compare other spurges.

(**i**) **Daisy** *Bellis perennis* L., family Compositae. A very common perennial of grassland and lawns throughout the British Isles. Height to 6cm. The leaves may be eaten as salad. The name comes from 'day's eye' but actually it needs a bright day to open. Flowers March to Oct.

(**j**) **Coltsfoot** *Tussilago farfara* L., family Compositae. A native perennial of hard, bare places and shingle. Very common throughout the British Isles. Flowers to a height of 25cm. The leaves develop well after the flowers. The botanical name comes from tussis ago, to drive away a cough, as it was the apothecary's best herb for the lungs. Flowers March to April. See Leaves 134(j).

(**k**) **Creeping Speedwell** *Veronica filiformis* Sm., family Scrophulariaceae. A creeping perennial, introduced, but spreading fast. Found in gardens, lawns and grassy places with scattered distribution throughout the British Isles. Flowers March to July. See other speedwells.

(**l**) **Butterbur** *Petasites hybridus* (L.) Gaertn., Mey. & Scherb., family Compositae. A patch-forming perennial. The male flower which is shown here is the more common. Flowerheads to a height of 40cm. Grows in wet places. The leaves follow the flowers and grow to a great size by the summer, as much as 50cm. across. Tradition has it they were used for wrapping butter. Flowers March to May. See 26(a).

(**a**) **Chickweed** *Stellaria media* (L.) Vill., family Caryophyllaceae. A very common annual weed of roadsides, gardens and waste land throughout Great Britain. It may grow to 35cm. The leaves and shoots are pleasant to eat in a salad or lightly cooked. Flowers all year but mainly in the spring and autumn. See 22(m), 52(a), 78(a), 90(g).
**Bog Stitchwort** *S. alsine* Grimm. Native, found on stream sides. Has a square stem. Flowers May to June.
**Wood Stitchwort** *S. nemorum* L. Native, found in woods and stream sides in the north. It has hairs all over the stems. Flowers May to July.

(**b**) **Shepherd's Purse** *Capsella bursa-pastoris* (L.) Medic., family Cruciferae. A very common annual weed of gardens and waste places. Found throughout the British Isles. Height to 35cm. Named from the purse-shaped fruits. May be eaten but mainly known for its medicinal property

of stopping haemorrhage. Flowers all year. See 54(i).
**Shepherd's Cress** *Teesdalia nudicaulis* (L.) R.Br., family Cruciferae. A native annual of sand and gravel. Scattered throughout, rare in Ireland and Scotland. Height to 30cm. Similar to Shepherd's Purse but smaller and delicate looking. Flowers April to June.

(**c**) **Thale Cress** *Arabidopsis thaliana* (L.) Heynh., family Cruciferae. An annual weed of walls and banks. Fairly common throughout the British Isles. Height variable to 45cm. Flowers March to June.

(**d**) **Wavy Bittercress** *Cardamine flexuosa* With., family Cruciferae. A common annual weed of rocks, bare ground and gardens. May grow to 30cm. Found throughout the British Isles. Flowers March to Sept. Very similar to 26(c).

photograph taken 24 March ○ represents 1 centimetre

photograph taken 25 March

(**a**) **Sloe or Blackthorn** *Prunus spinosa* L., family Rosaceae. A common native shrub growing in hedges and scrub on all soils except acid peat; throughout the British Isles but uncommon in north Scotland. Height to 4m. Modern plum trees have been bred by crossing the Sloe with the Cherry-Plum 16(d). Flowers March to May. Fruits Sept. See Fruit 164(f), others 16(d), 24(k), 34(i).

(**b**) **Mezereon** *Daphne mezereum* L., family Thymelaeaceae. A native shrub found in woods on calcareous soils. Very rare and only found wild in a few locations in England and Wales, often in gardens. Height to 1m. The berries, not illustrated, are oval and bright red. Poisonous. Flowers Aug. to Sept. See 24(l).

(**c**) **Cornelian** Cherry *Cornus mas* L., family Cornaceae. A frequently planted introduction. Shrub or small tree to 8m. Our specimen is past the best of its flowering period. Flowers Feb. to March. Fruit, not shown, is scarlet. See 58(c).

(**d**) **Cherry-plum** or **Myrobalan** *Prunus cerasifera* Ehrh., family Rosaceae. Introduced, rare. Found only in southern England and East Lothian in hedges and woods. Shrub or small tree to 8m. in height. A native of Russia and Persia. The fruit, round and yellowish, is only produced in favourable years (not shown). Flowers March to April. See 16(a), 24(k), 34(i).

(**e**) **Lesser Celandine** *Ranunculus ficaria* L., family Ranunculaceae. A very common mat-forming native perennial found throughout the British Isles. Height to 20cm. The bulbous roots used in an infusion were traditionally effective in curing haemorrhoids. Flowers March to May. See Greater Celandine 42(f).

(**f**) **Lesser Periwinkle** *Vinca minor* L., family Apocynaceae. A possibly native, perennial trailing plant found locally in woods and hedgebanks throughout the British Isles; rare in Ireland and the north. Common in gardens. The stems, up to 60cm., root at intervals. Flowers may be white. Flowers March to May. See Greater Periwinkle 24(e).

(**g**) **Sweet Violet** *Viola odorata* L., family Violaceae. A native perennial common in the south, rare in the north and Ireland. Found on hedgebanks and wood edges especially on calcareous soils. This is the violet of violet scent. The name means modesty. Flowers are often white. Flowers Feb. to April. Two examples shown. See other violets 18(j), 20(i), 22(b), 26(e), 60(n), 66(g).
**Hairy Violet** *V. hirta* L. A native of fields and open woods. Has narrower leaves and no runners. Flowers rarely white. Flowers March to May.

(**h**) **Primrose** *Primula vulgaris* Huds., family Primulaceae. A native perennial common throughout the British Isles. Grows in woods, hedgebanks and grassy places. Height to 20cm. The name comes from *prima rosa*—first rose. Flowers March to May. See 20(n), 24(d), 32(b).

(**i**) **Narrow-leaved Lungwort** *Pulmonaria angustifolia* L., family Boraginaceae. Introduced perennial, commonly grown in gardens and sometimes escaping. Height to 40cm. Flowers March to May.
*P. longifolia* L., Native perennial, but very rare growing only in the New Forest area and the Isle of Wight. Height to 40cm. It has narrower, heavily spotted leaves and a more compact flowerhead. Flowers end of March to May.

(**j**) **Lungwort** *Pulmonaria officinalis* L., family Boraginaceae. An introduced perennial of woods and hedgebanks often grown in gardens. Rare, naturalised in England and Scotland and absent from Ireland. Height to 30cm. Its name comes from it being used in the treatment of lung diseases (*Pulmonaria*). Flowers March to May. See 16(i).

(**k**) **Stinking Hellebore** *Helleborus foetidus* L., family Ranunculaceae. A native perennial of woods on calcareous soil. Very rare, found only in the south. Height to 80cm. Poisonous and foetid-smelling. Flowers March to April. See 36(d).

photograph taken 26 March

(**e**) **Blue-eyed Mary** *Omphalodes verna* Moench, family Boraginaceae. An introduced perennial sometimes naturalised in woods and often cultivated. To a height of 30cm. Flowers March to May.

(**f**) **Lady's Smock** or **Cuckoo Flower** *Cardamine pratensis* L., family Cruciferae. A very common native perennial of damp meadows and stream sides found throughout the British Isles. Height to 55cm. The bottom leaves are like Watercress, with seven leaflets on a stem, and may be eaten as Watercress. Flowers April to July. See Watercress 90(l) and 40(a), 78(e), 82(h).

(**g**) **Spotted Dead-nettle** *Lamium maculatum* L., family Labiatae. An introduced perennial often grown in gardens; sometimes found as an escape. Flowers April to Sept. See 14(f), 14(g), 50(a).

(**h**) **Wild Daffodil** *Narcissus pseudonarcissus* L., family Amaryllidaceae. A native bulb found wild in England and Wales but not in Scotland or Ireland. Very plentiful in the larger garden forms. Height to 35cm. Flowers Feb. to April.

(**i**) **Stinking Iris** or **Gladdon** *Iris foe*. family Iridaceae. Fruit only shown. It forms in the autumn and lasts through until spring. See Flower and text 106(e).

(**j**) **Pale Wood Violet** *Viola reichenbachiana* Jord. ex Bor., family Violaceae. A native perennial of woods on calcareous soils. Quite common in England, rare in Wales and Ireland and not found in Scotland. Height to 15cm. Flowers March to May. See 16(g), 20(l), 22(b), 26(e), 60(h), 66(g).

(**k**) **Crocus** *Crocus purpureus* Weston, family Iridaceae. An introduced corm. Very rare in the wild, only found in a few places in England and Wales, but common in gardens and planted woods. Height to 25cm. Flowers March to April. See 168(a).

(**l**) **Yellow Star-of-Bethlehem** *Gagea lutea* (L.) Ker-Gawl., family Liliaceae. A rare native of damp woods and pastures. Found scattered in central England and southern Scotland but not in Ireland. Height to 25cm. Flowers March to May. See 64(c), 150(g).

(**m**) **Wood-sorrel** *Oxalis acetosella* L., family Oxalidaceae. A native perennial of woods and hedges common throughout the British Isles. Height to 15cm. The three-part leaves often fold up as in our picture. May be eaten as salad, the taste is like cultivated sorrel. Flowers April to June. See 60(e), 60(f).

(**n**) **Wood Anemone** or **Windflower** *Anemone nemorosa* L., family Ranunculaceae. A native perennial very common in woods throughout the British Isles except southern Ireland, where it is rare. Absent from the Shetlands, Orkneys and Hebrides. Height to 30cm. The flowers vary in colour and may be white, pink or even purple. Poisonous. Flowers March to May. See 20(k).

(**c**) **Ivy** *Hedera helix* L., family Araliaceae. Fruit only shown. These berries were once recommended as a cure for rheumatism. The fruit forms by November and ripens by Christmas. For text see Flowers 172(l).

(**d**) **Yew** *Taxus baccata* L., family Taxaceae. A native tree, much planted, especially in graveyards. Fairly common in the wild in England and Wales, otherwise rare. Height to 20m. May live to a very great age, perhaps 3,000 years. Traditionally used for making bows, It is thought that the association with graveyards is actually a pre-Christian association with holy places. Male and female flowers occur on separate trees. Only the males are shown, being more dramatic than the females, which are tiny, yellow and cup-shaped. Flowers March to April. See Fruit 160(k).

(**a**) **Butcher's Broom** *Ruscus aculeatus* L., family Liliaceae. A native, tiny shrub found only in southern England in dry woods and among rocks. Height to 80cm. Probably bunches of it were used by butchers to wipe off their blocks. Flowers Jan. to April. Not related to broom. See Fruit 174(a).

(**b**) **Box** *Buxus sempervirens* L., family Buxaceae. A native shrub of chalk woods and scrub. Rare in the wild and found only in one or two places in southern England. Height to 5m. The wood was used for making rulers, chessmen, engraving blocks and originally, small boxes. Flowers March to May. See Fruit 158(m).

photograph taken 5 April ○ represents 1 centimetre

photograph taken 5 April

**(g) Buttercup** *Ranunculus acris* L., family Ranunculaceae. The common native buttercup. Perennial, especially on damp meadows throughout the British Isles but common elsewhere. Height to 70cm. The flowers, rubbed on to a cow's udder, were thought to improve the milk. Hold a flower under your chin and if your skin turns yellow it is said to show you like butter. Poisonous. Flowers April to May. See other *Ranunculus* species and 30(j), 58(h), 88(d).

**(h) Cowslip** *Primula veris* L., family Primulaceae. A native perennial. Common in meadows and on banks in England, Wales and central Ireland; rare elsewhere. Height to 30cm. The flowers are popular for wine-making but picking has made it much rarer. Flowers April to May. See 16(h), 24(d), 32(b).

**(i) Dandelion** *Taraxacum officinale* Weber agg., family Compositae. A perennial native. Very common throughout, in waysides, fields and as a weed of lawns. The flowers only open in full sun. Height to 35cm. The leaves are delicious cooked, or eaten in a salad. The roots may be dried, roasted and then ground to make coffee. Medicinally, it is used to clear up urinary problems. Flowers March to Sept.
**Red-veined Dandelion** *T. spectabile* Dahlst. Native of marshes. Often reddish beneath florets. Flowers April to Aug.

**(j) Bird's-eye Primrose** *Primula farinosa* L., family Primulaceae. A native perennial. Only found wild in and around Yorkshire and Cumbria where it may be abundant. Grows in damp, grassy places on peaty soil. Height to 15cm. Flowers April to June. See Scottish Primrose 88(b).

**(k) Pasque Flower** *Pulsatilla pratensis* (L.) Mill. syn. *Anemone pulsatilla* L., family Ranunculaceae. A native perennial found on calcareous, grassy slopes and old earthworks. Rare, found only in central England. Height may be to 25cm. This lovely flower comes out traditionally at Easter, hence Pasch or Pasque Flower. Flowers April to May. See 18(n).

**(l) Pansy** *Viola arvensis* Murr. agg., family Violaceae. A native annual common throughout but less so in the west. Prefers sandy soils. Height to 15cm. The name comes from the French 'pensee'—a thought. Very variable in size, leaf formation and colour. Flowers April to Sept. See 16(g), 18(j), 22(b), 26(e), 60(h), 66(g).

**(m) Snake's Head** or **Fritillary** *Fritillaria meleagris* L., family Liliaceae. A native bulb. Rare, only found wild in southern counties otherwise often in gardens. Height to 50cm. Flowers April to May.

**(n) Loddon Lily** or **Summer Snowflake** *Leucojum aestivum* L., family Amaryllidaceae. A native bulb. Rare, found naturalised only in southern England, mainly near the Vale of the White Horse in wet meadows. Commonly cultivated. Height to 60cm. Flowers April to May. See Spring Snowflake 12(c).

**(a) Hornbeam** *Carpinus betulus* L., family Corylaceae. A native tree, most common in the south-east of England and rare in Ireland and Scotland. Height to 25m. Flowers April to May. See Fruit 108(h).

**(b) Yellow Whitlow Grass** *Draba aizoides* L., family Cruciferae. Perennial, possibly native. Height to 15cm. Very rare, found only on the Gower coast. Flowers March to May.

**(c) Gorse** or **Furze** *Ulex europaeus* L., family Leguminosae. A common shrub of heaths and embankments throughout the British Isles. Height to 2m. Flowers March to June. Other gorses flower later. See 152(a), 154(h).

**(d) Silver Birch** *Betula pendula* Roth, family Betulaceae. A native tree, common throughout the British Isles except the Shetland and Orkney Islands. Height to 25m. Male catkins hang down; female, small, erect. Flowers April to May. See 108(i).

**(e) Asarabacca** *Asarum europaeum* L., family Aristolochiaceae. Perennial, possibly native in woods but very rare and found only on a few sites in England and Wales. Height to 5cm. Flowers April to Aug.

**(f) Grey Alder** *Alnus incana* (L.) Moench, family Betulaceae. An introduced tree. Height to 20m. Male catkins hang down as shown; female, erect and mature fruit 'cone' also shown. Flowers Feb. to April. See 158(p).

photograph taken 27 April ○ represents 1 centimetre

photograph taken 27 April

(**f**) **Oxford Ragwort** *Senecio squalidus* L., family Compositae. Annual. Introduced in 1794 to Oxford. Common in central and southern England rare in Scotland and Ireland. Found on waysides, railway embankments and wasteplaces. Height to 30cm. Flowers April to Dec. See 104(g), 148(b).

(**g**) **Charlock** *Sinapis arvensis* L., family Cruciferae. Annual probably native. Common all over the British Isles. A weed of arable land and roadsides. Height to 80cm. Flowers April to July. See below and 51(d), 122(k).

(**h**) **Rape** or **Cole** *Brassica napus* L., family Cruciferae. Possibly introduced annual or biennial, cultivated as fodder but often naturalised on road and streamsides near arable land. Found throughout Britain but rare in Ireland. Height to 60cm. Flowers end of April to Aug. See 51(d), 122(k).

(**i**) **Sweet Cicely** *Myrrhis odorata* (L.) Scop., family Umbelliferae. A perennial, probably native. Common in northern England and west Scotland, otherwise rare. Found in hedges, woods and grassy places. Height to 1m. Flowers April to June.

(**j**) **Cow Parsley** *Anthriscus sylvestris* (L.) Hoffm., family Umbelliferae. A native biennial. Prolific throughout the British Isles on roadsides, banks and paths. Height to 1m. Flowers April to June. **Bur-chervil** *A. caucalis* Bieb. Native annual of waste places and sandy ground near the sea. Common in south east England. Height to 50cm. Similar to Cow Parsley, but smaller, and fruit with hooked bristles. Flowers May to June.

(**k**) **Sun Spurge** *Euphorbia helioscopia* L., family Euphorbiaceae. An annual native. Common all over England but scattered elsewhere. Grows on roadsides and cultivated ground. Height to 45cm. Poisonous. Flowers April to Oct. See other spurges.

(**l**) **Jack-by-the-hedge** or **Garlic Mustard** *Alliaria petiolata* (Bieb.) Cavara & Grande, family Cruciferae. A native biennial. Common in England but scattered in Scotland and Ireland. Found in wood edges, hedges and gardens. Height to 1m. The leaves may be boiled or eaten raw. If crushed, they smell of garlic. Flowers April to June.

(**m**) **Greater Stitchwort** or **Adders' Meat** *Stellaria holostea* L., family Caryophyllaceae. A native perennial. Common throughout the British Isles except in west Ireland where it is scattered. Found on roadsides and woods. Height to 50cm. Flowers April to June. See 14(a), 78(a). **Lesser Stitchwort** *S. graminea* L. A common native perennial of woods and grassland. Height to 80cm. Differs from Greater Stitchwort by having smooth-edged leaves. Flowers May to July. **Marsh Stitchwort** *S. palustris* Retz. A local native of marshes. Height to 50cm. Smaller and greyer than Greater Stitchwort. Flowers May to July.

(**n**) **Soft Comfrey** *Symphytum orientale* L., family Boraginaceae. An introduced perennial, naturalised in a few places in southern England. Found on hedgebanks. Height to 65cm. Flowers April to May. See 40(c), 42(l), 58(i).

(**a**) **Ground Ivy** *Glechoma hederacea* L., family Labiatae. A native perennial. Very common throughout the British Isles except in north Scotland. Grows in woods, hedges and waste places. Height to 25cm. The leaves spread and grow to form mats like ivy. Flowers March to May.

(**b**) **Common Dog Violet** *Viola riviniana* Rchb., family Violaceae. A native perennial. Very common throughout the British Isles. Found in woods, heaths and hedges. Height to 20cm. May grow in great clumps with 20 or 30 flowers. The flowers vary in colour, can be white. Flowers April to July. See 16(g), 18(j), 22(b), 26(e), 60(h), 66(g). **Heath Dog Violet** *V. canina* L. A perennial of heaths, dry grassland, dunes and fens. Scattered throughout Britain. Height to 20cm. The leaves do not form a tuft. Flowers are bluer than 22(b) with a yellowish spur.

(**c**) **Barren Strawberry** *Potentilla sterilis* (L.) Garcke, family Rosaceae. A perennial native. Common throughout the British Isles except in north Scotland. Grows in open woods. Large gaps between petals distinguish it from Wild Strawberry. Flowers Feb. to May. See 32(g), 72(e).

(**d**) **Goldilocks** *Ranunculus auricomus* L., family Ranunculaceae. A perennial native. Quite common in England, rare elsewhere. Found in woods, on wood edges and hedgebanks. Height to 40cm. Usually has unevenly sized petals. Flowers April to June. See 20(g).

(**e**) **Townhall Clock** *Adoxa moschatellina* L., family Adoxaceae. A native perennial. Quite common in England and southern Scotland. Grows in woods and thickets. Height to 10cm. Flowers April to May.

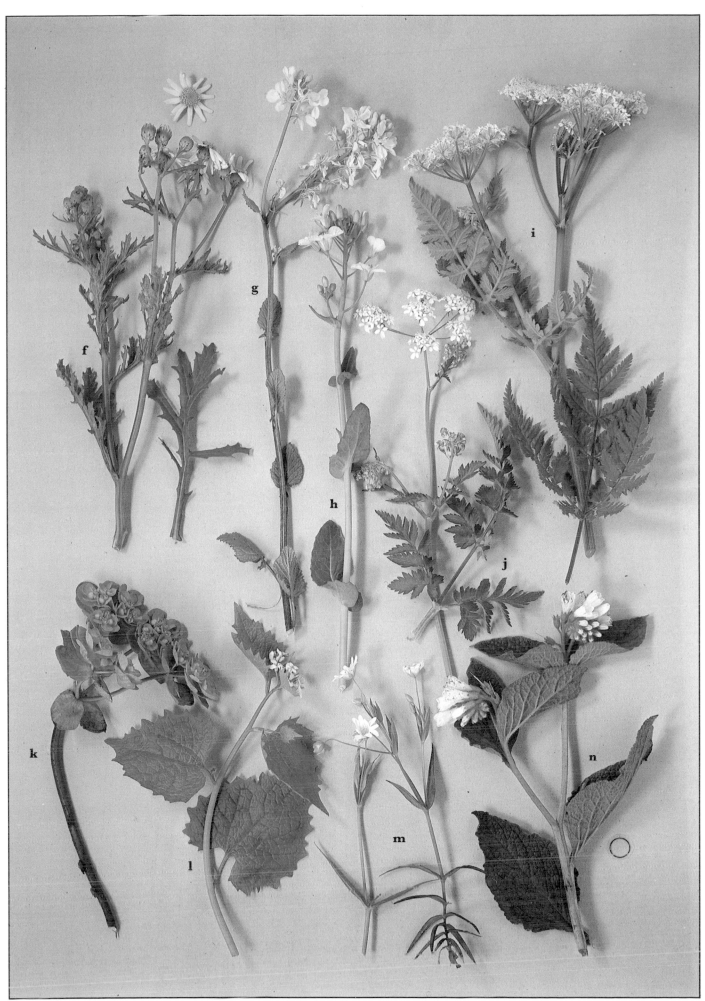

photograph taken 27 April ○ represents 1 centimetre

photograph taken 27 April

**(f) Beech** *Fagus sylvatica* L., family Fagaceae. A native tree found throughout the British Isles except Shetland and Orkney. In the south it is native, in the north planted. Dominant on chalk, to a height of 35m. The nuts may be eaten. Flowers April to May. See Nuts. 158(e).

**(g) Copper Beech** *F. sylvatica* L. There are several varieties of beech 24(f) with leaf colours shading from yellow through green to the purple leaved ones which are commonly known as Copper Beech. See Nuts: 158(f).

**(h) Wych Elm** *Ulmus glabra* Huds., family Ulmaceae. Photograph shows fruit. Note the fruit is larger and more oval than English Elm. For text see Flowers 12(k); Leaves 158(h).

**(i) English Elm** *Ulmus procera* Salisb., family Ulmaceae. Photograph shows fruit. Note the fruit is shorter and rounder than Wych Elm. For text see Flowers 12(l); Leaves 158 (g).

**(j) Walnut** *Juglans regia* L., family Juglandaceae. Introduced tree; to a height of 30m. As well as eating the nuts, you can pickle the young fruit in July. Flowers April to May. See Nuts 174(k).

**(k) Wild Cherry** *Prunus avium* L., family Rosaceae. A native tree. Fairly common all over the British Isles except Orkney and Shetland; to a height of 20m. The fruit which ripens in June is usually too bitter to eat. Flowers April to May.

**(l) Spurge Laurel** *Daphne laureola* L., family Thymelaeaceae. Native evergreen shrub. Found scattered over England rare in Wales, only found in Ireland and Scotland as an introduction. Grows mainly in calcareous soils, to a height of 1m. The leaves tend to grow only at the end of the rubbery stems. Flowers Feb. to April. See 16(b).

**(m) Crab Apple** *Malus sylvestris* Mill. ssp. *mitis* (Wallr.) Mansf., family Rosaceae. Introduced tree. Common in hedgerows, roadsides and scrub throughout the British Isles except Scotland, it becomes very rare in the north. There are two kinds of Crab Apple; this one descended from cultivated apples the other is the true wild one. Flowers April to May. For distinction, see Fruit 172(a) and (b).

**(n) Japanese Larch** *Larix kaempferi* (Lamb.) Carr syn. *L. leptolepis* (Sieb. et Zucc.) Gord., family Pinaceae. An introduced coniferous tree. Common in forestry plantations since it can maintain a good growth rate even on poor soils. Height to 30m. Both male and female flowers are shown, male on right, female on the left. Flowers March to April See Cones 168(h).

**(o) Mistletoe** *Viscum album* L., family Loranthaceae. A native parasite on trees. Found wild only in England and Wales. Common around the Severn and Wye valleys. Height up to 1m. A sacred plant of the Druids, who cut it with a golden sickle. Associated with fertility, from which developed our custom of kissing under it. Flowers Feb. to April. Fruit 174(d).

**(p) London Plane** *Platanus × hybrida* Brot. syns. *P. × hispanica* Muenchh., *P. × acerifolia* (Ait.) Willd., family Platanaceae. Tree originated in about 1650, a hybrid between *P. orientalis* and *P. occidentalis*. Very common in cities, especially London. Height to 35m. Distinctive flaking bark. Flowers March to May. See Leaves 160(j).

**(a) Wood Spurge** *Euphorbia amygdaloides* L., family Euphorbiaceae. A native perennial common in southern England and Wales, unknown elsewhere. Found in woods, particularly clearings. Height to 75cm. Flowers in the second year. Flowers March to May. See other spurges.

**(b) Evergreen Alkanet** *Pentaglottis sempervirens* Tausch, family Boraginaceae. Naturalised in hedgerows and at wood edges near gardens. Height to 80cm. Flowers April to June. See 84(k), 100(g), 124(g).

**(c) Ramsons** *Allium ursinum* L., family Liliaceae. Native. Bulb. Common over most of the British Isles, rare in Ireland and north Scotland. Grows in damp places and woods. Height to 40cm. Smells strongly of onions. Flowers April to June.

**(d) Oxlip** *Primula elatior* (L.) Hill, family Primulaceae. A perennial native. Common in a small area around Cambridge on the boulder clay. Height to 30cm. Flowers April to May. See 16(h), 20(h), 32(b).

**(e) Greater Periwinkle** *Vinca major* L., family Apocynaceae. Introduced. A trailing or climbing hedgerow plant, quite common in south England, rare in the rest of the British Isles. Flowers April to June. See 16(f).

photograph taken 30 April ○ represents 1 centimetre

(a) **Winter Heliotrope** *Petasites fragrans* (Vill.) C.Presl., family Compositae. A creeping rhizome and introduced. Fairly common in southern England and Ireland but rare in Scotland. It originally escaped from gardens but is now established on roadsides, waste places and stream sides. Height to as much as 20cm. Flowers Jan. to March. See 14(l).

(b) **Danish Scurvy-grass** or **Early Scurvy-grass** *Cochlearia danica* L., family Cruciferae. Native and an over-wintering annual. Rare around the east coast, more common on the west coast. Grows on sand, pebbles, banks and rocks near the sea. Height to 20cm. Tiny, dwarf forms have been found. Flowers Jan. to June. See 52(j), 148(i), 158(b).

(c) **Hairy Bitter-cress** *Cardamine hirsuta* L., family Cruciferae. A native annual of bare ground, rocks, scree, walls and wasteland. Common throughout Britain. Height to 20cm. Differs from Wavy Bitter-cress by having four rather than six stamens, many more basal leaves and a straight stem. Flowers April to Aug. See 14(d), 82(h).

(d) **Ash** *Fraxinus excelsior* L., family Oleaceae. A native tree. Very common all over the British Isles except for the Shetland Islands. Height to 25m. The Ash was a sacred tree of pre-Christian times for its protective powers. The Ashen spear was traditional and its wood burned specially at midwinter. Flowers before the leaves April to May. See Leaves and Fruit 174(f).

(e) **Marsh Violet** *Viola palustris* L., family Violaceae. A native perennial. Quite common all over the British Isles, except in central Ireland and central southern England where it is rather rare. Grows in bogs, marshes, fens and wet heaths. Height to 10cm. Flowers April to July. See 16(g), 18(j), 20(l), 66(g).

(f) **Spring Squill** *Scilla verna* Huds., family Liliaceae. A native bulb of dry coastal grassland. Mainly western but also on north coast of Scotland, Orkneys and Shetlands and in Ireland only on east coast. Height to 10cm. Flowers April to May. See 28(b), 168(b).

(a) **Lady's Slipper** *Cypripedium calceolus* L., family Orchidaceae. A native rhizome. Very nearly extinct, although it can still be found in Yorkshire, Durham and Cumbria in limestone woods. Height to 40cm. Once plentiful in the wild, this striking flower was so much in demand for gardens that it is now protected by law. Flowers May to June.

(b) **Green-winged Orchid** *Orchis morio* L., family Orchidaceae. A native tuber. Fairly common in south and central England, rarer in Wales and Ireland. Very rare in Scotland. It grows in meadows and pastures on calcareous soils. Height to 35cm. Flowers May to June. See 28(c).

(c) **Lesser Butterfly Orchid** *Platanthera bifolia* (L.) Rich., family Orchidaceae. A native root-tuber. Rare, except on the north west coast of Scotland. Apart from there, the best sites to find it are the North Downs, Cumbria and Devon. Grows in open woods and on grassy hillsides, especially on calcareous soils. Height to 30cm. Flowers May to July. See 96(b).

(d) **Fly Orchid** *Ophrys insectifera* L., family Orchidaceae. A native root-tuber. Rare, but quite common on the North and South Downs. It grows in copses, wood edges, scrub and on grassy hillsides, mainly on chalk or limestone. Height may be to 50cm. Quite difficult to see amongst the grass when you find it. At first, it looks just like a stray fly. Flowers May to July. See 94(d).

(e) **Long-leaved Helleborine** *Cephalanthera longifolia* (L.) Fritsch, family Orchidaceae. A native rhizome. Very rare, found in mainland Britain and Ireland in woods and shady places on calcareous soil. Height to 50cm. Similar to White Helleborine 96(a) but the leaves are twice as long. Flowers May to July.

(f) **Meadow Orchid** or **Early Marsh Orchid** *Dactylorhiza incarnata* (L.) Soó syn. *Dactylorchis incarnata* (L.) Vermeul., family Orchidaceae. A native root-tuber of scattered distribution all over the British Isles. Found in marshes, wet meadows and fens. This species has been divided into many subspecies, some spotted, some with yellowish or purple flowers. Flowers May to July.

photograph taken 4 May

(**a**) **Wood Speedwell** *Veronica montana* L., family Scrophulariaceae. A native perennial of damp woods. Quite common in the south less in the north and in Ireland. Height to 30cm. Flowers April to July. See other speedwells.

(**b**) **Bluebell** or **Wild Hyacinth** *Endymion non-scriptus* (L.) Garcke, family Liliaceae. A native bulb. Very common in England and Scotland less common in Ireland, not in Orkney or Shetland. Found in woods and shady places, often in dense patches. Height to 50cm. The flowers, also pink or white, have a wonderful, rich scent. Picking the flowers does not damage the plant, but treading down the leaves does. Flowers April to June. See 26 (f), 168 (b).

(**c**) **Early Purple Orchid** *Orchis mascula* (L.) L., family Orchidaceae. A native tuber. Quite common in the south. Scattered in Ireland and north Scotland. Found in woods and grassy places, often with bluebells. To a height of 50cm. The double ovoid tubers were thought quite wrongly to be an aphrodisiac and were much associated with fertility. Flowers April to June. See 27(b).

(**d**) **Bugle** *Ajuga repans* L., family Labiatae. A native perennial. Common throughout the British Isles except the Orkneys. Grows in woods and grassy places, to a height of 30cm. Each plant throws out creeping, rooting stems in all directions. Our specimen is early in the flowering period. It grows much taller. Flowers May to July. See 52(b), 138(d).

(**e**) **Ivy-leaved Speedwell** *Veronica hederifolia* L., family Scrophulariaceae. A native annual. Common in the south rare in Ireland and Scotland. Grows on cultivated ground and sprawls to a length of 45cm. Tiny, insignificant flowers may be lilac or white. Flowers April to July. See other speedwells.

(**f**) **Wall Speedwell** *Veronica arvensis* L., family Scrophulariaceae. A native annual. Common throughout the British Isles. Found on cultivated ground and grassland. To a height of 20cm. Flowers March to Oct. See other speedwells.

(**g**) **Field Speedwell** *Veronica agrestis* L., family Scrophulariaceae. A native annual. Scattered throughout the British Isles. Found on cultivated ground. Height to 15cm. Flowers Feb. to Oct. See other speedwells.

(**h**) **Thyme-leaved Speedwell** *Veronica serpyllifolia* L., family Scrophulariaceae. A native perennial common throughout the British Isles. Found in waste places and as a garden weed. Height to 25cm. Flowers March to Oct. See other speedwells.

(**i**) **Common Storksbill** *Erodium cicutarium* (L.) L'Hér., family Geraniaceae. A native annual. Common around the coasts inland it is fairly common in central and southern England. Found on dry ground, in waste places and arable land, especially near the sea. To a height of 50cm. Note the long seed pod. Flowers may be white. Flowers May to Aug.
**Sea Storksbill** *E. maritimum* (L.) L'Hér. A native annual of dunes and dry grassland near the sea, found mainly on south and south west coasts of England and Wales. Absent from north Scotland and rare in Ireland where it is found in the east and south. Height to 5cm. though trailing stems may reach 25cm. Much smaller than Common Storksbill with small undivided leaves and tiny, pink solitary flowers. Flowers May to Sept.

(**j**) **Germander Speedwell** *Veronica chamaedrys* L., family Scrophulariaceae. A native perennial. Very common all over the British Isles. Found in grassland and woods. Height to 35cm. The most striking speedwell. Flowers March to July. See other speedwells.

(**k**) **Chalk Milkwort** *Polygala calcarea*. F.W. Schultz, family Polygalaceae. A native perennial. Found on chalk grassland in south east England. Locally common in Salisbury Plain and the Mendips and the North Downs, otherwise very rare. Height to 15cm. Flowers May to July. See 56(f), 56(l).

(**l**) **Persian Speedwell** *Veronica persica* Poiret, family Scrophulariaceae. Introduced. A common annual over most of the British Isles, scattered in northern Ireland and west Scotland. A weed of gardens and cultivated land. To a height of 35cm. Introduced from Asia last century, but now one of the most common speedwells. Flowers Jan. to Dec. See other speedwells.

photograph taken 3 May ◯ represents 1 centimetre

photograph taken 4 May

(**e**) **Common Forget-me-not** *Myosotis arvensis* (L.) Hill, family Boraginaceae. A native annual, very common in woods, hedges and cultivated ground throughout the British Isles. Height to 25cm. Has smaller flowers than Wood Forget-me-not. Flowers April to Sept. See also 30(b), 90(h).
**Early Forget-me-not** *M. ramosissima* Rochel. A native annual, smaller than Common. Found on walls and banks. Flowers April to June.

(**f**) **Ox-eye Daisy, Dog Daisy** or **Marguerite** *Leucanthemum vulgare* Lam. syn. *Chrysanthemum leucanthemum* L., family Compositae. A very common native perennial of grassland and roadsides throughout. Height to 65cm. Once used as a cure for chest problems. Flowers May to Aug. See 112(g).

(**g**) **Sanicle** *Sanicula europara* L., family Umbelliferae. A native perennial. Common in England and Wales more scattered in Scotland and Ireland. Found in woods especially on chalk. Height to 50cm. Dried Sanicle, infused in a glass of wine overnight, is used for curing diarrhoea and dysentry and to assist the expulsion of the placenta. Flowers May to Aug.

(**h**) **Red Campion** *Silene dioica* (L.) Clairv., family Caryophyllaceae. A native biennial or perennial. Common everywhere except southern Ireland and the Hebrides where it is rare. Found in woods, hedges and shady places. Height to 80cm. Often hybridises with White Campion, 48(f) to give pink flowers. Flowers May to Nov. See 48(d), 48(f), 90(f), 137(b).

(**i**) **Leopard's Bane** *Doronicum pardalianches* L., family Compositae. An introduced perennial. Rare except in East Lothian. Found in woods and plantations. Height to 80cm. Flowers May to July.

(**j**) **King Cup** or **Marsh Marigold** *Caltha palustris* L., family Ranunculaceae. A native perennial. Common throughout the British Isles. Found in ditches, wet meadows and shady places. Height to 45cm. Hung upside down in doorways in May to ward off witches and also used as a protection against lightning. Flowers March to July. See 106(k).

(**k**) **Lily-of-the valley** *Convallaria majalis* L., family Liliaceae. Native, rhizome. Rare, scattered distribution in England and Wales, very rare in Scotland not in Ireland, of dry woods. Height to 30cm. A German folk story tells how it grew from Mary's tears, shed at the Cross. Flowers May to June. See Fruit 168(c).

(**l**) **Meadow Saxifrage** *Saxifraga granulata* L., family Saxifragaceae. A perennial native. Scattered distribution in England, Wales and southern Scotland, not in Ireland. Found on grassland and hills; not very common. Height to 45cm. Flowers April to June. See 44(b), 148(e).
**Rue-leaved Saxifrage** *S. tridactylites* L. A native annual of dry grassland or walls. Rare in Scotland but fairly common in lowland areas elsewhere. Height to 12cm. Smaller than Meadow Saxifrage, usually with more than one flowering stem, and without the group of bulbils at the base. Flowers April to June.

(**a**) **Mouse-tail** *Myosurus minimus* L., family Ranunculaceae. Annual. Probably native. Rare, found only in south west England and seems to be dying out. Found in damp fields and bare places. Height to 10cm. The English and Latin names both refer to the appearance of the fruit. Flowers May to July.

(**b**) **Wood Forget-me-not** *Myosotis sylvatica* Hoffm., family Boraginaceae. A native perennial. Locally common in woods mainly around the midlands otherwise rare. Height to 35cm. Flowers May to July. See 30(e), 90(h).
**Changing Forget-me-not** *M. discolor* Pers. Native annual, found on grassy places on light soil. Fairly common throughout Britain. Height to 20cm. A more slender plant than other forget-me-nots, with tiny flowers which start yellow and change to blue. Flowers May to Sept.

(**c**) **Golden Saxifrage** *Chrysoplenium oppositifolium* L., family Saxifragaceae. A native perennial. Fairly common throughout the British Isles, absent from the Orkneys and around the Wash. Found on stream sides and wet places. Height to 10cm. May be eaten as a vegetable. Flowers April to July.
**Alternate-leaved Golden Saxifrage** *C. alternifolium* L. As 30(c) above, except leaves alternate.

(**d**) **Bogbean** *Menyanthes trifoliata* L., family Menyanthaceae. Native rhizome. Common in north west Ireland and Scotland, scattered elsewhere but probably in large quantities when you find it. Grows in bogs and shallow water. Height to 30cm. A tea made from the dried leaves relieves headaches and migraine. Flowers May to July.

e f g h i j k l

photograph taken 10 May ○ represents 1 centimetre

photograph taken 4 May

(**e**) **Bush Vetch** or **Crow-peas** *Vicia sepium* L., family Leguminosae. A perennial native. Common throughout the British Isles. Grows in hedges, woods and as a garden weed to a height of 60cm. The flowers can be purple to blue; the pods contain many seeds and are black. Our specimen is fairly early in its flowering period; commonly has two or three spikes of flowers. Flowers April to Sept. See 56(e), 84(i), 116(e).

(**f**) **Salad Burnet** *Sanguisorba minor* Scop, family Rosaceae. A native perennial. Common in central England. Common in chalk grassland up to 30cm. in height. Sometimes grown as a garden herb, the leaves have a sharp chicory-like flavour which will add a kick to salad or garnish a summer drink. Flowers May to Aug. See 96(h).

(**g**) **Wild Strawberry** *Fragaria vesca* L., family Rosaceae. A native perennial. Common throughout the British Isles. Found on dry grassland and woods. The fruit is delicious with a stronger flavour than the cultivated strawberry. In France they are served as a delicacy. The flowers are similar to Barren Strawberry but the petals are close together and unnotched. Flowers April to July. Fruit end of June to Aug. See Fruits 92(h) and Barren Strawberry 22(c).

(**h**) **Herb Robert** *Geranium robertianum* L., family Geraniaceae. A native annual. Very common throughout the British Isles. Found in woods, hedgebanks, walls, stony places and as a garden weed. Height to 45cm. Identified by its distinctive flowers and leaf shape. Ours is a good specimen showing three normal leaf colours. Flowers end of April to Oct. See 36(i), 38(c), 44(k), 48(g), 52(h).

(**i**) **Toothwort** or **Corpse-flower** *Lathraea squamaria* L., family Scrophulariaceae. A native perennial. Scattered over England and Wales. Very rare in Scotland and Ireland. A parasite found growing on the roots of Hazel or other trees. Height to 30cm. All the flowers face one way. Thought in country areas to grow from buried bodies—hence Corpse-flower. Flowers April to May. Compare 96(c).

(**j**) **Lady's Mantle** *Alchemilla filicaulis* Buser ssp. *vestita* (Buser) M. E. Bradshaw, family Rosaceae. Lady's Mantle has been divided into many species. This one is a native perennial found quite commonly on grassland and open woods. Height to 35cm. Culpepper says women should drink distilled Lady's Mantle water for twenty days to encourage conception. Flowers May to Sept. See 50(b), 60(i), 60(j), 92(k).

(**k**) **Water Avens** or **Billy's Button** *Geum rivale* L., family Rosaceae. A native perennial. Common throughout the British Isles except the far north of Scotland. Grows in damp, shady places; less common in the south. Height to 60cm. The colour of the flowers is very subtle and difficult to describe. Flowers April to July. Check 32(l), 36(j).

(**l**) *Geum × intermedium* Ehrh., family Rosaceae. Quite common as a hybrid between Water Avens and Herb Bennet, when they both occur together. Height to 60cm. Flowers May to July. Check parents: 32(k), 36(j).

(**a**) **Pink Purslane** *Montia sibirica* (L.) Howell, family Portulacaceae. An introduced annual. Quite common in southern and eastern Scotland and down to Lancashire also near the Devon and Cornish border, otherwise rare. Found in damp woods and streamsides. Height to 30cm. Flowers April to July. See 40(l), 156(c).

(**b**) **False Oxlip** *Primula veris × vulgaris* Huds. family Primulaceae. This is a hybrid between Cowslip, *P. veris*, and Primrose, *P. vulgaris*, and occurs when they both grow together. Height to 30cm. Flowers April to June. See 16(h), 20(h), 24(d).

(**c**) **Herb Paris** *Paris quadrifolia* L., family Trilliaceae. Native. Rhizome. Scattered over England and east Wales rare elsewhere absent from Ireland. Found in damp woods on calcareous soils. To a height of 30cm. Very often has four leaves, hence its name, but may have three to eight; this specimen has five. Poisonous. Flowers May to July.

(**d**) **Woodruff** or **Sweet Woodruff** *Galium odoratum* (L.) Scop., family Rubiaceae. A native perennial. Common in England, Wales and southern Scotland, rare in the far north and in Ireland. Found in woods. Height to 40cm. When dried, this plant gives off a smell of new-mown hay. It may be added to scent summer drinks, and also used between linen. Flowers April to June. See 56(g), 78(d), 120(i).

photograph taken 10 May

(**e**) **Sessile Oak** or **Durmast Oak** *Quercus petraea* (Mattuschka) Liebl., family Fagaceae. A native tree. Fairly common throughout the British Isles tending more to the west. Found in woods and hedges. Height to 35m. To distinguish from English Oak, 34(f), the leaves have stalks and the acorns are unstalked. Flowers April to May. See below and 76(d); Acorns 174(i).

(**f**) **English Oak** or **Pedunculate Oak** *Quercus robur* L., family Fagaceae. Native tree. Very common throughout the British Isles. Found in woods aand hedges. To a height of 35m. Pre-eminent among sacred trees in pre-Christian times. Often they would be taken over by Christians and made Gospel Oaks or Boundary Oaks. Still highly thought of as a wood for chests and coffins. To distinguish from Sessile Oak, 34(e), the leaves have only very short stalks and the acorns long stalks. Flowers April to May. See above and 76(d); Acorns 174(j).

(**g**) **Sea Buckthorn** *Hippophae rhamnoides* L., family Eleagnaceae. A native shrub of fixed sand dunes and sea cliffs. Found on most British coasts but native only in the east. Often planted to stabilise dunes. Height to 2.5m. Flowers March to May. See Berries 164(j).

(**h**) **Cotoneaster** *Cotoneaster integerrimus* Medic., family Rosaceae. A native shrub found in the wild, only on Great Orme's Head, Wales; otherwise in gardens. Height to 1.5m. Flowers April to June.

(**i**) **Bird Cherry** *Prunus padus* L., family Rosaceae. A native tree of woods and stream sides, mainly on limestone in northern England and Scotland, very rare elsewhere. Sometimes planted for decoration. Height to 15m. Flowers, usually drooping, May. See 16(a), 16(d), 24(k) and Berries 147(e).

(**j**) **Sycamore** *Acer pseudoplatanus* L., family Aceraceae. Tree. Introduced about 400 years ago, now common all over the British Isles in woods, hedges and gardens and roadsides. It grows at a tremendous rate. Height to 30m. The Latin name of this genus *Acer* means sharp—maples were used for spears by the Romans. Flowers April to June. See others on this page and Fruits 108(l).

(**k**) **Norway Maple** *Acer platanoides* L., family Aceraceae. Tree. Introduced but readily naturalised Although it is not as common as the Sycamore, there are still a lot to be seen. In April when in full bloom, it is a very remarkable sight, seeming a mass of gold with its yellow flowers and the young leaves which are yellow at first. Height to 30m. The specimen is at the very end of the flowering period when the new leaves are quite advanced. Flowers March to beginning of May. See others on this page and Fruits 108(f).

(**l**) **Field Maple** *Acer campestre* L., family Aceraceae. Tree. This is our native maple. Common in the south as far north as Yorkshire and Lancashire. North of that found only as an introduction. Rare in Ireland. It grows in woods and scrub but mainly in hedges where it is sometimes kept trimmed so that it grows no bigger than a hedge shrub. Height to 20m. Flowers last of the maples, with the leaves, from May to June. See other maples this page and Fruits 108(g).

(**a**) **Laburnum** *Laburnum anagyroides* Medic., family Leguminosae. Introduced small tree. Commonly planted in gardens and on roadsides. Occasionally naturalized in waste places. Height to 7m. Poisonous. Flowers May to June.

(**b**) **Wayfaring Tree** *Viburnum lantana* L., family Caprifoliaceae. A native shrub. Common in southern England and Wales, absent from Ireland and the north. Found in hedges and chalk scrub. Height to 6m. Often planted in the past as an ornamental shrub on roadsides—hence its name. The leaves may be used to make a black hair dye. Flowers May to June. See Fruit 162(j) and also 58(b).

(**c**) **Broom** *Cytisus scoparius* (L.) Link, family Leguminosae. A native shrub. Common all over the British Isles except Orkney and Shetland. Grows on heaths, waste ground and embankments; not on chalk. Height to 2m. Used for making brooms but very commonly known as a magic shrub from which fairies often spoke. Flowers May to June. See 20(c).

(**d**) **Mountain Ash** or **Rowan** *Sorbus aucuparia* L., family Rosaceae. A native tree. Common all over the British Isles. Grows in woods and on mountains; much planted on roadsides and in gardens. To a height of 15m. A very significant tree in pre-Christian religions—normally used to protect man from evil. Flowers May to June.

photograph taken 11 May

(**e**) **Pignut** or **Earthnut** *Conopodium majus* (Gouan) Loret, family Umbelliferae. A native perennial. Common throughout the British Isles. Found in woods, fields and banks, but not on chalk. Height to 50cm. The plant used to be grubbed up by children and the 'nuts' or tubers eaten. Note normally no bracts below the umbels. Flowers May to July.

(**f**) **Hairy Tare** *Vicia hirsuta* (L.) S. F. Gray, family Leguminosae. A native annual. Common in England, scattered elsewhere. A trailing, climbing pea plant with tiny flowers found in grassy places and as a weed of cultivation. In fact, it is a pest of corn crops. Flowers May to Aug. See others 56(e), 81(c).

(**g**) **Wild Chamomile** or **Scented Mayweed** *Chamomilla recutita* (L.) Rauschert syns. *Matricaria chamomilla* L., *M. recutita* L., family Compositae. A native annual. Common in south England and around the Welsh border, rare elsewhere. Grows on roadsides, waste places and cornfields. Height to 50cm. Chamomile tea is made by drying the flower heads and then infusing in boiling water. The drink is taken for indigestion and insomnia and sold in most health food shops. Flowers May to Aug. See 78(c), 100(e), 120(b), 124(b).

(**h**) **Sheeps Sorrel** *Rumex acetosella* L., family Polygonaceae. A native annual. Common throughout the British Isles. Found on heaths, grassland, roadsides, cultivated land and as a garden weed. Height to 30cm. The leaves differ from common sorrel by having two lobes at the base. Flowers May to Aug. See 36(l), 116(j).

(**i**) **Mountain Cranesbill** or **Hedgerow Cranesbill** *Geranium pyrenaicum* Burm.f., family Geraniaceae. Perennial, possibly native. Fairly common in southern England, rare elsewhere. Grows in wood edges, waste places and hedgebanks. Despite its name this is not a mountain plant. Height to 55cm. Flowers May to Aug. See 32(h), 38(c), 44(k), 48(g), 52(h).

(**j**) **Herb Bennet** or **Wood Avens** *Geum urbanum* L., family Rosaceae. A native perennial. Common throughout except the north of Scotland. Grows on damp soils in woods, clearings, hedges or any shady places. Height to 60cm. Used medicinally by the Romans as a substitute for quinine. The roots give off a smell of cloves, said to repel evil spirits if hung by the door. Flowers May to Aug. See 32(k), 32(l).

(**k**) **Wild Mignonette** *Reseda lutea* L., family Resedaceae. A native biennial/perennial. Quite common in England and Wales, scattered in Ireland, rare in Scotland. Found on chalky soils, waste places, ploughed fields and disturbed ground. Although not in great quantities, it can often be seen at a distance as it stands above the grass. Height to 70cm. Flowers May to Aug. See 74(i), 96(e).

(**l**) **Sorrel** *Rumex acetosa* L., family Polygonaceae. A native perennial. Common throughout the British Isles. Found in grassland, roadsides and woods. Height to 1m. Larger than 36(h), with the top leaves clinging to the stalk. The leaves may be added to a salad to sharpen the taste; also nice in a sauce instead of lemon juice. Flowers May to June. See 36(h), 116(j).

(**a**) **Meadow Saffron** or **Autumn Crocus** *Colchicum autumnale* L., family Liliaceae. A native corm. Very rare except in the area around the Bristol Channel, may be quite prolific where found. Grows in damp meadows and woods. Height to 20cm. This photograph shows the fruit and leaves. See Flower 168(a).

(**b**) **Hedge Mustard** *Sisymbrium officinale* (L.) Scop., family Cruciferae. A native annual. Common over most of the British Isles except central and west Scotland and Orkney. Grows in waste places, roadsides and hedgebanks. Common except in north Scotland. Height to 80cm. Flowers May to Sept. See others 54(j), 94(j).

(**c**) **Yellow Rocket** or **Winter Cress** *Barbarea vulgaris* R.Br., family Cruciferae. A native biennial or perennial. Fairly common in England less in north Scotland. Found on roadsides, stream banks and waste places, if damp enough. Common in the south. Height to 80cm. The leaves start growing in the autumn and may be found all winter. May be cooked or eaten in salad. Flowers May to Sept. Compare with 90(l).

(**d**) **Green Hellebore** *Helleborus viridus* L., family Ranunculaceae. A native perennial. Rare, only in England and Wales. Found in calcareous woods or thickets. Height to 40cm. This plant is poisonous although in the Middle Ages it was used as a worm cure—it put the patient more at risk than the worms. Our specimen is right at the end of its flowering period. Flowers March to May. See 16(k).

e

f

g

h

i

j

k

l

photograph taken 12 May ◯ represents 1 centimetre

photograph taken 15 May

(**a**) **Birdsfoot-trefoil** or **Bacon and Eggs** *Lotus corniculatus* L., family Leguminosae. A native perennial. Very common throughout the British Isles. Found on grassland and roadsides and as a weed of lawns. Height may be to 35cm., but unlikely to get this high if free standing. About seventy local names for this plant have been recorded many, such as Tom Thumb, having an elfin connotation. Flowers May to Sept. See 100(f).
**Slender Birdsfoot-trefoil** *L. tenuis* Waldst. Kit. ex Willd. Native; dry grassy places. Height to 80cm. Much less common, the stems are more branched, the flowers, usually only four to a head, are smaller than 38(a). Flowers May to Aug.

(**b**) **Black Medick** *Medicago lupulina* L., family Leguminosae. A native annual. Common on roadsides and grass except in north west Scotland and northern Ireland. Height to 40cm. Black

because seeds are black when ripe. Flowers April to Aug. Also shown at 52(e). See 48(e), 52(f), 60(g), 84(d).

(**c**) **Shining Cranesbill** *Geranium lucidum* L., family Geraniaceae. A native annual. Scattered throughout the British Isles except Orkney, Shetland, Hebrides and Guernsey. Grows on paths, rocks, walls and hedgebanks; locally common. Height to 30cm. May be identified by its smooth, waxy leaves. Flowers May to Aug. See 32(h), 36(i), 44(k), 48(g), 52(h).

(**d**) **Horse-shoe Vetch** *Hippocrepis comosa* L., family Leguminosae. A native perennial. Locally common in southern England, not found in Scotland or Ireland. Found on dry, chalk grassland and cliffs. Height to 30cm. Note horse-shoe flower arrangement. Flowers May to July. See 38(a).

(**e**) **Elder** *Sambucus nigra* L., family Caprifoliaceae. A native shrub. Common throughout the British Isles. Found in woods, hedges and waste places especially disturbed ground. Height to 7m. Traditionally held in great awe; to burn Elder wood would allow bad spirits to enter the house. The flowers are used for wine and 'Champagne', berries also are used for wine. I have found that the berries boiled, and the juice preserved with sugar, makes a wonderful drink like blackcurrant juice. Serve watered with a dash of lemon. Flowers May to June. See Fruit 162(e) and 118(k).

(**f**) **Holly** *Ilex aquifolium* L., family Aquifoliaceae. Native; a small tree or shrub. Common throughout the British Isles in woods, hedges, scrub and rocks. Height to 12m. A mystical tree of winter, the red berries protecting the house since pre-Christian times. The very fine wood has been used for chessmen, inlays and wood engraving. Trees are planted near houses to ward off lightning. Male and female flowers are, except rarely, on separate trees. Flowers May to Aug. For Fruit see 174(c).

(**g**) **Hawthorn, May-tree** or **Whitethorn.**
*Crataegus monogyna* Jacq., family Rosaceae. A native shrub. Very common throughout the British Isles except the far north of Scotland. Found in woods, hedges and scrub, except on peat. Height to 8m. The May Tree signified the oncoming spring, the end of winter and the rebirth or Life. Some say Christ wore a crown of Hawthorn. It is considered very unlucky to cut down a Hawthorn. It is also the flower of lovers—the strong smell often having been associated with sex. Fruits Aug. to Nov. Flowers May to June. See Berries 162(h).

**Midland Hawthorn** *C. laevigata* (Poiret) DC., syn. *C. oxyacanthoides* Thuill., differs from Hawthorn in that it normally has two styles and the leaves are less deeply cut but more rounded in outline.

(**h**) **Horse Chestnut** or **Conker Tree** *Aesculus hippocastanum* L., family Hippocastanaceae. Tree. Introduced as a decorative tree in avenues and gardens but now commonly naturalised in woods throughout the British Isles. Height to 25m. Flour made from ground conkers was added to the food of horses that had difficulty in breathing—hence Horse Chestnut. The nut is called conker because the game played with them is the game 'conquer'. Flowers May to June. See Nuts 174(l).

(**i**) **Red Horse Chestnut** *Aesculus carnea* Hayne, family Hippocastanaceae. Tree; introduced and not common. Height to 25m.; very noticeable when planted with leaves generally darker than 38(h). Flowers May to June. See Nuts 174(m).

(**j**) **Lilac** *Syringa vulgaris* L., family Oleaceae. Shrub; introduced and much planted in greens and gardens. Occasionally naturalised. Height to 7m. May have white flowers as well as lilac. Strong, sweet, attractive smell. Flowers May.

(**k**) **Azalea** *Rhododendron luteum* Sweet, family Ericaceae. Shrub; introduced and common in gardens and parks. Sometimes naturalised. Height to 2m. Flowers May to June. See 62(c).

photograph taken 16 May ◯ represents 1 centimetre

photograph taken 16 May

**(a) Large Bittercress** *Cardamine amara* L., family Cruciferae. A native perennial. Scattered over south west England, the Midlands and southern Scotland, rare elsewhere. Found in wet places, stream sides, springs and ditches; often in woods. Height to 50cm. Flowers April to June. See 78(e), 82(h), 90(l).

**(b) Lords and Ladies** or **Cuckoo Pint** *Arum maculatum* L., family Araceae. A native perennial. Common in England, Wales, scattered in southern Scotland and Ireland. Rare in the far north. Grows in deep shade to a height of 45cm. Lords and Ladies and other male/female local names are descriptive of the flower and its likeness to male and female genitalia. Thought to be symbolic of copulation. Flowers April to May. See 76(g) and Fruit 134(d).

**(c) Comfrey** *Symphytum officinale* L., family Boraginaceae. A native perennial. Common in England and south Scotland, rare elsewhere. Grows in damp places, river banks, ditches and wet woods. Height to 1m. Very hairy, and sand-papery to the touch. The flowers can be white, mauve or pink. Flowers May to Sept. See others 22(n), 42(l), 58(i).

**(d) Hoary Cress** or **Hoary Pepperwort** *Cardaria draba* (L.) Desv., family Cruciferae. Perennial. Introduced. Fairly common in southern England, rare elsewhere. Found on roadsides and arable land. Height to 80cm. Flowers May to July.

**(e) Bearberry** *Arctostaphylos uva-ursi* (L.) Spreng., family Ericaceae. Native. Small shrub. Common in the Scottish Highlands, rare in Ireland and northern England, absent elsewhere. Found on moors and rocks. Cultivated in gardens. Height to 50cm. Contains tannin and the green leaves have been used for bladder and kidney trouble, particularly cystitis. Flowers May to July. See 40(f), 40(g), 66(i).

**(f) Bog Rosemary** or **Marsh Andromeda** *Andromeda polifolia* L., family Ericaceae. A native shrub. Rare, found mainly around Cumbria, and central Ireland. Grows in bogs. Height to 30cm. Flowers May to Aug.

**(g) Cowberry** or **Red Whortleberry** *Vaccinium vitis-idaea* L., family Ericaceae. A native evergreen shrub. Common in the Scottish Highlands, rare elsewhere. Found on moors and woods on acid soil. Height to 30cm. The flowers may be pink or white, the berries eaten and made into a good jelly. Flowers May to Aug. See Fruit 154(k) and also 66(i), 80(f).

**(h) Whitlow Grass** *Erophila verna* (L.) Chevall., family Cruciferae. A native annual. Fairly common all over the British Isles except Shetland. Found on rocks, walls and in dry places. Height to 15cm. May be very variable in appearance. Flowers March to June.

**(i) Arctic Stone Bramble** *Rubus arcticus* L., family Rosaceae. Once found in the Scottish Highlands but now thought to be extinct. Our specimen came from a garden. Flowers May to Aug.

**(j) Chickweed Wintergreen** *Trientalis europaea* L., family Primulaceae. A native perennial. Locally common in the Scottish Highlands, rare in north England, absent elsewhere. Grows in mossy pine woods. Height to 20cm. Flowers May to July.

**(k) Yellow Pimpernel** *Lysimachia nemorum* L., family Primulaceae. A native perennial. Fairly common all over the British Isles. Found in woods and shady hedgebanks. A creeping plant, the flowers opening fully whereas in Creeping Jenny, they only half open, see 92(m). Flowers May to Sept.

**(l) Spring Beauty** *Montia perfoliata* (Donn ex Willd.) Howell, family Portulacaceae. Introduced. An annual. Scattered over England, rare elsewhere. Cultivated or naturalised in waste ground on sandy soil. Height to 25cm. The word perfoliata means that the stem goes through the leaf. Flowers May to July. Compare 32(a).

photograph taken 16 May ◯ represents 1 centimetre

photograph taken 17 May

(**e**) **Solomon's Seal** *Polygonatum multiflorum* (L.) All., family Liliaceae. A native rhizome found locally in woods in England and Wales; grown commonly in gardens. Height to 70cm. Medicinally the roots were used to heal bruises. Gerard says: 'it takes many bruises of women's wilfullness in stumbling upon their hastie husbands' fists'. Also the flowers, distilled as a toilet water, were used to remove spots from the skin. Flowers May to June.
**Angular Solomon's Seal** *P. odoratum* (Mill.) Druce. Native but rare. Found limestone woods in north west England and Wales. Height to 18cm. Only one or two unwaisted flowers in each cluster. Flowers June to July.

(**f**) **Greater Celandine** *Chelidonium majus* L., family Papaveraceae. Perennial, probably native. Common in the south, rare in Scotland and Ireland. Grows on hedgebanks and roadsides. To a height of 75cm. It is thought to be named after swallows. The Greek word is *khelidon*, a swallow. Used medicinally for internal use but dangerous as it is poisonous. For external use, the yellow juice of the stem, applied to warts, is said to clear them up in eight days. Flowers May to July.

(**g**) **Alexanders** *Smyrnium olusatrum* L., family Umbelliferae. Introduced. Biennial. Common around the coast. Height to 1.75m. The whole plant may be eaten; the leaves to make a white sauce or as a herb, the soft stems cooked as asparagus, the roots as a substitute for parsnips and the flower buds in salads. Flowers April to June. See 94(g), 118(i).

(**h**) **Caraway** *Carum carvi* L., family Umbelliferae. Biennial. Possibly native. Very rare all over the British Isles, seems to be decreasing in the wild. Found in gardens or naturalised in waste places. Height to 50cm. The dried seeds are used to flavour cakes and sauerkraut. Flowers May to July.

(**i**) **Red Valerian** *Centranthus ruber* (L.) DC., family Valerianaceae. Introduced. A perennial. Fairly common in the south, getting less and less further north. Found on dry banks, walls and cliffs. Often cultivated. Height to 70cm. The young leaves may be used in salads but they are rather bitter. Flowers May to July. See 54(c), 106(g).

(**j**) **Caper Spurge** *Euphorbia lathyrus* L., family Euphorbiaceae. Possibly native. Biennial. Found commonly as a garden weed or wild in a few waste places mainly in the south. Height to 1.20m. Named caper from the capers we eat but the seeds, which look like edible capers, are in fact poisonous. Flowers May to June. See other spurges.

(**k**) **Woad** *Isatis tinctoria* L., family Cruciferae. Biennial or perennial. Thought to be introduced but certainly a very long time ago. Very rare, found in gardens and wild, near the Severn Valley, and in cornfields in the south. Height to 1.20m. Once used to make a blue dye, now superseded by indigo. Flowers May to July.

(**l**) **Tuberous Comfrey** *Symphytum tuberosum* L., family Boraginaceae. A native perennial. Fairly common in south and west Scotland, rare elsewhere. Found in damp meadows and by streams. Height to 45cm. The leaves are smaller than Common Comfrey and the root stalk is tuberous. Flowers May to July. See 22(n), 40(c).

(**a**) **Fairy Foxglove** or **Alpine Erinus** *Erinus alpinus* L., family Scrophulariaceae. Introduced. A small perennial grown in gardens and naturalised in a few places on walls and rocky woods. Height to 12cm. Flowers May to Oct.

(**b**) **Ivy-leaved Toadflax** *Cymbalaria muralis* Gaertn., Mey & Scherb., family Scrophulariaceae. Introduced. First recorded in 1640 but now common in England, Wales and Ireland, rare in north Scotland. Found on walls. A creeping plant, the stems can reach 70cm. in length. Flowers May to Sept. See 118(c), 128(f).

(**c**) **Spring Cinquefoil** *Potentilla tabernaemontani* Aschers., family Rosaceae. A native perennial. Rare, and only found in England and Scotland on dry, rocky grassland. Height to 15cm. Flowers April to June. See other cinquefoils 46(i), 104(d), 142(f), 142(g).

(**d**) **White Rockrose** *Helianthemum apenninum* (L.) Hill., family Cistaceae. A native annual. Very rare, only found in two places on limestone rocks: Brean Down, Somerset and Torbay, Devon; otherwise in gardens as a rockery plant. Straggly stems to 25cm. in length. It is distinguished from Common Rockrose by having white flowers. Flowers May to July. See 47(c).

e   f   g   h   i   j   k   l

photograph taken 18 May

(**e**) **Wood Cranesbill** *Geranium sylvaticum* L., family Geraniaceae. A native perennial, common in Scotland but very rare elsewhere. Grows in meadows, hedgebanks, damp woods and on mountain ledges. Height to 70cm. Flowers May to July. See others on this page and 66(a).

(**f**) **Blue Gromwell** *Buglossoides purpurocaerulea* (L.) I. M. Johnston, syn. *Lithospermum purpurocaeruleum* L., family Boraginaceae. A native perennial. A very rare plant of wood edges on chalk in the south west. The stems creep and the flowering stems are erect to a height of 50cm.; worth searching for in the Mendips. Flowers May to June. See 128(d).

(**g**) **Dusky Cranesbill** *Geranium phaeum* L., family Geraniaceae. An introduced perennial and a garden plant which has been naturalised in many places. Scattered throughout the British Isles, found wild on hedgebanks and roadsides. Height to 50cm. Worth finding for its lovely deep coloured flowers. Flowers May to June. See others on this page and 104(a).

(**h**) **Bloody Cranesbill** *Geranium sanguineum* L., family Geraniaceae. A native perennial. Rare; mainly found on the coasts of northern England on dry, rocky places, on limestone, sand dunes, grassland and woods. Height to 30cm. The single large flowers may be white or pink. Flowers May to Aug. See others on this page and 66(a), 104(a).

(**i**) **Herb Robert** *Geranium robertianum* L., family Geraniaceae. A native annual, common in woods, hedgebanks, walls, stony places and as a garden weed, throughout Britain. Height to 45cm. Identified by its distinctive flowers and leaf shape. Flowers end of April to Oct. See other geraniums 36(i), 38(c), 48(g), 52(h).

(**j**) **Small-flowered Cranesbill** *Geranium pusillum* L., family Geraniaceae. A native annual found on dry grassland; fairly common in east England and around Inverness, rare in Ireland, on cultivated ground and waste land. Height to 30cm. It can have more flowers than our specimen; blue to lilac in colour. Flowers May to Aug. See others this page and 52(h).

(**k**) **Round-leaved Cranesbill** *Geranium rotundifolium* L., family Geraniaceae. A native annual found on hedgebanks and walls. Rare; found only in southern England. Height to 30cm. Flowers May to July. See others this page and 32(h), 38(c), 48(g), 52(h).

(**l**) **Rock Cranesbill** *Geranium macrorrhizum* L., family Geraniaceae. A garden escape. Perennial. Found wild only in south Devon where it grows on walls. Height to 25cm. Flowers May to Aug. See others on this page and 104(a).

(**a**) **Kidney Vetch** or **Lady's Fingers** *Anthyllis vulneraria* L., family Leguminosae. A native perennial. Scattered throughout the British Isles on dry grassland often near the sea. Height to 50cm. The seed pods on this plant are minute and the flowers may be yellow, red or purple. Flowers May to Sept.

(**b**) **Dovedale Moss** *Saxifraga hypnoides* L., family Saxifragaceae. A native perennial. Rare except in Cumbria and Scotland where the distribution is scattered in hilly districts, on rocks and grassy places. Height to 15cm. Flowers May to July. Compare with 47(b).

(**c**) **Common Wild Thyme** *Thymus praecox* Opiz ssp. *arcticus* (E. Durand) Jalas syn. *T. drucei* Ronn., family Labiatae. Tiny native shrub, common on dry grassland, normally calcareous soil; more plentiful in the north and west. The straggling stems are up to 7cm. long. Common Wild Thyme is much milder than the garden variety and so, if used in cooking, remember to be lavish. Flowers May to Aug. See 120(e), 124(k).

(**d**) **Sea Campion** *Silene vulgaris* ssp. *maritima* (With.) A. & D. Löve, family Caryophyllaceae. A native perennial, locally common on shingle and sea cliffs throughout the British Isles; can also be found occasionally inland on mountains. Height to 20cm. Flowers May to July. See 28(h), 48(f), 66(b).

photograph taken 18 May ○ represents 1 centimetre

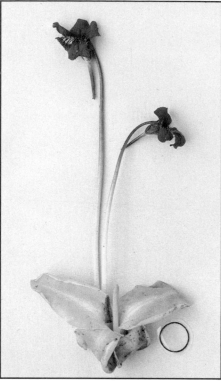

**(a) Coral Necklace** *Illecebrum verticillatum* L., family Caryophyllaceae. A native annual. Very rare, found only at the far end of Cornwall and near Portsmouth. Creeping stems to a length of 15cm. Flowers May to Sept. Photographed May 15.

**(b) Large-flowered Butterwort** *Pinguicula grandiflora* Lam., family Lentibulariaceae. Native perennial. Common on bogs and wet rocks in west Cork and Kerry. Height to 15cm. Flowers May to June. Photographed May 15.
**Pale Butterwort** *P. lusitanica* L. Native perennial of bogs and wet heaths. Common in west Scotland, west Ireland and south west England. Height to 12cm. Flowers June to Oct.

**(c) Basil-thyme** *Acinos arvensis* (Lam.) Dandy, family Labiatae. Native, usually annual. Fairly rare; found mainly in south east England on grassland or rocks, normally on chalk. Creeping stems can be as long as 20cm. May be used as wild thyme for flavouring. Note its distinguishing white marks on the lower lip of the flower. Flowers May to Aug. Photographed May 25.

**(d) Scarlet Pimpernel** or **Shepherd's Weatherglass** *Anagallis arvensis* L., family Primulaceae. A native annual, Common in England and Ireland rather rare in Scotland. Found on roadsides, cultivated land and dunes. Stems often straggling, to a length of 25cm. The flowers open in the morning and close at mid-afternoon. Flowers May to Aug. Photographed May 20.

**(e) Water-crowfoot** *Ranunculus aquatilis* L. agg., family Ranunculaceae. A native annual or perennial found in ponds, streams and ditches. Common except in Scotland. An underwater plant, the flower floats on the surface or sticks out a little. The solid leaves float and the fine leaves are submerged. Poisonous. Flowers May to June. Photographed May 15.

**(f) Adder's Tongue** *Ophioglossum vulgatum* L., family Ophioglossaceae. A native rhizome. Fairly common in the south. Found in grassland, fens and scrub; mainly in damp areas but tolerant of drier soils. Height to 12cm. This is not a flowering plant but a fern. It is included in the book as it may be mistaken for a flower. See 40(b), 96(g). Photographed May 15.

(a) **Spring Gentian** *Gentiana verna* L., family Gentianaceae. A native perennial, very rare in the wild except in the Burren and Teesdale where it is common, found on stony limestone turf. Height to 5cm. This is a protected plant and must not be picked. This is a garden specimen. Flowers April to June. See 146(f), 157(a), 157(b), 157(c). Photographed May 5.

(b) **Spring Sandwort** *Minuarta verna* (L.) Hiern, family Caryophyllaceae. A native perennial. Rare except Cumbria, Yorkshire, north Wales and the Pennines. Found on rock, screes and old mine workings. Height to 12cm. Does not actually grow on sand as its name suggests. Flowers May to Aug. See 44(b), 160(b). Photographed May 20.

(c) **Common Rockrose** *Helianthemum nummularium* (L.) Mill., family Cistaceae. A native undershrub. Common over most of the British Isles, very rare in Ireland. Found on grassland and scrub, mainly on calcareous soil. Straggling to a length of 25cm. Varieties are commonly grown on rockeries from whence its common name is derived. Flowers May to Aug. See 42(d). Photographed May 28.

(d) **Water Starwort** *Callitriche stagnalis* Scop., family Callitrichaceae. An annual to perennial native. Common throughout the British Isles. A water weed of ponds, ditches and streams. Stems can be up to 50cm. in the water. Flowers May to Aug. Photographed May 20.

(e) **Sweet Alison** or **Sweet Alyssum** *Lobularia maritima* (L.) Desv., family Cruciferae. Introduced. An annual or perennial grown in gardens as an edging plant. Naturalised as an escape in a few places, mainly near the sea and on waste places. Height to 20cm. Flowers May to Aug. Photographed May 28.

(f) **Procumbent Pearlwort** *Sagina procumbens* L., family Caryophyllaceae. A native perennial. Very common throughout the British Isles. Found on waste places, verges, lawns and between flagstones and bricks on paths. The creeping stems will often reach 12cm. in length. Very insignificant weed often thought of as moss. Flowers May to Aug. Photographed May 15.

photograph taken 18 May

**(e) Hop Trefoil** *Trifolium campestre* Schreb., family Leguminosae. A native annual. Grows on roadsides and grassy places; common except in Scotland and north Ireland. Height to 30cm. The English name describes the way the little yellow flowers resemble the fruit of the hops. Flowers May to Aug. See 52(e), 52(f), 60(g), 172(e).

**(f) White Campion** *Silene alba* (Mill.) E.H.L. Krause, family Caryophyllaceae. A native perennial. Common all over, except near the west coasts and in Ireland. It grows on roadsides, waste places and cultivated land. Height to 80cm. It commonly hybridises with Red Campion giving pink coloured intermediate flowers about two weeks later than Red Campion. Flowers May to Aug. See 30(h), 44(d), 66(b).

**(g) Cut-leaved Cranesbill** *Geranium dissectum* L., family Geraniaceae. A native annual. Common in the south, more scattered in the north. Found on roadsides, hedgebanks, waste and cultivated ground. Height to 50cm. The leaves of this geranium are much more deeply cut than the others. The flowers on our specimen do not show well as they have closed up. Flowers May to Aug. See 32(h), 38(c), 44(k), 52(h), 68(i).

**(h) Wallflower** *Cheiranthus cheiri* L., family Cruciferae. Introduced. Perennial. Now naturalised throughout lowland Britain, the distribution is scattered in the south, rare in Ireland and the north. Found on walls and rocky places. The Avon Gorge is a mass of them at the end of April. Height to 50cm. Flowers April to June.

**(i) Perennial Cornflower** *Centaurea montana* L., family Compositae. An introduced perennial grown widely in gardens and found as an escape on waste places and roadsides. Height to 60cm. Flowers May to Aug. See 84(h), 100(h), 110(d).

**(j) Bittersweet** or **Woody Nightshade** *Solanum dulcamara* L., family Solanaceae. A native perennial. Common in England, scattered in Scotland and Ireland. Found in hedges, woods and on waste ground. A sprawling plant, the stems up to 1.75m. in length. The name Deadly Nightshade is commonly used for this plant but is an error. The real Deadly Nightshade is another plant and quite distinct. The berries of this plant have been revered for thousands of years and a necklace of them was found in the tomb of Tutankhamun. There are two leaf shapes—the second shape is shown with Berry photograph 172(h). See 72(h), 116(g).

**(k) Rose Garlic** *Allium roseum* L., family Liliaceae. An introduced bulb, naturalised on sandy or rocky ground. In the few places where found, it may be quite profuse. Height to 60cm. May be a deeper pink than our specimen. Flowers April to June. See 122(a), 130(b).

**(a) Yellow Fumitory** or **Yellow Corydalis** *Corydalis lutea* (L.) DC., family Papaveraceae. Introduced. Perennial. This is a garden plant which is now naturalised. Quite common throughout England, Wales and southern Scotland. It grows on old walls. Height to 25cm. Flowers May to Aug.

**(b) Yellow Vetchling** *Lathyrus aphaca* L., family Leguminosae. A native annual. Rare in the south of England and Wales. Found on dry sand, gravel or chalk. A climbing plant, the stems can be up to 75cm. long. Flowers May to Aug.

**(c) Silverweed** *Potentilla anserina* L., family Rosaceae. A native perennial. Common throughout the British Isles. Found on all types of soil on roadsides, waste places, dunes and fields. Height normally to about 15cm. The roots can be cooked and eaten. Tea made from the leaves can be drunk to help diarrhoea or bleeding piles. Flowers May to Aug.

**(d) Sticky Catchfly** or **Red German Catchfly** *Lychnis viscaria* L., family Caryophyllaceae. A native perennial but very rare only on rocks in a few places in Wales and Scotland. Height to 50cm. Flowers May to Aug. See 30(h), 90(f).

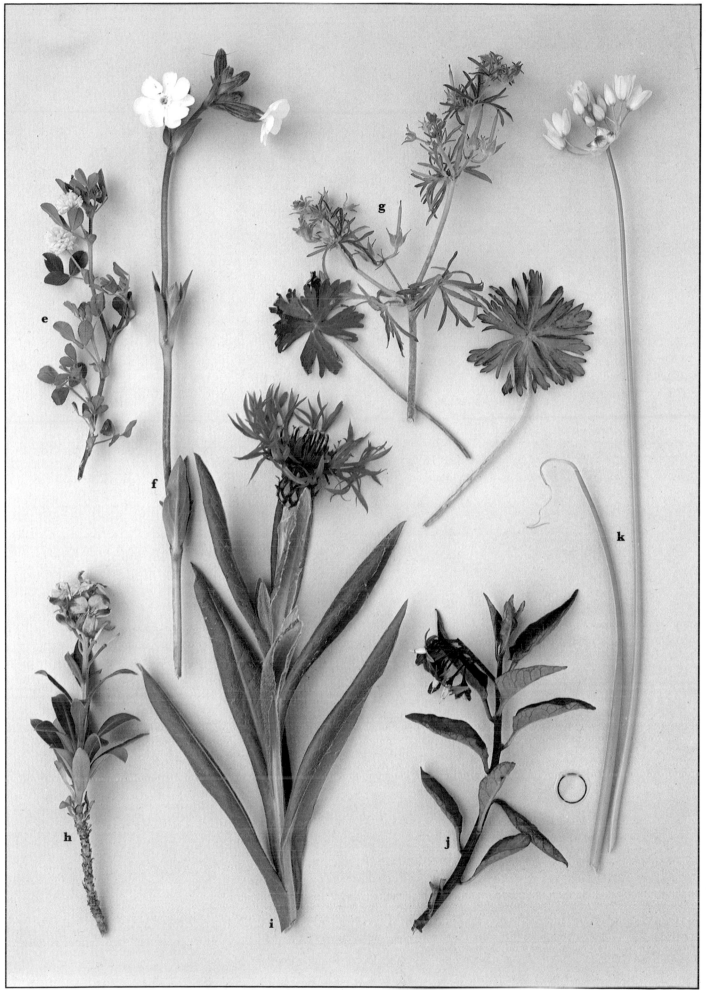

photograph taken 18 May ◯ represents 1 centimetre

(**a**) **Henbit Deadnettle** *Lamium amplexicaule* L., family Labiatae. A native annual. Fairly common up the east side of England and Scotland, rare elsewhere. Found on cultivated ground, normally on dry soils. Height to 25cm. Henbit means Hen's bite. Flowers April to Aug. See 14(f), 18(g).

(**b**) **Parsley Piert** *Aphanes arvensis* L., family Rosaceae. A native annual of bare ground and arable land. Fairly common throughout Britain. Stems may reach 15cm. Parsley Piert was traditionally used to cure kidney stones and was also pickled or eaten raw in the Hebrides. Not to be confused with Lady's Mantle. Flowers April to Oct. See 32(j), 60(i), 60(j).

(**c**) **Field Woundwort** *Stachys arvensis* (L.) L., family Labiatae. A native annual, found scattered over most of the British Isles. More common in Wales and Devon and Cornwall. Rare in Scotland and northern Ireland. Grows in arable fields, not on calcareous soils. Height to 25cm. Flowers April to Nov. See 58(l), 96 (j), 102(f), 128(c), 128(j).

(**d**) **Burnet Rose** *Rosa pimpinellifolia* L., family Rosaceae. A native shrub. Fairly common around the coast except the south east area. Rare inland. Found on dunes and sandy heaths. Height to 40cm., in rare cases to 1m. The flowers are creamy white, rarely pink and the stems densely prickly and the leaves small. Flowers May to July. See 70(d), 76(b), 86(a) and Hips 164(k).

(**e**) **Pyrenean Lily** *Lilium pyrenaicum* Gouan, family Liliaceae. A bulb, introduced as a garden flower and sometimes found as an escape near houses. In north Devon and elsewhere, it has become naturalised. Height to 75cm. Flowers May to July. See 157(e).

(**f**) **Knotted Clover** *Trifolium striatum* L., family Leguminosae. A native annual. Rare, found scattered throughout the British Isles. The distribution is mainly around south west England. Grows on well-drained soils in open places. Height to 35cm. Flowers May to July.

(**a**) **Butterwort** or **Bog Violet** *Pinguicula vulgaris* L., family Lentibulariaceae. Native, it overwinters as a rootless bud. Common in mountain areas, Wales, north England, Scotland and north west Ireland; rare elsewhere. It grows on wet heaths, rocks and in bogs. Height to 12cm. Milk from a cow that had eaten Butterwort was said to protect a newborn child. Flowers May to July. See 46(b).

(**b**) **Snowdon Lily** *Lloydia serotina* (L.) Rohb., family Liliaceae. A native bulb, found only in Snowdonia. It is protected and must not be picked. Height to 15cm. Flowers June.

(**c**) **Coral-root** *Corallorhiza trifida* Chatel., family Orchidaceae. A native rhizome. Very rare, found in damp, mossy woods of pine, birch or alder, in Scotland and north England. Absent from Wales, Ireland and south England. The rhizomes resemble branched coral and grow in the decaying moss or peat of the forest floor. Flowers May to Aug.

(**d**) **Turnip** *Brassica rapa* L., family Cruciferae. Probably an introduced annual or biennial. Commonly cultivated, naturalised on arable land. Height to 80cm. The lower leaves are lobed. Flowers May to Aug. See 22(h), 122(k).
**Black Mustard** *B. nigra* (L.) Koch. Probably native annual. Grows wild on sea cliffs, roadsides and stream sides. Height to 1m. Flowers June to Aug.

(**e**) **Rose-root** or **Midsummer-men** *Rhodiola rosea* L., *Sedum rosea* (L.) Scop. syn. family Crassulaceae. A native perennial. Quite common in the north west of Scotland and rarely in other mountain areas. Grows in rock crevices on mountains and sea cliffs. Height to 30cm. Flowers May to Aug.

(**f**) **Birdsfoot** *Ornithopus perpusillus* L., family Leguminosae. A native annual. Fairly common in south west England, scattered elsewhere and rare in Scotland and Ireland. Grows in gravel and dry, sandy places. Height to 40cm. Flowers May to Aug.

photograph taken 20 May

(**a**) **Field Mouse-ear Chickweed** *Cerastium arvense* L., family Caryophyllaceae. A native perennial found on grassland and roadsides. Fairly common. Height to 25cm. Flowers April to Aug. See 22(m), 78(a), 90(g).
**Little Mouse-ear Chickweed** *C. semidecandrum* L. Native annual of dry sandy or limestone soils. Common in south east England, rare elsewhere. Height to 15cm. Smaller than Field Mouse-ear. Flowers April to May.

(**b**) **Pyramidal Bugle** *Ajuga pyramidalis* L., family Labiatae. A native perennial. Very rare; found in rock crevices mainly in north Scotland and the Hebrides. Also recorded in west Ireland. Height to 25cm. Flowers May to July. See 28(d), 138(d).

(**c**) **Mountain Avens** *Dryas octopetala* L., family Rosaceae. Named after Dryad, the wood-nymph of oaks since the leaves slightly resemble oak leaves. A native undershrub found in rock crevices. Very rare except in north west Scotland and the Burren of the west coast of Ireland. Height of the flowering stalk to 10cm. Flowers May to July. See 148(f).

(**d**) **Pheasant's Eye** *Adonis annua* L., family Ranunculaceae. An introduced annual found in gardens but also naturalised in a few places in southern England as a cornfield weed. Height to 30cm. In Welsh, it is called Llygad y bwgan, Sprite's Eye, as the devil as well as the pheasant is said to have a red eye. Flowers May to July.

(**e**) **Black Medick** *Medicago lupulina* L., family Leguminosae. A common native annual. See 38(b) for full text. See also 48(e), 52(f), 60(g).

(**f**) **Spotted Medick** *Medicago arabica* (L.) Huds., family Leguminosae. A native annual found on sandy places, grass and waysides in southern England. Not in Scotland or Ireland. Height to 50cm. Note the black spots on the leaflets. Flowers April to Aug. See 48(e), 52(e), 60(g).

(**g**) **Sea Sandwort** *Honkenya peploides* (L.) Ehrh., family Caryophyllaceae. A native perennial found commonly on all British coasts on sand dunes and shingle. Height to 20cm. Flowers May to Aug.

(**h**) **Dove's-foot Cranesbill** *Geranium molle* L., family Geraniaceae. A native annual. Common, found on grassland, dunes and waste places throughout. Height to 35cm. According to Gerard it is miraculous against ruptures if powdered and drunk in claret. The flowers can vary to almost white. Flowers April to Sept. See 32(h), 38(c), 44(k), 48(g), 52(h).

(**i**) **Red Clover** *Trifolium pratense* L., family Leguminosae. A native perennial growing on grassy places, fields and lawns throughout. Height, if erect, to 30cm. A good fodder crop; perhaps the expression 'living in clover' comes from the contented cattle fed on clover. Also a great source of delectable honey. Flowers May to Sept. See 50(f), 54(f), 80(d), 104(c).

(**j**) **Long-leaved Scurvy-grass** or **English Scurvy-grass** *Cochlearia anglica* L., family Cruciferae. A native biennial or perennial found on muddy estuaries, very rare in Scotland and uncommon elsewhere. Height to 30cm. Scurvy-grass keeps well and so was used by sailors to supply vitamin C to protect themselves from scurvy. True of Common Scurvy-grass, 158(b), and of the others too. Flowers April to July. See 26(b), 148(i).

(**k**) **Sea Arrow-grass** *Triglochin maritima* L., family Juncaginaceae. Native; annual or perennial. Common all round the coasts of the British Isles on salt marshes and rocky shores. Height to 45cm. Flowers May to Sept. See 90(a), 126(d).

(**l**) **Common Fumitory** *Fumaria officinalis* L., family Papaveraceae. A native annual. Quite common throughout on disturbed roadsides and cultivated ground, but rare in north west Scotland and west Ireland. Height to 50cm. Used medicinally for liver complaints especially jaundice: 25 grammes of the dried, whole plant infused in 2 pints of water for fifteen minutes, thereafter 2 cupfuls a day before meals for a week is recommended. Flowers May to Oct. See 78(f), 104(b).
**Wall Fumitory** *F. muralis* Spender ex Koch. Native annual found on cultivated and waste ground, old walls and hedgebanks. Rather uncommon, occurring most in south and west England and Wales, east Scotland and south west Ireland. Stronger-looking than Common Fumitory with larger, paler flowers. Flowers May to Oct.

photograph taken 20 May ◯ represents 1 centimetre

photograph taken 20 May

**(f)** **White Clover** or **Dutch Clover** *Trifolium repens* L., family Leguminosae. A native perennial. Common, found in grassland, waste places and lawns throughout the British Isles. The length of the stems which creep along the ground can be up to 50cm. The flower stems which stand up can be up to 25cm. It roots at the nodes of the stem. Olwen of Welsh mythology left a track of white clover wherever she walked. Flowers May to Sept. See 52(i).

**Alsike Clover** *T. hybridum* L. Introduced perennial naturalised by roadsides throughout Britain but rare in the north west and Ireland. Height to 60cm. Flowers are short stalked and whitish pink; the leaves unmarked. Used to be a forage crop. Flowers May to Sept.

**(g)** **White Melilot** *Melilotus alba* Medic., family Leguminosae. Introduced annual or biennial. Naturalised in fields and waste places, frequently found in south east England. Rare elsewhere. Height to 1.25m. It grows to the size of a small bush. Flowers May to Sept. See 72(f).

**(h)** **Mouse-ear Hawkweed** *Hieracium pilosella* L., family Compositae. A native rhizome. Grows everywhere except the Shetland Isles. Height to 25cm. These plants vary a great deal in hairiness and leaf shape. The solitary flowers are normally touched with red underneath. It was used as a herbal remedy for jaundice. Flowers May to Sept.

**(i)** **Shepherd's Purse** *Capsella bursa-pastoris* (L.) Medic., family Cruciferae. A very common annual weed of gardens and waste places throughout. Height to 35cm. Named from the purse-shaped seeds. May be eaten, but mainly known for its medicinal property of stopping haemorrhage. Flowers all year.

**(j)** **Eastern Rocket** *Sisymbrium orientale* L., family Cruciferae. An introduced annual. Established on waste ground mainly in the south of England. Rare elsewhere. Height to 80cm. Note the long stem-like seed pods. Flowers May to Aug. See 36(b), 94(j).

**(k)** **Ribwort** or **Ribgrass** *Plantago lanceolata* L., family Plantaginaceae. A native perennial. Very common plant of roadsides, meadows and as a lawn weed throughout. Height to 50cm. Children play a game with the flower heads, striking one against the other until one falls and the other wins. From this, the flowers are called Soldiers or Fighting Cocks. Flowers April to Aug. See 68(k), 79(c), 90(a).

**(l)** **Beaked Hawk's Beard** *Crepis vesicaria* L., family Compositae. Introduced. A biennial found in waste places. Common in south-east England; rare in Wales and southern Ireland and not found in Scotland and northern England. Height to 70cm. Flowers May to July. See 68(b), 82(g).

**Rough Hawk's Beard** *C. biennis* L. Probably native biennial of arable land, roadsides and waste places. Fairly common in central and south east England, rare in Ireland and Wales and absent from north Scotland. Height to 1m. There are fewer, but larger flowerheads than on Beaked Hawk's Beard. Flowers June to July.

**(m)** **Three-nerved Sandwort** *Moehringia trinervia* (L.) Clairv., family Caryophyllaceae. A native annual. Grows in woods and woodland clearings. Rather common except in Scotland and Ireland. A straggling plant with stems up to 30cm. long. Flowers May to June. See 14(a).

**(a)** **Sainfoin** *Onobrychis viciifolia* Scop., family Leguminosae. A native perennial found only on calcareous grassland in south east England. Often as an escape from cultivation. Height to 50cm. Culpepper thinks it may be used for increasing the milk of nursing mothers. Flowers May to Aug.

**(b)** **Buck's-horn Plantain** *Plantago coronopus* L., family Plantaginaceae. A native biennial. Common, found near the sea all round British coasts on sandy or rocky soil. Height to about 10cm. The plant grows out from the centre and then up around the edges like a basket. Flowers May to July. See 90(a).

**(c)** **Red Valerian** *Centranthus ruber* (L.) DC. family Valerianaceae. This is the white flowered form of the Red Valerian. The white form is quite common and apart from the colour is the same as 42(i).

**(d)** **Seakale** *Crambe maritima* L., family Cruciferae. A native perennial found on the coastal shingle sand and rocks, often on the tide line. Not common except along the east end of the south coast. Height to 50cm. The large brown root stock looks like an old washed-out kale stump when you find it in winter. Flower May to Aug.

**(e)** **Sea Pea** *Lathyrus japonicus* Willd., family Leguminosae. A native perennial of shingle beaches; rare, except on the Suffolk coast. Creeping stems to 80cm. long. Where you find it may be in large patches. Flowers May to Aug.

photograph taken 22 May ◯ represents 1 centimetre

photograph taken 22 May

(**e**) **Common Vetch** *Vicia sativa* L., family Leguminosae. A native annual of hedges, wood edges and grassy places. More common in the south-east; rare in the north-west and west Ireland. A climbing plant, with stems up to 1m. long. Despite its name this is not the most common of the vetches. Flowers April to Sept. See 32(e). **Spring Vetch** *V. lathyroides* L. A rare native annual of grassy, sandy places, mainly near the east coast. Stems sprawl to 15cm. The tendrils are always unbranched. Flowers May to June.

(**f**) **Common Milkwort** *Polygala vulgaris* L., family Polygalaceae. A native perennial, fairly common on grassland, heaths and dunes throughout the British Isles. Height can be to 25cm. but normally smaller. The lower leaves are alternate rather than opposite as in 56(l). The flowers vary from white to blue to deep purplish pink, in fact you may find all the colours growing together. In Ireland it is believed to be used as soap by fairies. Flowers May to Sept. See 28(k), 56(l).

(**g**) **Heath Bedstraw** *Galium saxatile* L., family Rubiaceae. A native perennial. Common throughout on grassland, moors, heaths and woods. Height to 20cm. Flowers May to Aug. See 32(d), 78(d), 86(g), 112(a), 120(i).

(**h**) **Bitter Vetch** *Lathyrus montanus* Bernh., family Leguminosae. A native perennial. Grows on hedgebanks and in woods. Quite common throughout but absent from East Anglia. Height to 35cm. Flowers April to July. See 32(e), 102(g).

(**i**) **Tormentil** *Potentilla erecta* (L.) Rausch., family Rosaceae. A native perennial. Very common on grassland, mountains, heaths and bogs throughout Britain. Height to 25cm. The plant is used to cure colic, diarrhoea and even cystitis. The roots contain tannin and if chewed occasionally may keep the mouth clear of mouth complaints and harden the gums. Flowers May to Oct. See 42(c), 56(i), 104(d), 142(f), 142(g). **Trailing Tormentil** *P. anglica* Laicharding. A native perennial, scattered in south England and Ireland; rare elsewhere. The trailing stems are up to 65cm. and the flowers are larger than Tormentil. It may root at the leaf junctions. Flowers May to Sept.

(**j**) **Lousewort** *Pedicularis sylvatica* L., family Scrophulariaceae. A native perennial. Found in marshes, bogs and damp heathland. Quite common, especially in Scotland and Wales. Height to 20cm. It may have many unbranched stems from the root which has only one branched stem. In Germany, Lousewort was believed to give lice and liverworms to cattle. Flowers April to July. See 128(a).

(**k**) **Petty Whin** *Genista anglica* L., family Leguminosae. A native shrub of dry heaths and moors. Rather rare. More common in Scotland; unknown in Ireland. Very small, rarely over 40cm high. Flowers May to June. See 34(c), 102(i).

(**l**) **Heath Milkwort** *Polygala serpyllifolia* Hose, family Polygalaceae. A native perennial of heaths and grassy places. Fairly common throughout but less so in the south. Height to 25cm. The lower leaves are in opposite pairs. Flowers May to Aug. See 28(k), 56(f).

(**c**) **Jacob's Ladder** *Polemonium caeruleum* L., family Polemoniaceae. A native perennial; very rare, found only in the Pennines. Otherwise common in gardens and as a garden escape. Height to 75cm. The English name comes from the ladder-like leaves. Flowers May to July.

(**d**) **Bistort** or **Easter-ledges** *Polygonum bistorta* L., family Polygonaceae. A native perennial. Common in the Lancashire area, scattered elsewhere. Rare in Ireland. Grows on roadsides and meadows often in large patches. Height to 20cm. Bistort may be eaten; indeed, in Yorkshire and the Lake District Ledger Pudding is made at Easter. It consists of fresh, edible, wild plants with hard-boiled eggs. Bistort is the most important ingredient. In our specimen the flower is not fully open. Flowers May to Aug. See 134(h), 162(c), 170(b), 170(e).

(**a**) **Cypress Spruge** *Euphorbia cyparissias* L., family Euphorbiaceae. Perennial, probably native, on calcareous grassland and scrub. Rare but found in many parts of England and Wales. Recorded on north coast of Scotland and absent from Ireland, poisonous. Height to 25cm. Flowers May to Aug. See other spurges.

(**b**) **Irish Spurge** *Euphorbia hyberna* L., family Euphorbiaceae. A native perennial. Rare, except in south-west Ireland. Found in only one or two places elsewhere. Height to 50cm. Poisonous. Flowers April to July. See other spurges.

photograph taken 23 May ◯ represents 1 centimetre

photograph taken 25 May

(**e**) **Honesty** *Lunaria annua* L., family Cruciferae. Introduced, normally biennial. Very common in gardens and often found as an escape nearby. Height to 1m. The flower heads with dried seed pods are kept for decoration. Flowers April to June.

(**f**) **Field Penny-cress** *Thlaspi arvense* L., family Cruciferae. Possibly native. Annual. Found on disturbed ground, roadsides and arable land. Common in the south east but rare in Ireland and west Scotland. Height to 50cm. As with Honesty, 58(e), the dried stem and seeds pods make attractive winter decoration. Flowers May to July.

(**g**) **Corn Salad** or **Lamb's Lettuce** *Valerianella locusta* (L.) Laterrade, family Valerianaceae. A native annual found on arable land, hedge banks and roadsides. Its distribution is scattered; more common in the south than the north and Ireland. Height to 35cm. May be eaten as a salad. This is not a good specimen. The tiny flowers at the top are white to purple. Flowers April to June.

(**h**) **Bulbous Buttercup** *Ranunculus bulbosus* L., family Ranunculaceae. A native perennial. Common in England but scattered in Ireland and Scotland. It grows in meadows and grassy places. Height to 35cm. The bulbous tubers and the way the sepals bend back distinguish it from other Buttercups. Flowers April to June. See 20(g).
**Hairy Buttercup** *R. sardous* Crantz. Native annual of damp arable and waste ground. Rather uncommon, found most frequently in the south and east. Absent from Ireland and west Scotland. Stems may reach 40cm. in height. Very similar to Bulbous Buttercup but lacks the tubers and is covered with hairs. Flowers June to Oct.

(**i**) **Comfrey** *Symphytum officinale* L., family Boraginaceae. The flowers may be white or mauve-pink or purple as this specimen. Flowers May to Sept. See main text at 40(c).

(**j**) **Crosswort** *Cruciata laevipes* Opiz., family Rubiaceae. A perennial native found on roadside fields, hedges and open woodland. Common in England especially on chalk, absent from Ireland, west Wales and north Scotland. Height to 50cm. Named Crosswort because of the way the four leaves form crosses up the stem. Flowers May to June. See 56(g), 64(a), 78(d), 86(g).

(**k**) **Yellow Archangel** *Lamiastrum galeobdolon* L. Ehrend & Polatschek, family Labiatae. A native perennial found in woods and clearings; common in southern and central England, rare elsewhere. Height to 50cm. Flowers May to June.

(**l**) **Hedge Woundwort** *Stachys sylvatica* L., family Labiatae. A perennial native. Very common throughout the British Isles, in woods, hedges and shady places. Height to 80cm. The leaves are used for healing wounds, containing a volatile oil with antiseptic qualities. Flowers May to Aug. See 50(c), 96(j), 102(f), 128(c), 128(j).

(**m**) **Stinging Nettle** *Urtica dioica* L., family Urticaceae. A native perennial. Very common throughout, in woods, ditches, grassy places and especially disturbed ground and rubbish tips. Height to 1.5m. Painful stings from the hairs may be relieved by rubbing with dock leaves. Young shoots steamed and served with pepper and butter make an excellent vegetable. Flowers May to Sept.
**Small Nettle** *U. urens* L. A native perennial found on similar soil to the stinging nettle. Distinguished from the Stinging Nettle by the lower leaves being shorter than their stalks. Flowers May to Sept.

(**a**) **Spindle-tree** *Euonymus europaeus* L., family Celastraceae. A native shrub, found in woods and hedges mainly on chalk. Quite common in England and Wales, less so in Ireland and absent from Scotland. Height to 5m. The wood is very hard and used to be used for making skewers and spindles. Poisonous. Flowers May to June. See Fruit 172(c).

(**b**) **Guelder Rose** *Viburnum opulus* L., family Caprifoliaceae. A native shrub found in damp hedges, woods and scrub. Common throughout but rarer in north Scotland. Height to 5m. The outer flowers of the bunch open first; they are sterile and larger than the inner ones. Flowers May to July. See Fruit 162(g) and also 34(b).

(**c**) **Dogwood** *Cornus sanguinea* L., family Cornaceae. A native shrub found in scrub and woods. Very common on chalk; it only extends as far north as the Midlands, and is rare in Ireland. Height to 3m. In the past the hard wood was used for arrows, toothpicks, ramrods, pestles, millcogs and wedges. Flowers May to July. See Fruit 164(i) and also 16(c).

(**d**) **White Beam** *Sorbus aria* (L.) Crantz, family Rosaceae. Native tree. May be quite common on chalk in England, but rare elsewhere. Height to 15m. Called White Beam because the underside of the leaves are covered with hair and look white. Flowers May to June. See Fruit 174(e) and also 34(d).
**Wild Service Tree** *S. torminalis* (L.) Crantz. Native tree found on clay or limestone. Rare, found in south England and Wales. Height to 25m. The fruit is brown rather than red as in White Beam. Flowers May to June. Fruits Sept.

e

f

g

h

i

j

k

l

m

**(a) Bog Myrtle** or **Gale** *Myrica gale* L., family
Myricaceae. A native shrub found in bogs and wet
heaths. Uncommon in England except around
Lancashire and the Cumbrian coast. Common in
west Ireland and Scotland. Height to 2m. Has a
lovely aromatic smell, rather like eucalyptus.
Flowers April to May. Photographed May 10.

**(b) Barberry** *Berberis vulgaris* L., family
Berberidaceae. A shrub. Probably introduced;
occasionally found wild in hedges, often grown in
gardens for ornament. Height to 2m. Flowers May
to June. The sausage-shaped fruits, Sept. to Oct.,
hang in red clusters and have been used to make
jellies, jams, candy and pickles.
Photographed May 17.

**(e) Yellow Sorrel** *Oxalis corniculata* L., family
Oxalidaceae. Introduced, annual or perennial.
Found as a garden weed and in waste places.
Rather uncommon found mainly in the south of
England. Leaves often purplish. Height to 12cm.
Flowers May to Sept. See 18(m), 60(f).

**(f) Upright Yellow Sorrel** *Oxalis europaea* Jord.,
family Oxalidaceae. An introduced perennial.
Found occasionally as a garden weed and in waste
places. Rare, except in the Surrey area. Height to
12cm. Distinguished from 60(e) by not rooting at
the leaf junctions. The flower on this specimen is
not out. Flowers May to Aug. See 18(m), 60(e).

**(g) Hairy Medick** or **Toothed Medick** *Medicago
polymorpha* L., family Leguminosae. A native
annual. Very rare, found near the sea on sandy soil
in the south. A piece of black Medick has crept in
behind this specimen by accident. The Hairy
Medick is the specimen on right with coiled spiny
fruit and few tiny flowers. Height to 45cm.
Flowers May to Aug. See 38(b), 52(f), 48(e).

**(h) Wild Pansy** or **Heartsease** *Viola tricolor* L.,
family Violaceae. A native annual or perennial.
Quite common throughout Britain on grassland
and wasteland but rarer in Ireland. Height to
30cm. In Midsummer Night's Dream, Oberon
squeezes the juice of this pansy into Titania's eyes
so that she will fall in love with Bottom. It has been
commonly associated with love. Flowers April to
Sept. See 16(g), 18(j), 20(l), 22(b), 26(e), 66(g).

**(i) Lady's Mantle** *Alchemilla xanthochlora* Rothm.,
family Rosaceae. A native perennial of grassland
found at lower altitudes than 60(j) or 32 (j). Height
to 35cm. Flowers May to Sept. For further details,
see 32(j), 60(j), 92(k).

**(j) Lady's Mantle** *Alchemilla glabra* Neygen,
family Rosaceae. A native perennial of grassland
open woods and rocky ledges. This is the most
common species of Lady's Mantle on mountains
and rare in lowland areas. Height to 35cm.
Flowers May to Sept. For further details, see 32(j),
60(i), 92(k).

**(k) Shrubby Cinquefoil** *Potentilla fruticosa* L.,
family Rosaceae. A native shrub. Very rare, found
wild only on rocks near Helvellyn and the Burren
in Ireland. Height to 1m. Flowers May to July.
See 56(i), 42(c), 142(f), 142(g).

**(l) Rough Hawkbit** *Leontondon hispidus* L., family
Compositae. A native perennial found on meadows
and grassy slopes, especially on chalk. Common
in England, scattered in southern Scotland, rare
elsewhere. Height to 50cm. Flowers May to Sept.
See 137(e).
**Lesser Hawkbit** *L. taraxacoides* L. Native
perennial of dunes and dry grassland. Fairly
common throughout Britain but rare in Scotland
and north Ireland. Height to 25cm. Much smaller
than Rough Hawkbit, and the outer flowerheads
are grey-violet beneath. Flowers June to Sept.

**(c) Buckthorn** *Rhamnus catharticus* L., family
Rhamnaceae. A native shrub, thorny. Found in
scrubland, hedges and woods on chalk. Quite
common in the south east; rare in Ireland and
not found in Scotland. The berries may be used as
a purgative but are very strong. Flowers May to
June. See Fruit 164(l) and also 76(a).
Photographed May 25.

**(d) Black Pine** *Pinus nigra* Arnold, family
Pinaceae. An introduced tree. Much planted and
occasionally found naturalised. Height to 45m.
Flowers May to June. See Cones 170(f), others
62(d), 168(g), 170(g). Photographed May 25.

photograph taken 26 May ○ represents 1 centimetre

photograph taken 25 May

(**a**) **Dewberry** *Rubus caesius* L., family Rosaceae. Native shrub. Common in the south and east of England, scattered elsewhere and absent in north Scotland. Trailing stems may reach 3m. in length. Similar to the Bramble but has weaker stems with fewer prickles, the leaves all have 3 leaflets and the flowers always white. The most striking difference, however, is between the fruit. Flowers end of May to Sept. See Fruit 147(d) and Bramble 108(o).

(**b**) **Raspberry** *Rubus idaeus* L., family Rosaceae. A native shrub, common. Found in woods, scrub heaths and hedges throughout Britain. Height to 1.5m. This is the wild Raspberry from which the cultivated garden varieties have been bred. The petals are tiny and drop off at the slightest touch. Flowers May to Aug. See Fruit 108(j) and Bramble 108(o).

(**c**) **Wild Rhododendron** *Rhododendron ponticum* L., family Ericaceae. An introduced, evergreen shrub commonly planted in woods and gardens, it has now become naturalised in many places and is often regarded as a troublesome weed. Height to 3m. Flowers May to June. See 38(k).

(**d**) **Scots Pine** *Pinus sylvestris* L., family Pinaceae. A native tree. Commonly planted and naturalised all over the country but the true wild ones are found only in north Scotland. Height up to 30m. The bark is a distinctive golden orange and the needles are always in pairs. Flowers May to June. For cone see 168(j), other Pines 60(d), 168(g), 170(g).

(**e**) **Giant Hogweed** *Heracleum mantegazzianum* Somm. & Lev., family Umbelliferae. Recently introduced. Biennial. An escape from gardens it is rapidly spreading in waste places, near streams and roads. Once established, if allowed to flourish, it may become a dominant species. Grows to a height of 3.5m. and may be seen from a great distance; the stems may be up to 10cm. in diameter. Children should be warned against cutting them especially if they then use the stems for blow pipes or telescopes, as the juice may cause severe blisters after the skin has been exposed to sunlight. It has a most powerful smell and if kept indoors, becomes almost overpowering. The dried stems and fruits are quite popular for giant flower arrangements. Flowers June to July. See Hogweed 62(f).

(**f**) **Hogweed** or **Cow Parsnip** *Heracleum sphondylium* L., family Umbelliferae. A native biennial. Very common all over the British Isles. Found in grassy places, on roadsides, hedges, woods and wasteplaces. Height to 1.75m. Up until recently the plants were gathered for pig fodder which gives it the name Hogweed. The young shoots are quite pleasant to eat, rather like asparagus. Flowers June to Aug. See 62(e) above.

(**g**) **Angelica** *Angelica archangelica* L., family Umbelliferae. An introduced perennial. This is the garden angelica; it has escaped in a few places and naturalised on river banks and deserted river islands. Once established, it may quickly become dominant. A good example of this is at the tidal Chiswick Eyot on the Thames. Height to 2m. The confectionery angelica is made from this plant by candying the stems. The roots have been widely used medicinally for treatment of the digestion and anaemia, loss of appetite and migraines. An infusion is made of one ounce of crushed root to one pint of boiling water, strained and then sweetened with a little honey. Flowers June to Aug. See Wild Angelica 148(c).

e

f

g

photograph taken 1 June ◯ represents 1 centimetre

photograph taken 25 May

**(e) Hemlock Water Dropwort** *Oenanthe crocata*
L., family Umbelliferae. A native perennial.
Common to the west and south of England, the
west of Scotland and in the south of Ireland; fairly
rare elsewhere. Grows in wet places, marshes and
wasteland, often near the sea. Height to 1.5m.
Very poisonous. Its smell is very strong. Flowers
May to Aug. See 110(f), 126(b), 156(f).

**(f) Ground Elder, Bishop's-weed** or
**Goutweed** *Aegopodium podagraria* L., family
Umbelliferae. Perennial. Possibly introduced by
the Romans but now very common all over the
British Isles in waste places, roadsides and as a
garden weed. Height to 90cm. The leaves are
similar to that of the Elder shrub, hence its name.
Although thought of as a pest by gardeners, the
leaves in fact are very good to eat; cooked as
spinach and served with butter. Flowers May to
July.

**(g) Horse-radish** *Armoracia rusticana* P. Gaertn.,
B. Meyer & Scherb., family Cruciferae. An
introduced perennial. Common in the south east
of England, rare in Scotland and Ireland. This
plant is often cultivated but has become widely
naturalised. Height to 1m. The lovely glossy leaves
stand out when you see them on a roadside or
bank. The root of this plant is used for horseradish
sauce. Flowers May to June. Compare with 116(e).

**(h) Hemlock** *Conium maculatum* L., family
Umbelliferae. A native biennial. Common in
England, less common elsewhere. Grows mainly in
damp places but also on disturbed ground. Height
to 2m. This plant is very poisonous and is said to
have been the drug used to poison Socrates.
Children should be warned against making blow
pipes or whistles from the smooth, hollow stem.
The distinguishing features are the purple blotches
on the stem, its great height and attractive
feathery leaves. Flowers May to July.

**(i) Rough Chervil** *Chaerophyllum temulentum* L.,
family Umbelliferae. A native biennial. Common
in England and Wales, not common in Scotland,
rare in Ireland. Found on roadsides, hedges and
grassy places. Height to 80cm. The name
*temulentum* is from the Latin for drunkenness as this
is a symptom of poisoning by this plant. Flowers
May to July.

**(j) Broad-leaved Dock** *Rumex obtusifolius* L.,
family Polygonaceae. A native perennial. Very
common all over the British Isles. Grows on
roadsides, hedges, waste ground and fields and as a
garden weed. Height to 1m. There are two
common docks, this one, and the Curled Dock.
This one has much larger leaves and is the one
normally used for nettle stings. Flowers May to
Oct. See 106(i), 126(e), 126(i), 126(j), 126(k).
**Golden Dock** *R. maritimus* L. A native annual or
perennial found near ponds and near the sea. Rare
in England and Ireland, not found in Scotland.
Height to 75cm. The leaves turn golden yellow
when it is in fruit. Flowers June to Sept.
**Northern Dock** *R. longifolius* DC. A native
perennial found near rivers and damp grassy
places from Lancashire and Yorkshire northwards.
It has large, slightly crinkly leaves. Flowers June
to July.

**(a) Goosegrass, Cleavers** or **Sticky Willie**
*Galium aparine* L., family Rubiaceae. A native
annual. Very common all over the British Isles in
hedges, woods, scrub and waste places. Straggling,
climbing plant can have stems up to 1m. long. The
stem leaves and fruit have hooked bristles which
catch on animals and clothing. Flowers May to
Aug. See Fruit 134(a), see also 30(d), 56(g), 78(d),
86(g), 112(a).

**(b) Field Poppy** *Papaver rhoeas* L., family
Papaveraceae. A native annual. Most common in
south England and south west Ireland; less
common in east Wales, Scotland and northern
Ireland. Grows on disturbed ground, roadsides,
arable fields and waste places. Height to 50cm.
Ceres the corn goddess is depicted with a crown of
poppies. Flowers May to Aug. See 71(a), 82(c).

**(c) Star-of-Bethlehem** *Ornithogalum umbellatum*
L., family Liliaceae. Probably native. Bulb.
Unknown in Ireland, uncommon in Scotland,
most common in south east England. Found on
grassy places. Height to 25cm. Star-of-Bethlehem
because of the shape of the flowers. The flowers do
not open on dull days. Flowers April to June.

**(d) Marsh Horsetail** *Equisetum palustre* L., family
Equisetaceae. A native rhizome found on wet
land, marshes and bogs throughout the British
Isles. Height to 50cm. The horsetails are not
flowering plants, this one has been included for
comparison. There are many others with a similar
appearance, either larger or smaller, bushier or
less bushy. See 102(a).

photograph taken 1 June ◯ represents 1 centimetre

photograph taken 1 June

**Meadow Cranesbill** *Geranium pratense* L., family Geraniaceae. A native perennial found locally in limestone areas on roadsides and banks; more common in the south. Very rare in Ireland and north Scotland. Height to 60cm. One of the most striking cranesbills with its distinctive big blue flowers. Flowers May to Sept. See 44(e) and other geraniums.

(**b**) **Bladder Campion** *Silene vulgaris* (Moench) Garcke, family Caryophyllaceae. A native perennial. Common field and roadside plant, especially on limestone. Rare in north Scotland. Height to 80cm. It may be identified by its large bladder-like calyx. Believed in Scotland to be an aphrodisiac for cows. Flowers May to Sept. See 30(h), 44(d), 48(f), 72(c).

(**c**) **Thrift** or **Sea Pink** *Armeria maritima* (Miller) Willd., family Plumbaginaceae. A native perennial. Common on cliffs, salt marshes and sandy places also inland mountains throughout the British Isles. Height to 15cm. Thrift, known as the plant of sympathy, is a popular garden plant. It was featured on George VI brass threepenny bits. Flowers April to Aug.

(**d**) **Garden Catmint** *Nepeta × faassenii* Bergmans ex Stearn, family Labiatae. An introduced perennial. A common garden plant sometimes found as an escape. Height to 30cm. Cats love to roll in and eat this plant as they do Wild Catmint. Flowers May to Sept.

(**e**) **Yarrow** or **Milfoil** *Achillea millefolium* L., family Compositae. A native perennial. Very common all over the British Isles, on roadsides, disturbed ground, meadows, hedgebanks and as a garden weed. Height to 45cm. Its use in the treatment of wounds is said to go back to Achilles who used it for wounds made by iron weapons. The flowers may be tinged with pink or even as dark as purple. Flowers June to Nov. See 98(i).

(**f**) **Hairy Rock-cress** *Arabis hirsuta* (L.) Scop., family Cruciferae. A native biennial or perennial. Not very common; found on limestone and chalk slopes, rocks and walls scattered throughout Britain. Height to 50cm. The leaves vary a great deal; coastal ones can be tiny. Flowers May to Aug. See 72(i).

(**g**) **Mountain Pansy** or **Yellow Violet** *Viola lutea* Hudson, family Violaceae. A native perennial found on mountain grassland, not in southern England and very rare in Ireland. Height to 20cm. Modern garden pansies are said to have arisen from hybrids between this species and the Wild Pansy, 60(h). The flowers may be yellow, blue-violet, red-violet or a combination of these but always yellow at the base of the lower petal. Flowers May to Aug. See 16(g), 18(j), 20(l), 22(b), 26(e).

(**h**) **Cotton-grass** or **Hare's-tail** *Eriophorum vaginatum* L., family Cyperaceae. Native perennial common in damp, peaty areas and moorland bogs. Rare in south east England, common elsewhere. Height to 50cm. The white, fluffy, fruiting heads are a well-known sign of boggy ground. Flowers April to May. Fruits May to June.
**Common Cotton-grass** *E. angustifolium* Honck. Native, perennial. Found in bogs, bog-pools and acid fens. Common in north and west, rare in south due to drainage. Height to 60cm. Differs from 66(h) by having more than one flowering head. Flowers May to June. Fruits June to July.

(**i**) **Bilberry, Blaeberry** or **Whortleberry** *Vaccinium myrtilis* L., family Ericaceae. Native shrub. Very common on moors, mountains and in woods on acid soils; rare in south east. Height to 50cm. Dried leaves have been used in the Hebrides as a substitute for tea. Flowers April to June. See Fruits 154(g) and compare 40(g), 80(f), 154(g).

(**j**) **London Pride** *Saxifraga spathularis × umbrosa*, family Saxifragaceae. Perennial. Commonly grown in gardens sometimes escaping and becoming naturalised. Scattered distribution. Height to 40cm. This is a hybrid between St Patrick's Cabbage and Wood Saxifrage. Flowers June to Aug.

(**k**) **Pellitory-of-the wall** *Parietaria diffusa* Mert. & Koch, family Urticaceae. A native perennial of old walls and rocks; common in the south but rare in north England, Scotland and northern Ireland. Height to 70cm. As a medicinal herb, it has been used to relieve bladder stones as well as coughs and burns. Its colour may vary from green to bright red. Flowers June to Oct.

(**l**) **Hawkweed** *Hieraceum brittanicum* F. J. Hanb., family Compositae. Native perennial of rocks in mountain districts in England and Wales and Ireland. Not found in north Scotland. Height to 35cm. Flowers May to Aug. See 54(h), 130(d), 142(j).

photograph taken 25 May

(**e**) **Clary** *Salvia verbenaca* L., family Labiatae. A native perennial. Common on dry pastures and roadsides in south England; rare elsewhere and absent from north Scotland. Height to 65cm. The seeds may be soaked in water and the mucilage used to cleanse and soothe irritation in the eyes. Roots provide a snuff, and the leaves used as a herb with lemon or orange juice. Two white marks on the lower lip are a distinctive feature. Flowers May to Aug. See 68(h).

(**f**) **Purging Flax** or **Fairy Flax** *Linum catharticum* L., family Linaceae. A native annual very common on calcareous grassland but also common throughout Britain on grassland, heaths, rocks and dunes. Height to 25cm. An infusion of the dried plant is purgative but may be dangerous since large quantities are extremely poisonous. Flowers June to Sept. See 68(j).

(**g**) **Small Scabious** *Scabiosa columbaria* L., family Dipsacaceae. A native perennial. Common on dry calcareous pasture in England but absent from Scotland and Ireland. Height to 65cm. The name is derived from the Latin scabies meaning itch. Culpepper advises using the bruised herb and infusions of it in the treatment of sores and ulcers. Mixed with borax and samphire it clears the face of pimples and freckles, and the scalp of dandruff or itching. Flowers June to Aug. See 84(e), 138(g), 150(e).

(**h**) **Meadow Clary** *Salvia pratensis* L., family Labiatae. A native perennial. Rare, found only on calcareous grassland in south England. Height to 80cm. Flowers June to July. Compare 68(e).

(**i**) **Long-stalked Cranesbill** *Geranium columbinum* L., family Geraniaceae. A native annual. Most common in south England on dry grassland and scrub. Rare elsewhere. Height to 60cm. Flowers June to July. See others 32(h), 44(j), 44(k), 48(g), 52(h).

(**j**) **Perennial Flax** *Linum perenne* L., ssp. *anglicum* (Mill.) Ockendon, family Linaceae. A native perennial. Rare, found only on calcareous grassland in east England. Height to 40cm. Flowers June to July. See 68(f).
**Pale Flax** *L. bienne* Mill. A native annual, biennial or perennial; common on dry grassland on southern coasts and south east Ireland. Height to 40cm. The flower is a paler blue than 68(j), and the cultivated flax which yields linseed oil was possibly derived from this species. Flowers May to Sept.

(**k**) **Hoary Plantain** *Plantago media* L., family Plantaginaceae. A native perennial. Most common in southeast England in grassland, waste places and roadsides, also as a garden weed; less common in north England and rare in Scotland and Ireland. Height to 25cm. Leaves may be used in similar ways to *P. major* and *P. lanceolata*. Flowers May to Aug. See 54(k), 70(c), 90(a).

(**l**) **Spotted Cat's Ear** *Hypochoeris maculata* L., family Compositae. A native perennial. Very rare on calcareous grassland in very scattered localities in England and Wales. Height to 50cm. The leaves have distinctive dark purple spots. Flowers June to Aug. See 74(g).

(**a**) **Common Speedwell** *Veronica officinalis* L., family Scrophulariaceae. A native perennial of grassland, heath and open woods on drier soils. Common throughout Britain. Height to 30cm. An infusion of the whole plant, taken 3 times a day is said to relieve bronchitis, whooping-cough, indigestion, gout, bladder-stones, rheumatism and liver complaints. Flowers May to Aug. See other speedwells.

(**b**) **Purple Milk-vetch** *Astragalus danicus* Retz., family Leguminosae. A native perennial. Grows among short grass on dunes and calcareous soils. Rare except in the east, where it is frequently found near the coast. In Ireland, only on Aran islands. Height to 30cm. A very attractive blue-purple flower, not to be confused with the clovers. Flowers May to July. See 81(f), 98(g).

(**c**) **Smooth Hawk's-beard** *Crepis capillaris* (L.) Wallr., family Compositae. A native, usually annual, of grassland heaths, walls, waste places and roadsides. Common throughout Britain, but not on mountains. Height to 75cm. Flowerheads often reddish underneath. Flowers May to Sept. See 54(l), 82(g).

(**d**) **Cat's foot** or **Mountain Everlasting** *Antennaria dioica* (L.) Gaertner., family Compositae. Native perennial. Common on heaths, dry pastures and dry mountain slopes in the Scottish Highlands and in west Ireland; less common elsewhere, rare in the south. Height to 20cm. Male and female flowers are on separate plants; the illustrated male white, and the female usually rose-pink. Flowers May to July.

e

f

g

h

i

j

k

l

photograph taken 4 June ○ represents 1 centimetre

(a) **Portland Spurge** *Euphorbia portlandica* L., family Euphorbiaceae. A natural annual or biennial. Rare, found on the west coast of England and Wales and around the Irish coast on sand. Height to 35cm. Flowers May to Aug. See other spurges.

(b) **Venus's Looking Glass** *Legousia hybrida* (L.) Delarbre, family Campanulaceae. Native annual found in arable fields. Fairly common in south and east England, absent from Ireland and Scotland. Height to 25cm. Flowers May to Aug.

(c) **Great Plantain** or **Rat's Tail** *Plantago major* L., family Plantaginaceae. Native perennial of open places by roads, on cultivated ground and wasteland. Very common throughout Britain. Height to 15cm. It has ancient magical associations, its power being suggested by its resistance to rough treatment. Flowers May to Sept. See 54(k), 68(k), 90(a).

(d) **Field Rose** *Rosa arvensis* Huds., family Rosaceae. A native shrub. Quite common in southern and central England and Wales and also in the south east corner of Ireland; in Scotland it is only found as an introduction. May be found in hedges, woods and scrub. Height to a maximum of 1m. Smaller than the Dog Rose. Flowers June to July. See 50(d), 76(b), 86(a).

(e) **Musk Orchid** *Herminium monarchis* (L.) R.Br., family Orchidaceae. A native root-tuber. Very rare and found on chalk downs and pastures in southern England. Height to 15cm. Flowers June to July.

(f) **Tall Broomrape** *Orobanche elatior* Sutton, family Orobanchaceae. A native parasite. Locally common in Salisbury Plain and the Cambridge area, very rare elsewhere and absent in Wales, Scotland and Ireland. It grows as a parasite, mainly on the roots of Greater Knapweed in dry, calcareous areas. Height to 65cm. Flowers June to July. See 94(a).

**(a) Long-headed Poppy** *Papaver dubium* L., family Papaveraceae. A native annual. Common and found throughout the British Isles; rare in the east. Grows on waste places and arable land. Height to 50cm. Flowers June to July. See 64(b), 82(c).
**Prickly Poppy** *P. argemone* L. Native or introduced annual. Fairly common in south east England. Height to 40cm. The seed heads are long and covered with bristles. Flowers June to July.

**(b) Dark Red Helleborine** *Epipactis atrorubens* (Hoffm.) Schult., family Orchidaceae. A native rhizome. Very rare, found in the Midlands, the north Wales coast, the coast of northern Scotland and near the Burren in Ireland. Grows on limestone rocks and screes, sometimes in woods, sometimes in the open. Height to 30cm. Flowers June to July. See 89(c), 94(b), 132(a), 132(b), 156(a).

**(c) Hoary Whitlow Grass** *Draba incana* L., family Cruciferae. A native annual to biennial. Rare, found in the Midlands, Scotland, northern Ireland and near Caernarvon. Grows on cliffs, rocks and screes. Height to 45cm. Flowers June to July. See 20(b).

**(d) Northern Marsh Orchid** *Dactylorhiza purpurella* (T. & T. A. Steph.) Soó syn. *Dactylorchis purpurella* (T. & T. A. Steph.) Vermeul., family Orchidaceae. A native root-tuber fairly common in Scotland and northern England but rare in Wales and Ireland. Found in marshes, fens, and damp pastures. Height to 25cm. Sometimes has spotted leaves. Flowers June to July.

**(e) Water Soldier** *Stratiotes aloides* L., family Hydrocharitaceae. A native herb of ponds and ditches in calcareous regions. Rather rare, most often found in east England but also recorded in Wales and probably introduced in Ireland and south Scotland. Height above water to 25cm. The plant is normally submerged but rises to the surface at flowering time. Flowers June to Aug.

**(f) Oyster Plant** *Mertensia maritima* (L.) S. F. Gray, family Boraginaceae. A native perennial found on shingle by the sea. Rather rare, found mainly on the west coast from north Wales northwards and on north Scottish coasts; in Ireland on the north and east coasts. Height to 50cm. Sadly, this beautiful seaside plant is decreasing. Flowers June to Aug.

photograph taken 4 June

**(e) Rock Cinquefoil** *Potentilla rupestris* L., family Rosaceae. A native perennial. Very rare, but found on basic rocks in 2 localities in Wales and one in north Scotland. Height to 50cm. Distinguished by its large white flowers in a loose cluster. Flowers May to June. See 22(c).

**(f) Common Melilot** *Melilotus officinalis* (L.) Pall., family Leguminosae. Introduced biennial. Common in south east England, in meadows, waste places and roadsides. Height to 130cm. It was widely used by the ancient Egyptians who included it in their incantation to ward off death. The lower petal is shorter than the upper ones. Flowers June to Sept. See 54(g).
**Tall Melilot** *M. altissima* Thuill. Possibly introduced biennial or perennial. Common in south east England in waste places and woods. Height to 150cm. Differs from Common Melilot in that the parts of the yellow flowers are all equal in length. Flowers June to Aug.
**Small-flowered Melilot** *M. indica* (L.) All. An introduced annual. Less common and scattered through England. Similar to Common Melilot but much smaller flowers. Flowers June to Oct.

**(g) Welsh Poppy** *Meconopsis cambrica* (L.) Vig., family Papaveraceae. A native perennial. Grows in damp, rocky sites in south west England and Wales. Extensively grown in gardens throughout Britain, frequently escaping and becoming naturalised. Height to 50cm. Flowers June to Aug.

**(h) Deadly Nightshade** *Atropa bella-donna* L., family Solanaceae. Native, an annual or biennial plant. Fairly common on chalk in the south east, rare elsewhere. It grows in scrub, woods, wood-edges and thickets. Height to 1.25m. This is the true Deadly Nightshade. The whole plant is very poisonous and children should be warned against the attractive berries. A child may be killed by eating two. The drug atropine, which is used to dilate the pupils for optical examination comes from this plant. The name *bella-donna* means 'beautiful lady', the juice once being used as a cosmetic. Flowers June to Aug. Fruit see 162(i) and other nightshades 48(j), 116(g).

**(i) Tower Mustard** *Arabis glabra* (L.) Bernh., family Cruciferae. A native biennial. A rare plant, mainly of east England, absent from Scotland and Ireland, rare in Wales. Grows on dry banks, roadsides, waste places, rocks and cliffs. Height to as much as 1m. Flowers May to July.

**(j) Field Fleawort** *Senecio integrifolius* (L.) Clairv., family Compositae. A native perennial. Rare, it is found on chalk grassland in central and southern England; not found in Scotland or Ireland and very rare in Wales. Height to 30cm., except the variety *maritimus* which may grow to 60cm. This variety is only found on Holyhead Island and in Westmorland. Flowers June to July.

**(k) Navelwort** or **Pennywort** *Umbilicus rupestris* (Salisb.) Dandy, family Crassulaceae. A native perennial. Common in west England, Wales and southern Ireland. It is rare in the east and north of England and Scotland. Grows on rock crevices and walls. Height to 30cm. Flowers May to Aug.

**(l) Swinecress** or **Wartcress** *Coronopus squamatus* (Forsk.) Aschers., family Cruciferae. A native annual or biennial. Found on waste ground tracks and paths. Common in south and south east England, rather rare elsewhere. The sprawling stems may be up to 30cm. long. Flowers June to Sept. See 92(e).

**(a) Columbine** *Aquilegia vulgaris* L., family Ranunculaceae. A native perennial. Uncommon. Found in woods, damp places and fens throughout England and Wales, mainly in the south. Often grown as a garden plant. Height to 70cm. An infusion has been used to treat a sore mouth or throat and as a lotion for rheumatism. However, this plant is poisonous. Flowers May to June.

**(b) Astrantia** *Astrantia major* L., family Umbelliferae. Introduced perennial. Rare but naturalised in woods, wood-edges and meadows in a few places. Height to 60cm. Flowers May to July.

**(c) Sand Catchfly** *Silene conica* L., family Caryophyllaceae. A native annual. Rare, but found on sand dunes in south east England and north east Scotland and a few other scattered localities. Height to 30cm. Flowers May to June. See 66(b).

**(d) Corn Crowfoot** or **Corn Buttercup** *Ranunculus arvensis* L., family Ranunculaceae. Possibly native, annual. A cornfield weed, particularly on calcareous soils in south east England. Rare or absent elsewhere. Height to 50cm. Poisonous. Flowers June to July. See 20(g), 22(d), 100(i).
**Small-flowered Buttercup** *R. parviflorus* L., Native annual of dry grassy or bare places especially on lime. Uncommon. Erect or spreading stems may reach 35cm. Flowers May to June.

e

f

g

h

i

j

k

l

photograph taken 4 June

(e) **Celery-leaved Crowfoot** *Ranunculus sceleratus* L., family Ranunculaceae. Native annual or over-wintering plant. Common in and near slow streams, ditches and muddy ponds, common in south east England and rare elsewhere. Poisonous. Flowers May to Sept. Compare 20(g).

(f) **Common Mallow** *Malva sylvestris* L., family Malvaceae. A native perennial. Very common on waste places and roadsides in England and Wales particularly the south; rarer in Scotland and Ireland. Height to 50cm. This plant has long been used as a soothing agent in treating inflammation of the skin, eyes, and respiratory, gastric and urinary systems. Chewing fresh flowers relieves toothache and crushed in olive oil they relieve bee and wasp stings. Flowers June to Sept. See 96(f), 122(h).

(g) **Cat's Ear** *Hypochoeris radicata* L., family Compositae. A native perennial. Common in meadows, dunes, roadsides and waste places and as a garden weed throughout Britain. Height to 50cm. The leaves may be used in salad and can be gathered practically all year round. Flowers May to Sept. See 68(l).

(h) **Wild Carrot** *Daucus carota* L., family Umbelliferae. A native biennial. Common on fields, grassy and waste places, especially near the sea or on chalky soil. Uncommon in central and east Scotland. Height to 90cm. The flowers are frequently tinged a pinkish-purple which can make them look quite different from the illustrated specimen. Flowers June to Aug.

(i) **Weld, Dyer's Rocket** *Reseda luteola* L., family Resedaceae. A native biennial. Common on disturbed ground, roadsides, arable land, walls, particularly on calcareous soils. Found throughout the British Isles but less common in Ireland and rare in the north. This plant provides one of the most ancient dyes and used to be cultivated in England for this purpose. Its flavone dye gives a bright yellow colour to fabric. Flowers June to Aug. See 36(k), 96(e).

(j) **Great Yellow-cress** *Rorippa amphibia* (L.) Besser, family Cruciferae. A native perennial. Common by ponds, ditches and rivers in south east England, rare or absent elsewhere; scattered in Ireland. Height to 1m. Flowers June to Aug.
**Marsh Yellow-cress** *R. islandica* (Oeder) Borbas A native annual or biennial of most places throughout Britain but rare in the north. Height to 50cm. Flowers are paler yellow than Great Yellow-cress and slightly smaller. Flowers June to Sept.
**Creeping Yellow-cress** *R. sylvestris* (L.) Besser. A native perennial of moist ground near streams. Less common than Marsh Yellow-cress; rare in north and west. Height to 45cm. Leaves are deeply cut and lower ones have stalks. Flowers June to Aug.

(k) **Water Figwort** or **Water Betony** *Scrophularia auriculata* L. syn. *S. aquatica* auct., family Scrophulariaceae. A native perennial. Common by streams, pools and in damp woods in England but absent in the north. Rare in Wales and Ireland. Height to 85cm. Mixing the crushed leaves with lard forms an ointment which soothes swellings. The two small ears or wings at the base of the leaves is a common distinguishing feature. Flowers June to Sept. See 98(h), 162(d).

(a) **Brooklime** *Veronica beccabunga* L., family Scrophulariaceae. A native perennial. Grows in streams, marshes, ponds, ditches and wet places. Very common except in north west Scotland. Height to 60cm. Often found together with watercress, it may also be eaten as salad although has a bitter taste. It was one of the plants recommended against scurvy. Flowers May to Aug. See 90(i).

(b) **Lesser Spearwort** *Ranunculus flammula* L., family Ranunculaceae. A perennial native. Common in wet places throughout the British Isles. Height to 70cm. The root was pounded then applied to the skin in a limpet shell to produce

blistering which was thought to extract disease, a practice much used on plague sores. Poisonous. Flowers May to Sept. See 106(k).

(c) **Marsh Pea** *Lathyrus palustris* L., family Leguminosae. A native perennial of fens. Rare and scattered mostly in east England and central Ireland; absent from Scotland. Height to 1.20m Flowers May to July. See 56(h), 102(k), 138(h).

(d) **Water Violet** *Hottonia palustris* L., family Primulaceae. A native perennial which grows in ponds and ditches. Fairly common in east England rare in the west and Wales and absent from Scotland and Ireland. Height to 40cm. above water. This specimen is rather pale in colour, the flower more usually being lilac with a yellow throat. Flowers May to June.

photograph taken 7 June

**(a) Alder Buckthorn** or **Black Dogwood**
*Frangula alnus* Mill., family Rhamnaceae. A native shrub or small tree found on fens, bog margins, heaths, limestone scrub and in open woods, usually on moist, peaty soils. Fairly common through England and Wales, rare in Ireland absent in Scotland. Height to 5m. Poisonous. Flowers May to June. See Fruits 164(m) and 60(c).

**(b) Dog Rose** *Rosa canina* L., family Rosaceae. A native shrub, common in woods, scrub and hedgerows throughout Britain, though not on mountains. Height to 3m. An extremely variable species. Over 60 varieties and forms have been recognised and the flowers may vary from pink to white. Flowers June to July. See Fruits 172(k) and 50(d), 70(d), 86(a).

**(c) Tutsan** or **Sweet Amber** *Hypericum androsaemum* L., family Guttiferae. A native, shrubby perennial. Fairly common in damp woods and hedgerows and frequently grown in gardens. Rare in the east and north. Height to 1m. The leaves are slightly aromatic and used to be pressed between the pages of the Bible for luck. Flowers June to Aug. See Fruits 162(h) and compare 104(e), 108(k).

**(d) Holm Oak** or **Evergreen Oak** *Quercus ilex* L., family Fagaceae. An introduced tree, commonly planted and sometimes naturalised in the south of England. Height to 30m. This tree differs from other British Oaks by being evergreen. The leaves are also darker green and have a harder texture. Flowers May to June. Fruits Sept. See Fruit 174(h) and 34(e), 34(f).

**(e) Monkshood** *Aconitum napellus* L., family Ranunculaceae. A native perennial of shady stream banks in south Wales and south west England, although, together with other varieties, it is often grown in gardens. Height to as much as 1m. Although Monkshood has been used medicinally to treat neuralgia, gout, arthritis, rheumatism and measles, it is extremely poisonous. Only a small amount may cause death within a very short time. Flowers May to July.

**(f) Tree Lupin** *Lupinus arboreus* Sims, family Leguminosae. Introduced shrub, which has become naturalised on waste places mostly on coasts in south and east England. Height to 3m. The name lupin is derived from the Latin for 'wolf' indicating 'wolf pea', a pea fit only for wolves. Flowers end of May to Sept.

**(g) Large Cuckoo Pint** *Arum italicum* Mill., family Araceae. A native perennial which grows only on the south coast of England and in the Channel Isles. It prefers light shade and often stony ground. Height to 25cm. The main distinguishing features from the more common Lords and Ladies are the unmarked leaves and slightly later flowering time. Bright red berries similar to those of Lords and Ladies are produced in autumn. Flowers April to June. Fruits Aug. to Sept. See 40(b).

**(h) Milk-thistle** *Silybum marianum* Adanson, family Compositae. An introduced annual or biennial. Uncommon and found naturalised or casually throughout lowland Britain; rare in Scotland. Height to 2m. The milky-white veins on these stunning leaves give this plant its name. Legend has it they were formed by milk which fell from the Virgin Mary's breast as she suckled Jesus. The leaves may be boiled like spinach and the stems soaked to remove bitterness and then stewed as rhubarb. Flowers June to Aug.

**(i) Yellow Flag** *Iris pseudacorus* L., family Iridaceae. A native perennial of marshes, wet woods and wet ground by rivers and ditches. Common throughout the British Isles. Height to 1.20m. Iris is the Greek word for 'rainbow'. To the Greeks it symbolised life and resurrection and is associated with Osiris, the first Pharaoh to become immortal. Also thought to be the source of the fleur-de-lys symbol of French royalty, although it is not clear to which species this refers. Flowers May to July. See Fruit 140(i) and 18(i).

**(j) Welted Thistle** *Carduus acanthoides* L., family Compositae. A native biennial of stream sides, damp hedgerows, waste places and road sides. Common in the south, rarer in the north and west. Height to 1m. The stems have distinct wavy-edged, spiny wings or welts which provide its common name. The flower heads are also smaller than the other species. Flowers June to Aug. Compare 86(j), 98(l), 112(c).

e

f

g

h

i

j

photograph taken 7 June ○ represents 1 centimetre

photograph taken 7 June

(**e**) **Dame's Violet** *Hesperis matronalis* L., family Cruciferae. Introduced biennial or perennial found as a garden escape and sometimes naturalised in hedgerows and meadows. Scattered throughout Britain. Height to 80cm. Flowers May to July. Compare 18(f).

(**f**) **Nottingham Catchfly** *Silene nutans* L., family Caryophyllaceae. A native perennial. Rare, though found on dry slopes, rocks, walls, cliff-ledges and shingle in certain isolated localities in England, Scotland and Wales. Height to 50cm. The illustrated flowers are a bit shrivelled. Flowers May to July. See 48(b), 66(b).

(**g**) **Broad-leaved Willowherb** *Epilobium montanum* L., family Onagraceae. A native perennial found in woods, hedgerows, walls, roadsides and as a garden weed. Very common throughout Britain. Height to 50cm. The leaves are distinctly oval shaped and pointed. Flowers June to Aug. See 94(h), 104(n).
**Short-fruited Willowherb** *E. obscurum* Schreb. A native perennial which grows in marshes, damp woods and by streams and ditches. Fairly common throughout Britain. Similar to Spear-leaved Willowherb but has unstalked leaves and short seed pods. Flowers June to Aug.
**Marsh Willowherb** *E. palustre* L. Native perennial of marshes, ditches and acid fens. Common throughout Britain. Height to 50cm. Rather slender with pairs of narrow, unstalked leaves up the stem. Flowers July to Aug.
**Square-stemmed Willowherb** *E. tetragonum* L. A native perennial of damp woods, ditches, marshes and hedgerows. Fairly common in south England and Wales; rare in north and Ireland. It has a square stem and strap-shaped, unstalked leaves. Flowers June to Aug.

(**h**) **Thale Cress** *Arabidopsis thaliana* (L.) Heynh., family Cruciferae. An annual weed of walls and banks. Fairly common throughout the British Isles. Height variable to 45cm. Flowers March to June.

(**i**) **Ramping Fumitory** *Fumaria capreolata* L., family Papaveraceae. A native annual of waste ground, hedgerows and cultivated ground. Uncommon, except in scattered localities, especially near sea. Climbs to a height of 1m. Flowers May to Sept. See 52(l), 109(b).

(**j**) **Melancholy Thistle** *Cirsium helenioides* (L.) Hill, family Compositae. A native perennial of hilly grasslands and scrub and by streams. Fairly common in Scotland and north England; rare or absent elsewhere. Height to 70cm. The flower heads droop at first, hence the name Melancholy. Flowers June to Aug. See 86(j).

(**k**) **Hare's-foot** *Trifolium arvense* L., family Leguminosae. A native annual of dunes and sandy grassland. Most common in south east England; rare in Scotland and Ireland. Height to 20cm. The soft, furry flower heads give this plant its name as they look like hare's or rabbit's feet. Flowers June to Sept. See 52(i), 54(f).

(**l**) **Blue-eyed Grass** *Sisyrinchium bermudiana* L., family Iridaceae. A native perennial of marshes and lakesides. Fairly common in western Ireland. Introduced and sometimes naturalised elsewhere in Britain. Often grown as a garden plant. Height to 40cm. Flowers June to July.

(**a**) **Water Chickweed** *Myosoton aquaticum* (L.) Moench., family Caryophyllaceae. A native perennial of marshes, fens, riversides, ditches and damp woods. Common in south east England, rare in north and west and absent in Scotland. Height to as much as 1m. Flowers June to Aug. See 14(a), 22(m), 52(a), 90(g).

(**b**) **Bindweed** *Convolvulus arvensis* L., family Convolvulaceae. A native perennial of roadsides, waste places, railway banks, cultivated ground, hedgerows and short grassland, especially near the sea. Very common in England but less so in Scotland and rather rare in Ireland. Height to 70cm. Flowers June to Sept. See 90(c), 134(b).

(**c**) **Pineapple Weed** or **Pineapple Mayweed** *Chamomilla suaveolens* (Pursh.) Rydb., syn. *Matricaria matricarioides* (Less.) Porter, family Compositae. An introduced, annual weed of road-sides, waste places and particularly trampled ground. Very common throughout Britain. Height to 20cm. Thought to have been introduced from Oregon in 1871. The cone-shaped heads are hollow and the plant is strongly aromatic. Flowers June to July. See 36(g).

(**d**) **Hedge Bedstraw** *Galium mollugo* L., family Rubiaceae. A native perennial. Common in hedgerows, open woods, and scrub throughout England; rare in Wales, Ireland and Scotland. Height to 1m. A red dye used to be obtained from the roots. Flowers June to Sept. See 32(d), 56(g), 64(a), 112(a), 120(i).

e

f

g

h

i

j

k

l

photograph taken 7 June ◯ represents 1 centimetre

(a) **Maiden Pink** *Dianthus deltoides* L., family Caryophyllaceae. A native perennial of dry grasslands. Rare but scattered throughout Britain but absent from Ireland. Height to 40cm. A very attractive flower, said to have received its English name since its colour is that of a blushing maiden. Flowers June to Sept. See 80(b), 136(d). Photographed June 18.

b) **Cheddar Pink** *Dianthus gratianopolitanus* Vill., family Caryophyllaceae. A native perennial. Extremely rare, growing wild only on the limestone cliffs of Cheddar Gorge. Frequently grown in gardens. This plant is now protected by The Wild Creatures and Wild Plants Act (1975) and must not be picked. This is a garden specimen. Flowers June to July. See 80(a), 136(d). Photographed June 10.

(c) **Grass Poly** *Lythrum hyssopifolia* L., family Lythraceae. A native annual of damp, bare ground and hollows which hold water in winter. Rare and scattered, mostly in south east England; absent from Ireland and north Scotland. Height to 20cm. Flowers June to July. See 96(g). Photographed June 10.

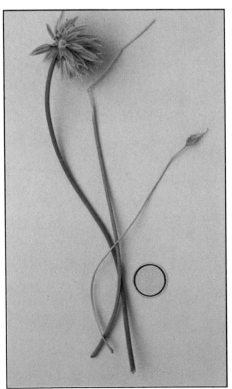

(d) **Zigzag Clover** *Trifolium medium* L., family Leguminosae. A native perennial of grassy places. Fairly common throughout Britain but more so in northern England. Rare in north Scotland and Ireland. The straggling stems can reach 40cm. in length. Flowers June to Sept. See other clovers 52(i), 54(f), and also 50(f), 104(c). Photographed June 15.

(e) **Chives** *Allium schoenoprasum* L., family Liliaceae. A native bulb. Rarely found growing wild, but usually on limestone. Height to 20cm. Chives are a popular garden herb used particularly in salads. It has a high iron content and has been used to treat anaemia. Flowers June to July. See 48(k), 122(a), 128(i), 130(f), 130(g). Photographed June 7.

(f) **Cranberry** *Vaccinium oxycoccus* L., family Ericaceae. A native undershrub of bogs and wet heaths. Fairly common in north England, Wales and Ireland; rarer, and scattered elsewhere. The trailing stems may reach 30cm. The berries are eaten as a fruit in pies and jellies. Flowers June to Aug. See Fruit 154(f) and also 40(g), 66(i). Photographed June 10.

(**a**) **Perennial Knawel** *Scleranthus perennis* L., family Caryophyllaceae. A native perennial. Very rare, growing only in Norfolk and Suffolk. Height to 15cm. Flowers June to Aug. Photographed June 15.
**Annual Knawel** *S. annuus* L. Native annual of dry sandy places. Common. Has lighter green, delicate leaves. Flowers June to Aug.

(**b**) **Cliff Sand Spurrey** *Spergularia rupicola* Lebel ex Le Jolis, family Caryophyllaceae. A native perennial of sea cliffs, rocks and walls on the west coasts of mainland Britain and all coasts of Ireland. Height to 10cm. Flowers June to Sept. See 106(b). Photographed June 18.

(**c**) **Smooth Tare** *Vicia tetrasperma* (L.) Schreb., family Leguminosae. A native annual of grassy places. Common throughout England and Wales but rare or absent in Ireland and Scotland. Height to 40cm. Distinguished from Hairy Tare by having four seeds in each pod. Flowers May to Aug. See 36(f). Photographed June 7.

(**d**) **Snowberry** *Symphoricarpos rivularis* Suksdorf, family Caprifoliaceae. An introduced shrub naturalised in hedgerows throughout Britain though rarer in the north. Commonly planted as cover for game birds. Height to 3m. The name is derived from its soft, white berries which persist through the winter. Flowers June to Sept. See Fruits 164(g). Photographed June 17.

(**e**) **Jack-go-to-bed-at-noon** or **Goat's-beard** *Tragopogon pratensis* L., family Compositae. A native annual and sometimes perennial of dunes, meadows, waste places and roadsides. Height to 60cm. Very common in England and parts of Wales, rare in Ireland and north Scotland. The flowers open early and close at noon. Flowers June to July. See 20(i). Photographed June 15.

(**f**) **Purple Beaked Milk-vetch** *Oxytropis halleri* Bunge ex Koch, family Leguminosae. A native perennial of dry, rocky pastures. Rare, found only in Scotland particularly on north coast. Height to 10cm. Flowers June to July. See 68(b, 102(l). Photographed June 10.

photograph taken 11 June

(**a**) **White Bryony** or **Red Bryony** *Bryonia cretica* L. ssp. *dioica* (Jacq.) Tutin, syn. *Bryonia divica* Jacq., family Cucurbitaceae. A native perennial of hedgerows, scrub and woodland. Very common in south west and central England, rare or absent elsewhere. The climbing stems may reach 3m. in length. The male flowers are illustrated, the unstalked female ones being on separate plants. Flowers May to Sept. See Fruits 172(j).

(**b**) **Perennial Wall Rocket** *Diplotaxis tenuifolia* (L.) DC., family Cruciferae. A possibly native perennial which grows on old walls, roadsides and waste places in south east England; rare and casual elsewhere; absent from Ireland and north Scotland. Height to 60cm. Flowers May to Sept. See 111(b).

(**c**) **Opium Poppy** *Papaver somniferum* L., family Papaveraceae. An introduced annual, scattered through Britain, often on waste ground as a garden escape. Height to 50cm. This lilac subspecies was grown to yield poppy-seed oil. A white subspecies yields the drug opium but this is not grown in Britain. Flowers June to Aug. Compare 64(b).

(**d**) **Everlasting Pea** *Lathyrus latifolius* L., family Leguminosae. An introduced perennial, naturalised in a few localities. Climbing stem may reach 2m. This pea is very similar to Narrow-leaved Everlasting Pea but distinguished by its broader leaves. Flowers June to Aug. See 102(k), 138(h).

(**e**) **Shepherd's Needle** *Scandix pecten-veneris* L., family Umbelliferae. A native annual growing as an arable weed in south and east England; rare elsewhere. Height to 40cm. The distinctive needle-like fruits are the reason for the English name. Flowers April to July.

(**f**) **Black Bryony** *Tamus communis* L., family Dioscoreaceae. A native perennial of wood edges, scrub and hedgerows. Common in England and Wales but absent in the north and in Ireland. Climbing stems do not have tendrils and may reach 3m. Poisonous raw, its roots may be boiled and eaten. Flowers May to July. See Fruits 172(i).

(**g**) **Marsh Hawk's Beard** *Crepis paludosa* (L.) Moench, family Compositae. A native perennial of wet meadows, fens and stream sides. More common in the north, absent in south England. Height to 70cm. Flowers June to Sept. See 54(l), 68(b).

(**h**) **Narrow-leaved Bittercress** *Cardamine impatiens* L., family Cruciferae. A native biennial or sometimes annual, found in shady woods, particularly ash, and on moist limestone. Rather rare and mainly in the west; absent from Ireland. Height to 40cm. Flowers May to Aug. See 18(f), 40(a), 90(l).

(**i**) **Red Horned Poppy** *Glaucium corniculatum* (L.) Rudolph, family Papaveraceae. An introduced annual which was once naturalised but now only occurring as a casual near sea ports. Height to 25cm. Flowers June to July. See 114(b).

(**j**) **Spignel, Meu** or **Baldmoney** *Meum athamanticum* Jacq., family Umbelliferae. A native perennial of grassy, mountain areas in Scotland and Wales. Rather rare and absent in lowland regions, and Ireland. Flowers June to July.

e

f

g

h

i

j

photograph taken 11 June ◯ represents 1 centimetre

photograph taken 11 June

(**e**) **Field Scabious** or **Gypsy Rose** *Knautia arvensis* (L.) Coult., family Dipsacaceae. A native perennial growing on dry grassland, waste places, hedgerows and roadsides. Common throughout Britain except in the north of Scotland. Height to 80cm. Flowers June to Sept. Compare 68(g), 138(g), 150(e).

(**f**) **Self-heal** *Prunella vulgaris* L., family Labiatae. A native perennial, very common throughout Britain on grassland, waste places, woodland clearings, roadsides and as a garden weed. Height to 20cm. Flowers June to Sept.

(**g**) **Skullcap** *Scutellaria galericulata* L., family Labiatae. A native perennial found on wet meadows, fens and stream sides. Common throughout Britain except in Ireland and east Scotland. Height to 35cm. North American Indians used it to ease menstruation. Flowers June to Sept.
**Lesser Skullcap** *S. minor* Huds. A native perennial found on wet heaths in the south of England and on western coasts. Height to 10cm. Similar to Skullcap but smaller and less common, and the flower is pinkish-purple with dark spots rather than blue or violet. Flowers July to Nov.

(**h**) **Lesser Knapweed** or **Hardheads** *Centaurea nigra* L., family Compositae. A native perennial herb of grassland, roadsides, hedgerows and waste places. Very common throughout Britain except in the Highlands. Height to 50cm. The flower tops mixed with an alum mordant give a pale yellow/green dye. It has been used medicinally to treat bruises, scabs and wounds. The dried flower heads make a very pretty addition to a winter bouquet. Flowers June to Sept. See 100(h), 142(e).

(**i**) **Tufted Vetch** *Vicia cracca* L., family Leguminosae. A native perennial of grassland scrub and hedgerows. Common throughout Britain except on mountains. The straggling stems may reach 2m. and climb by clinging to bushes with branched tendrils on the ends of the leaves. Flowers June to Aug. See 32(e), 116(c).

(**j**) **Goat's Rue** or **French Lilac** *Galega officinalis* L., family Leguminosae. An introduced perennial naturalised in waste places in the south. Height to 1m. Not to be confused with the melilots. Flowers June to July. See 54(g).

(**k**) **Viper's Bugloss** *Echium vulgare* L., family Boraginaceae. A native biennial found on grass places on dry soils, sea cliffs, dunes and chalky areas. Common in south east England but rare in Scotland and Ireland. Height to 70cm. A decoction, made by boiling the seeds in wine and taken daily, was reputed to help the flow of mother's milk. Flowers June to Sept.

(**l**) **Black Horehound** *Ballota nigra* L., family Labiatae. A native perennial common in waste places and roadsides throughout England and Wales; rare or absent elsewhere. Height to 1m. This plant has a strong, unpleasant smell which has given it one of its English names, Stinking Roger. It has been used to treat the bites of mad dogs. Flowers June to Oct.

(**a**) **Common Cow-wheat** *Melampyrum pratense* L., family Scrophulariaceae. A native annual common in damp woods and heaths throughout Britain, but rarer in Ireland and east England. Height to 50cm. This is an extremely variable species. Pregnant women used to eat Cow-wheat flour in the belief that their children would be male. Flowers May to Oct. See 144(a).
**Wood Cow-wheat** *M. sylvaticum* L. A native annual, occurring only in mountain woods, mostly in Scotland. Height to 50cm. Flowers June to Aug.

(**b**) **Meadow Vetchling** *Lathyrus pratensis* L., family Leguminosae. A native perennial common in hedgerows, roadsides and grassy places throughout Britain. Height to 1m. Not to be confused with Birdsfoot-trefoil or Horseshoe Vetch. Flowers May to Aug. Compare with 38(a), 38(d), 48(b).

(**c**) **Wallpepper** *Sedum acre* L., family Crassulaceae. A native perennial of dry grassland, walls, shingle and dunes. Common throughout Britain but rarer in Scotland and Ireland. Height to 8cm. In Dorset and Suffolk this was known as 'Welcome home husband, though never so drunk'. Flowers June to July.

(**d**) **Lucerne** or **Alfalfa** *Medicago sativa* L., family Leguminosae. An introduced perennial naturalised on waste ground and roadsides. Common in the south west; rare elsewhere. Height to 80cm. Originally planted as fodder crop. Flowers June to July.

e f g h i j k l

photograph taken 15 June

(**e**) **Wild Radish** or **White Charlock** *Raphanus raphanistrum* L., ssp. *raphanistrum*, family Cruciferae. Possibly native annual. A common weed of arable land and roadsides throughout England. Height to 50cm. Rarer in Scotland and Ireland. The white or lilac petals have distinctive purple veins but may sometimes be yellow. The seed pods are distinctively beaded. Flowers May to Sept. **Sea Radish** *R. raphanistrum* ssp. *maritimus* (Sm.) Thell. A native biennial or perennial of cliffs and shore margins. Rather rare but mostly on western and southern coasts. Height to 70cm. Taller than Wild Radish, the petals are always yellow and the seed pods unbeaded. Flowers June to Aug.

(**f**) **Sea Beet** *Beta vulgaris* L., ssp. *maritima* (L.) Arcangeli, family Chenopodiaceae. A native annual, biennial or perennial. Common at the edges of salt marshes and on sea shores on English, Welsh and Irish coasts. Rare in Scotland and northern England. Height to 1m. This is the wild version of beet, another subspecies, providing the beetroot, sugar-beet, chard, spinach and mangold of cultivation. These do escape and become naturalised in the wild. Flowers June to Sept.

(**g**) **Lady's Bedstraw** *Galium verum* L., family Rubiaceae. A native perennial. Very common throughout the British Isles. Grows on roadside hedgebanks, sandy places and as a lawn weed. Height to 75cm. Legend has it Mary gave birth to Jesus on a bed made from this plant—hence Lady's Bedstraw. Flowers June to Aug. See 56(g), 58(k).

(**h**) **Nipplewort** *Lapsana communis* L., family Compositae. A native annual common throughout Britain except in the extreme north. Found on waste places, roadsides, wood edges, hedges and as a garden weed. Height to 90cm. The flowers only open on sunny mornings and close in the afternoon. Flowers June to Aug.

(**i**) **Toadflax** *Linaria vulgaris* Mill, family Scrophulariaceae. A native perennial. Common in England and Wales, becoming rare in the north west of Scotland and rare in Ireland. Found on roadsides, wasteplaces, grassy places, cultivated fields and even woods. Height to 60cm. Flowers June to Oct. See 86(i), 92(j), 128(f).

(**j**) **Creeping Thistle** *Cirsium arvense* (L.) Scop., family Compositae. A native perennial. Very common throughout Britain on roadsides, waste places, hedgerows and fields and as a persistent weed. Height to 1m. Male and female flowers usually occur on separate plants. This plant is a serious weed in pastures, having persistent rootstock and being resistant to many weed killers. Flowers June to Sept. Compare with 98(l).

(**k**) **Prickly Sowthistle** *Sonchus asper* (L.) Hill, family Compositae. A native annual. Common throughout Britain, except in the Highlands. Found on waste places, roadsides and cultivated ground. Height to 1.5m. Similar to Smooth Sowthistle but leaves are usually undivided, have harder prickles and the base of the leaf, clasping the stem, is rounded. Flowers June to Aug. See 86(l), 104(l), 146(a).

(**l**) **Smooth Sowthistle** *Sonchus cleraceus* L., family Compositae. A native annual found on waste places, roadsides and cultivated ground. Common throughout Britain but less so in Scotland. Height to 1.5m. Similar to the Prickly Sowthistle but the base of the leaf clasping the stem is always slightly pointed. Flowers June to Aug. See 86(k), 104(l), 146(a).

(**a**) **Sweet Briar** or **Eglantine** *Rosa rubiginosa* L., family Rosaceae. A native shrub of scrub and hedgerows, mainly on calcareous soils. Scattered throughout Britain but rare in north west Scotland. Height to 2m. This rose is much less common than either Dog or Field Rose and is distinguished by its darker pink petals and small, round leaflets. Flowers June to July. See 50(d), 70(d), 76(b).

(**b**) **Honeysuckle** or **Woodbine** *Lonicera periclymenum* L., family Caprifoliaceae. A native shrub, very common in woods, hedges and scrub throughout Britain, climbing and trailing around bushes and trees. Stems may reach 6m. Flowers June to Sept. See Berries 162(k).

(**c**) **Common Privet** *Ligustrum vulgare* L., family Oleaceae. A native shrub commonly found in hedgerows and scrub, especially on calcareous soils throughout Britain though rare in Scotland. Height to 5m. Flowers June to July. See Fruit 172(d).

(**d**) **Silver Lace Vine** *Bilderdykia aubertii* (L. Henry) Moldenke syn. *Polygonum aubertii* L. Henry, Moldenke family Polygonaceae. An introduced perennial often planted on house walls and hedges. The flowers are white. Frequently confused with the Russian Vine (below) it also grows at an alarming rate. Stems may reach 20m. Flowers Jan. to Nov. See 134(f), 147(a).
**Russian Vine** *B. baldschuanica* (Regel) D. A. Webb syn. *Polygonum baldschuanicum* Regel. Similar to Silver Lace Vine (above) but with flowers tinged pink.

photograph taken 15 June ◯ represents 1 centimetre

(a) **Twinflower** *Linnaea borealis* L., family Caprifoliaceae. Very rare, found in Scotland and previously in Yorkshire. Found in woods, especially pine woods and in the shade among rocks. Height to 7cm. This plant is named after Linnaeus, the man who reorganised botanical naming into the two-name system we now use. Flowers June to Aug.

(b) **Scottish Primrose** *Primula scotica* Hook., family Primulaceae. A native perennial, found only on the north coast of Scotland, down the north west coast of Scotland to Helmsdale and in the Orkney Islands. Grows in damp pastures and can be common in these areas. Height to 11cm. Flowers June to Aug. Similar to Bird's-eye Primrose 20(j).

(c) **Cloudberry** *Rubus chamaemorus* L., family Rosaceae. Native, a creeping rhizome. Found in the Scottish Highlands and scattered in the Pennines otherwise very rare. Absent from southern England. Found in peat bogs and moors in mountains. Height to 18cm. Flowers June to Aug. See Fruit 157(f).

(d) **Globe Flower** *Trollius europaeus* L., family Ranunculaceae. A native perennial. Quite common in Scotland and northern England; scattered in Wales, rare in Ireland and absent from southern England. Grows in woods, scrub and wet pastures. Height to 50cm. Flowers June to Aug.

(e) **Common Wintergreen** *Pyrola minor* L., family Pyrolaceae. A native perennial with a creeping rhizome. Rare, found throughout the British Isles but mainly in Scotland. Grows mainly in woods but also on moors, rock-ledges and dunes. Height to 25cm. Flowers June to Aug. See 154(a), 154(b).

(f) **One-flowered Wintergreen** *Moneses uniflora* (L.) A. Gray, family Pyrolaceae. A native rhizome. Very rare, found only in north Scotland, mainly in the Spey Valley and near Brora. Grows in pinewoods. Height to 5cm. Flowers June to Aug.

(a) **Hound's-tongue** *Cynoglossum officinale* L., family Boraginaceae. A native biennial. Fairly common in central and south west England, diminishing to rare elsewhere. Found in grassy places and wood edges on dry soil, especially near the sea. Height to 80cm. Flowers June to Aug

(b) **Southern Marsh Orchid** *Dactylorhiza praetermissa* (Druce) Soó syn. *Dactylorchis praetermissa*, (Druce) Vermeul., family Orchidaceae. A native root-tuber found fairly commonly in southern England and Wales, not in Scotland or Ireland. Grows on wet, calcareous or base-rich peat, often in fens. Height to 20cm. Flowers June to Aug.

(c) **Narrow-lipped Helleborine** *Epipactis leptochila* (Godf.) Godf., family Orchidaceae. A native rhizome. Very rare, found in southern England and Wales. Grows in woods and on dunes. Height to 60cm. Flowers June to Aug. See 71(b), 94(b), 132(a), 132(b), 156(a).

(d) **Yellow Birdsnest** *Monotropa hypopitys* agg., family Pyrolaceae. A native saprophyte. Rare, found mainly in southern England on chalk. It grows in woods, especially beech or pine and on dunes. Height to 25cm. Flowers June to Aug.

(e) **Marshwort** *Apium inundatum* (L.) Rchb., family Umbelliferae. A native perennial. Floats on ponds, lakes and ditches and grows on wet mud by the water. Rather uncommon but scattered throughout Britain. Straggling stems to 30cm. Flowers June to Aug. See 90(j).

(f) **English Stonecrop** *Sedum anglicum* Huds., family Crassulaceae. A native perennial. Common on and near the west coast of England, Scotland and Ireland. Found on rocks and dry grassland, dunes and shingle, ascending to 1,000m. above sea level. Grows to a height of 5cm. Flowers June to Aug. See 90(d).

photograph taken 18 June

(**e**) **Enchanter's Nightshade** *Circaea lutetiana* L., family Onagraceae. A native perennial of damp woods, shady places and hedgerows on basic soils. Common throughout Britain though rare in north Scotland. Height to 60cm. Flowers June to Aug. **Alpine Enchanter's Nightshade** *C. alpina* L. Native perennial of mountain woods and shaded rocks. Most common in Scotland. Height to 25cm. Smaller than Enchanter's Nightshade with heartshaped toothed leaves. Flowers July to Aug.

(**f**) **Ragged Robin** *Lychnis flos-cuculi* L., family Caryophyllaceae. A native perennial of marshes, fens, damp meadows and woods. Common throughout Britain. Height to 70cm. Flowers May to June. See 30(h), 48(d), 48(g).

(**g**) **Common Mouse-ear Chickweed** *Cerastium fontanum* Baumg., family Caryophyllaceae. A native perennial. Very common in grassland, waste places, hedgerows and cultivated ground throughout Britain. Height to 40cm. Flowers April to Sept. See 14(a), 22(m), 52(e), 78(a), 154(c). **Sea Mouse-ear Chickweed** *C. diffusum* Pers. Native annual of sandy or stony ground near the sea. Fairly common on all coasts and sometimes inland on railway gravel. Height to 15cm. Smaller than Common Mouse-ear. Flowers May to July. **Sticky Mouse-ear Chickweed** *C. glomeratum* Thuill. Native annual of waste places, arable land. Common throughout Britain. Height to 40cm. Covered with sticky hairs. Flowers April to Sept.

(**h**) **Water Forget-me-not** *Myosotis scorpioides* L., family Boraginaceae. A native perennial. Common throughout Britain by rivers, streams and ponds. Height to 45cm. Flowers May to Sept. See also 30(b), 30(e), 160(a). **Tufted Forget-me-not** *M. caespitosa* C. F. Schultz. A native annual or biennial of marshes, streamsides and pondsides, fairly common throughout. Height to 40cm. It has smaller flowers with un-notched petals and the whole plant may be hairless. Flowers May to Aug. **Creeping Forget-me-not** *M. secunda* A. Murr. A native perennial of wet, peaty places. Fairly common in the north and west, rare in south east. Tends to avoid calcareous soils. Height to 50cm. Only the lower stem is hairy. Flowers May to Aug.

(**i**) **Water Speedwell** *Veronica anagallis-aquatica* L., family Scrophulariaceae. A native perennial sometimes annual, of ponds, ditches and stream sides. Fairly common throughout England and Ireland but rare elsewhere. Height to 30cm. Flowers June to Aug. See 74(a).

(**j**) **Fool's Watercress** *Apium nodiflorum* (L.) Lag., family Umbelliferae. A native perennial common in ditches and ponds throughout England, Wales and Ireland but rare or absent in Scotland. Height to 90cm. Flowers June to Aug. Compare with 90(l). **Wild Celery** *A. graveolens* L. Native biennial of damp places, especially by the sea. Common on most English and Welsh coasts. Height to 50cm. Similar to Fool's Watercress but erect and with a strong smell of celery. Flowers June to Aug.

(**k**) **Narrow-leaved Water Parsnip** *Berula erecta* (Huds.) Coville, family Umbelliferae. A native perennial of ponds, ditches, canals, marshes and fens. Common in south east England and the midlands. Height to 1m. This specimen is rather small. Flowers June to Sept.

(**l**) **Watercress** *Nasturtium officinale* R.Br., family Cruciferae. A native perennial common in ditches, streams and wet flushes throughout Britain but rare in mountain areas. Height to 60cm. Flowers May to Oct.

(**a**) **Sea Plantain** *Plantago maritima* L., family Plantaginaceae. A native perennial. Common on most British coasts in salt marshes and in short grass. Also inland on mountains. Height to 15cm. Not to be confused with the Arrow-grasses. Flowers June to Aug. See 52(k), 126(d).

(**b**) **Yellow Rattle** *Rhinanthus minor* L., family Scrophulariaceae. A native annual of grassland and waysides. Common throughout Britain. Height to 40cm. This is extremely variable and has been divided into several subspecies which are all fairly similar to each other but which grow in slightly different situations. Flowers May to Aug. See 58(k), 111(f).

(**c**) **Sea Bindweed** *Calystegia soldanella* (L.) R.Br., family Convolvulaceae. A native perennial of sand dunes and sea shores. May be common on most British coasts but rare in Scotland and north west Ireland. The trailing stems may reach 50cm. The funnel-shaped flowers open wide during the day and close at night. The photographed specimen is slightly closed. Flowers June to Aug. See 78(b), 134(b).

(**d**) **White Stonecrop** *Sedum album* L., family Crassulaceae. Possibly introduced perennial of walls and rocks. Uncommon and scattered through Britain. Height to 15cm. The flower may sometimes be tinged pink on the back of the petals and the whole plant tinged red, differing from English Stonecrop by having longer leaves and a more branched flower-head. Flowers June to Aug. See 89(f).

(a) **Common Spotted Orchid** *Dactylorhiza fuchsii* (Druce) Soó, syn. *Dactylorchis fuchsii* (Druce) Vermeul, family Orchidaceae. A native perennial of marshes, wet meadows, grassy slopes, woods and fens. Fairly common throughout Britain but rare in Scotland. Height to 50cm. Flowers June to Aug. Photographed June 10.

(b) **Fragrant Orchid** *Gymnadenia conopsea* (L.) R.Br., family Orchidaceae. A native perennial, fairly common on grassland and fens especially on chalk or limestone throughout Britain. Height to 40cm. This orchid, unlike the other British species, is very fragrant which is a distinctive feature. Flowers June to Aug. Photographed June 15.

(e) **Lesser Swinecress** *Coronopus didymus* (L.) Sm., family Cruciferae. An introduced annual or biennial. Common as a weed and on waste ground in the south of England; rare or absent elsewhere. Height to 30cm. Similar to the native Swinecress but smaller and finer. Flowers June to Sept. See 72(l).

(f) **Yellow-wort** *Blackstonia perfoliata* (L.) Huds., family Gentianaceae. A native annual. Common on calcareous grassland and dunes in south England; rarer elsewhere and absent in Scotland. Height to 45cm. One of the distinct chalkland flowers often found with the pink Common Centuary and Squinancy Wort. The flowers close in early afternoon. Flowers June to Oct.

(g) **Eyebright** *Euphrasia officinalis* L. agg., family Scrophulariaceae. A native annual of grassland and mountains, common throughout Britain. Height to 15cm. This group has actually been divided into many species but it is difficult, even for an expert, to distinguish them. The flowers are basically white but may be purple-tinged, purple veined and have yellow spots. Flowers June to Sept.

(h) **Wild Strawberry** *Fragaria vesca* L., family Rosaceae. The fruit of the wild strawberry is illustrated. These are tiny in comparison to the garden version but often have more flavour. Fruits June to Aug. See Flowers: 32(g), see also 22(i), 72(e).

(i) **Restharrow** *Ononis repens* L., family Leguminosae. A native perennial of grassy places throughout Britain. More common on calcareous soils and coasts; rare in Scotland and Ireland. Height to 50cm. Flowers June to Sept. See 106(a).

(j) **Purple Toadflax** *Linaria purpurea* (L.) Mill., family Scrophulariaceae. An introduced perennial frequently grown in gardens and often naturalised on walls and waste places. More common in England. Height to 80cm. Flowers June to Aug. See 86(i), 128(f).

(k) **Alpine Lady's Mantle** *Alchemilla alpina* L., family Rosaceae. A native perennial, common on mountain grassland in north Scotland and Cumberland, absent elsewhere, though often grown on garden rockeries. Height to 20cm. Flowers June to Aug. See 3(j), 60(i), 60(j).

(l) **Squinancy Wort** *Asparula cynanchica* L., family Rubiaceae. A native perennial, common on dry calcareous pastures and dunes in south England and Wales and on the west coast of Ireland; absent elsewhere. Height to 30cm. This is a characteristic chalkland flower which can be either white or pink. Flowers June to July.

(m) **Creeping Jenny** *Lysimachia nummularia* L., family Primulaceae. A native perennial of damp grassy places and hedgerows. Common in England and Wales; rare or absent elsewhere. The creeping stems may reach 60cm. This plant has been used medicinally for menstruation and against external bleeding. Flowers June to Aug. See 40(k).

(c) **Twayblade** *Listera ovata* (L.) R.Br., family Orchidaceae. A native perennial of damp woods, meadows and dunes on base-rich soil. Fairly common everywhere, except Scotland. Height to 60cm. Flowers June to Sept. Photographed June 19. **Lesser Twayblade** *L. cordata* (L.) R.Br. A native perennial. Common in Scottish pine woods. Height to 20cm. Smaller than Twayblade. Flowers July to Sept.

(d) **Pyramidal Orchid** *Anacamptis pyramidalis* (L.) Rich., family Orchidaceae. A native perennial of calcareous grassland and dunes. Fairly common throughout England and Ireland though rare in Scotland. Height to 50cm. This orchid is easily recognised by its distinct pink, conical-shaped flower-head. Flowers June to Aug. Photographed June 19.

(e) **Wall Lettuce** *Mycelis muralis* (L.) Dumort., family Compositae. A native perennial of walls, rocks and sometimes in woods on chalk. Common throughout England and Wales; rare elsewhere. Height to 1m. The leaves of this plant may be eaten in salads. Flowers July to Sept.

(f) **Foxglove** *Digitalis purpurea* L., family Scrophulariaceae. A native biennial or perennial common in woods, hedgerows and open places throughout Britain; it is often grown in gardens. Height to 1.5m. A well-loved plant of British hedgerows and extremely poisonous. A powerful drug, digitalin, which is used to treat heart disease, is extracted from the leaves. Flowers June to Sept.

(g) **Wild Parsnip** *Pastinaca sativa* L., family Umbelliferae. A native biennial of roadsides, hedgerows and waste places, mainly on chalky soils. Common in south east England; rare or absent elsewhere. Height to 15m. A strong smelling plant, very similar to the cultivated parsnip but without the swollen root. Flowers June to Aug. Compare with 42(g).

(h) **Rosebay Willowherb** *Epilobium angustifolium* L., family Onagraceae. A native perennial of rocks, scree, wood edges, gardens, roadsides, waste places and any disturbed ground. Very common throughout Britain, but rarer in Ireland. Height to 1.5m. A fast-spreading weed whose white, fluffy seeds are a familiar sight blowing in the wind in the autumn. An alternative name is Fireweed because it likes ground where there has been a fire. Flowers June to Sept. See 78(g), 104(h).

(i) **Bristly Ox-tongue** *Picris echioides* L., family Compositae. Possibly native annual or biennial. Common on waste places, roadsides, field edges and hedgerows in south England and Wales. Rare elsewhere. Height to 80cm. Looks similar to the sowthistles but has numerous distinctive bristles rising from small, white blisters all over the leaves and stem. The leaves used to be boiled and pickled. Flowers June to Oct. See 144(j).

(j) **Tall Rocket** *Sisymbrium altissimum* L., family Cruciferae. An introduced annual which has been naturalised on waste places throughout Britain. Uncommon. Found more frequently in England than elsewhere. Height to 1m. Flowers June to Aug. See 36(b), 54(j).

(k) **Aaron's Rod** *Verbascum thapsus* L., family Scrophulariaceae. A native biennial. Common on sunny banks and waste places throughout Britain though rarer in Scotland and Ireland. Height to 2m. Once used to treat bronchial troubles and smoked in a pipe as a herbal tobacco. Flowers June to Aug. See 98(l).

(l) **Treacle Mustard** *Erysimum cheiranthoides* L., family Cruciferae. Probably introduced annual established as a weed of cultivation and waste ground. Fairly common in south east England and midlands; rare elsewhere. Height to 60cm. Flowers June to Aug.

(a) **Lesser Broomrape** *Orobanche minor* Sm., family Orobanchaceae. A native annual to perennial parasite growing on roots of plants in the pea and daisy families. Fairly common in the south. Height to 50cm. Flowers June to Sept. See 70(f), 96(c). Photographed June 20.
**Greater Broomrape** *O. rapum-genistae* Thuill. A native annual to perennial, parasitic on the roots of shrubby peas. Flowers May to July.

(b) **Broad-leaved Helleborine** *Epipactis helleborine* (L.) Grantz, family Orchidaceae. A native perennial of woods and hedgerows. Fairly uncommon but scattered throughout England and Wales; rare elsewhere and absent in north Scotland. Height to 70cm. Flowers June to Oct. See 71(b), 89(c), 132(a), 132(b), 156(a). Photographed June 25.

(c) **Man Orchid** *Aceras anthropophorum* (L.) Ait.f., family Orchidaceae. A native perennial of field edges and grassy slopes on chalk and old chalk pits. Rather rare, found only in the south east of England. Height to 40cm. The individual flowers are thought to be man-shaped with head, arms and legs—hence the plant's name. Flowers June to July. Photographed June 18.

(d) **Bee Orchid** *Ophrys apifera* Huds., family Orchidaceae. A native perennial of field edges, pastures and grassy slopes on calcareous ground especially on recently disturbed ground. Fairly common in south east England and midlands; less common elsewhere and absent in north Scotland. Height to 45cm. Flowers June to July. See 27(d). Photographed June 18.

(m) **Musk Thistle** *Carduus nutans* L., family Compositae. A native biennial of pasture, fields waste places, hedgerows and roadsides. Common in England but rare or absent in Scotland and Ireland. Height to 1m. The stems have prickles for most of their length but are bare for some distance just below the solitary, nodding flower-heads. Flowers May to Aug.

(a) **White Helleborine** *Cephalanthera damasonium* (Mill.) Druce, family Orchidaceae. A native perennial of woods and shady places. Fairly common on calcareous soil in the south of England. Height to 40cm. Flowers May to June. See 27(e). Photographed June 20.
**Red Helleborine** *C. rubra* (L.) Rich. A native perennial. Very rare. It has rose-red flowers.

(b) **Butterfly Orchid** *Platanthera chlorantha* (Cust.) Rchb., family Orchidaceae. A native perennial of woods and grassy banks on calcareous or base-rich soil. Fairly common in south England and west Scotland; rarer elsewhere. Height to 40cm. Flowers May to July. See 27(c). Photographed June 24.

(e) **White Mignonette** *Reseda alba* L., family Resedaceae. An introduced annual or perennial. Frequently found naturalised on waste ground in the south of England or as a casual near ports. Height to 70cm. Distinguished from the other mignonettes by white rather than yellow flowers. Flowers June to Aug. See 36(k), 74(i).

(f) **Musk Mallow** *Malva moschata* L., family Malvaceae. A native perennial of pastures, grassy banks, hedgerows and roadsides and sometimes grown in gardens. Common throughout England and Wales; rare elsewhere. Height to 70cm. The flowers may occasionally be white and the leaf shape may vary considerably being either more or less deeply cut. It used to be used, like Common Mallow, for poultices and in cough mixtures. Flowers June to Aug. See 74(f), 122(h).

(g) **Purple Loosestrife** *Lythrum salicaria* L., family Lythraceae. A native perennial found in marshes, reed swamps and beside lakes, slow rivers and canals. Common throughout Britain except in Scottish highlands where it is absent in the north. Height to 1m. Purple Loosestrife appears as the 'long purples' described by Shakespeare in Millais' painting of Ophelia. In fact, Shakespeare was referring to another plant, the Early Purple Orchid. Flowers June to Aug. See 80(c).

(h) **Great Burnet** *Sanguisorba officinalis* L., family Rosaceae. A native perennial of damp grassland. Common in north England and the midlands; rare elsewhere and absent in north Scotland. Height to 1m. Like the Salad Burnet, this plant was used medicinally to staunch bleeding. Flowers June to Sept. See 32(f).

(i) **Sweet William Catchfly** *Silene armeria* With., family Caryophyllaceae. An introduced perennial grown in gardens but sometimes escaping and becoming established in south England. Height to 50cm. Flowers June to July. See 30(h).

(j) **Limestone Woundwort** *Stachys alpina* L., family Labiatae. A native perennial. Very rare, found only in open woods in Gloucestershire and Denbigh but sometimes grown in gardens. Height to 1m. Flowers June to Aug. See 50(c), 58(l), 102(f), 128(j).

(k) **Vervain** *Verbena officinalis* L., family Verbenaceae. A native perennial of roadsides and waste places especially on chalky soils. Common in south of England and Wales; rare elsewhere and absent in Scotland. Height to 50cm. Vervain has had many herbal uses, including treatment of nervous disorders, staunching blood and aiding childbirth. It has also been used as a charm against witchcraft and devils. Flowers June to Sept.

(c) **Bird's Nest Orchid** *Neottia nidus-avis* (L.) Rich., family Orchidaceae. A native perennial of woods, particularly beech, on calcareous soil. Fairly common in south England; rare elsewhere. Height to 40cm. Not to be confused with the broomrapes. Flowers June to July. See 32(i), 70(f), 94(a). Photographed June 24.

(d) **Moorland Spotted Orchid** *Dactylorhiza maculata* (L.) Soó. syn. *Dactylorchis maculata* (L.) Vermeul. ssp. *ericetorum* (E. F. Linton) P. F. Hunt & Summerhayes, family Orchidaceae. A native tuber of moist, acid soils. Fairly common throughout Britain though rare in south east Ireland, south east England and the midlands. Height to 30cm. Flowers June to Aug. Photographed June 28.

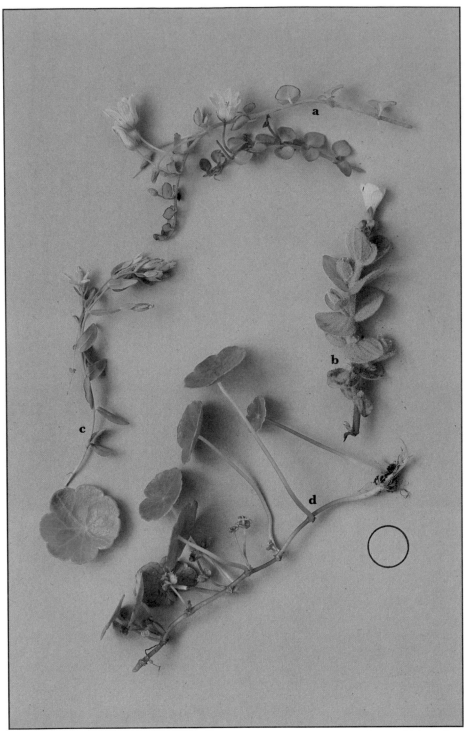

photograph taken 29 June

(**e**) **Common Agrimony** *Agrimonia eupatoria* L., family Rosaceae. A native perennial. Common in the south, petering out to rare in the north. Found on roadsides, grassland, hedge banks and field edges. Height to 50cm. Agrimony has a long history in medicine and is still used for liver complaints and to aid digestion. Flowers June to Aug.

(**f**) **Larkspur** *Delphinium ambiguum* L., family Ranunculaceae. An introduced annual commonly grown in gardens and which was once naturalised in parts of England and often found as a casual weed in cornfields. Height to 50cm. All Larkspurs are very poisonous. Flowers June to July.

(**g**) **Wild Liquorice** or **Milk-vetch** *Astragalus glycophyllos* L., family Leguminosae. A native perennial found on rough, grassy places on chalky soil. Uncommon and scattered throughout Britain but more frequent in England and absent in north Scotland and Ireland. Height to 1m. Flowers June to Aug. See 48(b).

(**h**) **Figwort** *Scrophularia nodosa* L., family Scrophulariaceae. A native perennial, common to damp woods and hedgerows throughout Britain though rare in the north of Scotland. Height to 80cm. This herb was used to treat piles, ulcers, itching and many other skin complaints. Flowers June to Sept. See 74(k), 162(d).

(**i**) **Sneezewort** *Achillea ptarmica* L., family Compositae. A native perennial which grows in marshes, by streams, in damp meadows and roadsides. Common throughout Britain though less frequent in south England and rare in south Ireland. A form of Sneezewort is commonly grown in gardens. Height to 50cm. Flowers July to Aug. See 66(a).

(**j**) **Marsh Thistle** *Cirsium palustre* (L.) Scop., family Compositae. A native biennial of marshes, damp hedgerows, woods and grassland. Common throughout Britain. Height to 1.5m. In some parts of Europe, young stems are peeled (removing prickles) then eaten raw in salad or boiled. Flowers July to Aug. See 86(j), 110(e).

(**k**) **Tansy** *Tanacetum vulgare* L., family Compositae. A native perennial found in hedgerows, roadsides and waste places. Fairly common throughout Britain but rarer in Ireland. Height to 1m. Still a very popular herb in modern herb gardens, it has traditionally been used to flavour eggs. The name Tansy is derived from an old name for herb-flavoured omelettes. Flowers July to Sept.

(**l**) **Dark Mullein** *Verbascum nigrum* L., family Scrophulariaceae. A native biennial of grassy banks, hedgerows and roadsides on calcareous soils. Rather uncommon in south east England and rare or absent elsewhere. Height to 1.20m. Very similar to the Great Mullein but generally smaller and lacking the thick, white downy covering. Flowers June to Oct. See 94(k).

(**m**) **Burdock** *Arctium minus* Bernh., family Compositae. A native biennial common in waste places, hedgerows, roadsides, scrub and wood edges throughout Britain except in the Scottish Highlands. Height to 1.30m. Burdock is well-known to children, since the old, dried flower heads cling by hooked bristles to clothes and animals. Flowers July to Sept. See 137(d).

(**a**) **Bog Pimpernel** *Anagallis tenella* (L.) L., family Primulaceae. A native perennial in bogs and damp, peaty places. Fairly common on the western parts of Britain and Ireland; rare in the Midlands, the east and the south. The creeping stems may reach 10cm. Flowers June to Aug. See 46(d).
**Chaffweed** *A. minima* (L.) E. H. L. Krause. A native annual of damp sandy places near the sea. Rather uncommon, found on western and southern coasts and inland in the south. Height to 5cm. Much smaller than Bog Pimpernel; stalkless pink flowers, 1mm., hidden at the base of the leaves. Flowers June to July.

(**b**) **Marsh St John's Wort** *Hypericum elodes* L., family Guttiferae. A native perennial found in bogs and by streams and ponds on acid soils. Rather rare, occurring mostly on the west coasts of Britain and Ireland. Absent in north Scotland. The creeping stems may reach 30cm. Flowers June to Sept. See other St John's Worts 98(c), 104(e), 104(f), 126(a), 128(k).

(**c**) **Trailing St John's Wort** *Hypericum humifusum* L., family Guttiferae. A native perennial growing on dry moors and heaths and open woods, avoiding calcareous soils. Fairly common throughout Britain; rarer in Ireland and north Scotland. Height to 15cm. Flowers June to Sept. See 98(b), 104(e), 104(f), 126(a), 128(k).

(**d**) **Pennywort** or **White-rot** *Hydrocotyle vulgaris* L., family Umbelliferae. A native perennial of bogs, fens and marsh, mostly on acid soils. It may sometimes float in shallow water. Rather common throughout Britain. The stems may reach 20cm. Flowers June to Aug.

photograph taken 1 July

**(e) Corn Chamomile** *Anthemis arvensis* L., family Compositae. A native annual of arable fields and waste places on chalky soils. Rare or absent in Scotland and Ireland but fairly common in the Midlands, Wales and the south. Height to 20cm. Corn Chamomile is aromatic, having a similar smell to the cultivated Chamomile. Flowers June to July. See 36(g), 120(b), 124(b).

**Stinking Chamomile** *A. cotula* L. A native annual of waste and arable land. Common in south England, less common in Wales and north England and rare in Scotland and Ireland. Height is 50cm. This plant has a stronger sicklier smell than Corn Chamomile and broader leaf segments. Flowers July to Sept.

**(f) Large Birdsfoot-trefoil** *Lotus pedunculatus* Cav., family Leguminosae. A native perennial of damp, grassy places. Common throughout Britain but rare in the Scottish and Irish Highlands. Height to 70cm. Differs from the Common Birdsfoot-trefoil by being larger and having hollow stems. Flowers June to Aug. See 38(a).

**(g) Bugloss** *Lycopsis arvensis* L., family Boraginaceae. A native annual or biennial. Fairly common in fields on sandy and chalky soils, on dry heaths and by the sea around most British coasts. Rare in Ireland and inland Scotland. Height to 40cm. The bright blue flower-tube has a distinctive bend halfway down. Flowers June to Sept.

**(h) Greater Knapweed** *Centaurea scabiosa* L., family Compositae. A native perennial of hedgerows, roadsides and dry grassland. Common in the south and east of England, rarer elsewhere. Height to 80cm. Flowers July to Sept. See 48(i), 84(h), 142(e).

**(i) Creeping Buttercup** *Ranunculus repens* L., family Ranunculaceae. A native perennial, common throughout Britain in wet fields, woods and waste places and as a persistent garden weed. The creeping stems may reach 50cm. This may be distinguished from other buttercups by its creeping habit. The middle of the three leaflets is typically stalked and all leaves have light spots. Flowers May to Aug. See 20(g), 58(h), 72(d).

**(j) Feverfew** *Tanacetum parthenium* (L.) Bernh., family Compositae. Possibly introduced perennial found on walls, waste places, hedgerows and roadsides. Fairly common throughout Britain but rather rare in Ireland. Height to 50cm. Feverfew was a popular herb of physic gardens and has been used against fever. Infusions are taken to ease colic, to aid digestion and as a tonic. Flowers July to Aug.

**(k) Dropwort** *Filipendula vulgaris* Moench, family Rosaceae. A native perennial of calcareous grassland. Fairly common in the south and east of England; rare elsewhere and absent in Ireland and north Scotland. Height to 70cm. Flowers June to Aug. See 112(d).

**(l) Stinking Groundsel** or **Sticky Groundsel** *Senecio viscosus* L., family Compositae. Probably native, an annual of waste ground, roadsides, tracks, sea shores and sea walls. Fairly common throughout Britain but rare in Ireland and north Scotland. Height to 50cm. This groundsel is sticky and has a strong, very unpleasant smell. Flowers July to Sept. See 14(e), 152(h).

**(a) Reflexed Stonecrop** *Sedum reflexum* L., family Crassulaceae. An introduced perennial frequently grown in gardens and naturalised on rocks and old walls in south England but rather uncommon. Height to 20cm. Flowers June to Aug.

**(b) Pepperwort** *Lepidium campestre* (L.) R.Br., family Cruciferae. A native annual or biennial which grows on walls, dry banks and fields, waste places and roadsides. Rare in Scotland and Ireland, scattered throughout England and Wales and most common in the south east. Height to 50cm. Flowers May to July. See 116(e), 118(b).

**Narrow-leaved Pepperwort** *L. ruderale* L. Native annual or biennial of roadsides and wasteplaces, often near the sea. Common only in south east England, rare in Scotland and absent from Ireland. Height to 25cm. Smaller than Pepperwort, with narrow leaves and tiny, usually petalless flowers. Flowers May to July.

**(c) Wild Candytuft** *Iberis amara* L., family Cruciferae. A native annual of hillsides and cornfields on dry calcareous soils only in south England. Height to 30cm. Flowers July to Aug.

**(d) Sea Rocket** *Cakile maritima* Scop., family Cruciferae. A native annual of sand and shingle, common around most British coasts. Height to 40cm. This is a rather variable plant and has been divided into further groups. Flowers June to Aug.

photograph taken 1 July ○ represents 1 centimetre

photograph taken 2 July

**(e) Grass Vetchling** *Lathyrus nissolia* L., family Leguminosae. A native annual of grassland and bushy places. Found only in the south of England and Wales, more common in the east. Absent in Ireland and Scotland. Height to 90cm. When not flowering it is easily mistaken for a grass. Flowers May to July.

**(f) Betony** *Stachys officinalis* (L.) Trevisan, family Labiatae. A native perennial of open woods, hedgerows, grassland and heaths on light soil. Common in England and Wales but rare in Scotland and Ireland. Height to 50cm. Betony was an invaluable medicinal herb, known to the Romans, and used for headaches, liver and bronchial complaints. It was also thought to be a safeguard against witchcraft and has been used in herbal tobacco mixtures. Flowers June to Sept. See 50(c), 58(l), 96(j), 128(c), 128(j).

**(g) Black Pea** *Lathyrus niger* (L.) Bernh., family Leguminosae. A native or introduced perennial. Once common in rocky woods and mountain valleys in Scotland; now very rare. Height to 50cm. The Black Pea takes its name from the shrivelled black pods. Flowers June to July.

**(h) Wild Basil** *Clinopodium vulgare* L., family Labiatae. A native perennial of hedgerows, wood edges and scrub. Common in England and Wales, becoming rare in the north and in Ireland. Height to 60cm. A pleasant smelling herb, Wild Basil is said to have been strewn with rushes on medieval floors. Flowers July to Sept. See also 104(j).

**(i) Dyer's Greenwood** *Genista tinctoria* L., family Leguminosae. A native shrub found in rough pasture. Fairly common in England and Wales but rare in south Scotland and absent in Ireland and north Scotland. Height to 60cm. A prostrate form is found on the Lizard in Cornwall. The flowering tops provide a yellow dye or a green, when dyed again with blue from Woad, or vice versa – hence the name 'Greenwood'. Flowers July to Sept. See 56(k).

**(j) Crown Vetch** *Coronilla varia* L., family Leguminosae. An introduced perennial naturalised on grassy places in a few localities throughout Britain, though more frequent in the south. Height to 50cm. An extremely attractive flower which varies from purple to pink to white. Flowers June to July. Compare 84(j).

**(k) Tuberous Pea** or **Earth-nut Pea** *Lathyrus tuberosus* L., family Leguminosae. An introduced perennial naturalised in hedgerows and cornfields. Uncommon but most frequently found in the south of England. Height to 1m. Similar to the everlasting peas but has smaller, round leaflets. Flowers July. See everlasting peas 82(d), 138(h).

**(l) Yellow Beaked Milk-vetch** *Oxytropis campestris* (L.) DC., family Leguminosae. A native perennial. Very rare and found only on mountain rock ledges in Scotland. Height to 20cm. Flowers June to July. See Purple Beaked Milk-vetch 81(f).

**(c) Bulrush, Cat's-tail** or **Great Reedmace** *Typha latifolia* L., family Typhaceae. A native perennial of reed swamps by lakes, ponds, slow moving rivers and canals. Common throughout Britain but rare in north Scotland. Height to 2.5m. The Lesser Reedmace differs by having the two parts of the flowerhead (male and female) separated by a section stem. Flowers June to July. See 140(g), 140(h).

**(a) Marestail** *Hippuris vulgaris* L., family Hippuridaceae. A native perennial of lakes, ponds and slow streams especially in base-rich water. Scattered throughout Britain but most common in the south and east. Flowers June to July. See 64(d).

**(b) Broad-leaved Pondweed** *Potamogeton natans* L., family Potamogetonaceae. A native perennial of ponds, rivers, lakes, ditches, usually in shallow water on a highly organic mud. Common throughout Britain. The stems may grow to 1m. There are many other species of pondweeds which vary in leaf shape and habitat. Flowers May to Sept.

**(d) Water-plantain** *Alisma plantago-aquatica* L., family Alismataceae. A native perennial found on muddy ground by ponds, slow rivers, canals and ditches. Common in Britain, except north Scotland. Height to 1m. Water-plantain is unrelated to the better known plantains, species of *Plantago*. Flowers June to Aug. See 115(d).

photograph taken 2 July

(a) **French Cranesbill** *Geranium endressii* Gay, family Geraniaceae. An introduced perennial. Often grown in gardens, sometimes escaping and becoming naturalised on waste places and roadsides. Scattered throughout Britain. Height to 70cm. Flowers June to July. See 36(i), 44(h), 122(j).

(b) **Small Fumitory** *Fumaria parviflora* Lam., family Papaveraceae. A native annual. Rather rare, found on arable land, usually on chalk, in south England and a few other localities. Absent in Ireland. Trailing stems to a length of 20cm. Flowers June to Sept. See other fumitories 52(l), 78(i).

(c) **Strawberry Clover** *Trifolium fragiferum* L., family Leguminosae. A native perennial of grassy places on clay soils. Fairly common in south and east England and by the sea elsewhere. Rare in Scotland and Ireland. Height to 25cm. Our specimen has nearly finished flowering and has dead flowers round the base. Flowers July to Sept. See 50(f), 52(i), 54(f).

(d) **Creeping Cinquefoil** *Potentilla reptans* L., family Rosaceae. A native perennial. Common on waste places, hedgerows and grassy places throughout Britain except in Scotland where it becomes rare in the north. Creeping stems may reach 1m. in length. Each leaf has five leaflets which distinguishes it from Tormentil which has three leaflets. Egyptians used it medicinally against malaria. Flowers June to Sept. See tormentils and cinquefoils 42(c), 56(i), 142(g).

(e) **Common St John's Wort** *Hypericum perforatum* L., family Guttiferae. A native perennial of hedgerows, open woods and grassy banks. Common throughout Britain except in Scotland where it is absent in the north. Height to 50cm. Associated with the Knights of St John and the Crusades and hung around houses on St John's Eve to ward off evil spirits. Flowers June to Sept. See 104(f), 126(a), 128(k).

(f) **Hairy St John's Wort** *Hypericum hirsutum* L., family Guttiferae. A native perennial found in woods and damp grassland, particularly on basic soils. Throughout Britain but rare in Ireland and Scotland and in the west. Height to 80cm. Flowers July to Aug. See 104(e), 126(a), 128(k).
**Pale St John's Wort** *H. montanum* L. A native perennial of woods, hedgerows and scrub on calcareous soil. Uncommon throughout England and Wales; absent in Scotland and Ireland. Height to 70cm. Differs from other St John's Worts by its paler, yellow flowers. Flowers June to Aug.

(g) **Ragwort** *Senecio jacobaea* L., family Compositae. A native biennial to perennial. Common throughout Britain on waste ground and roadsides and as a weed of grazing land. Height to 1.5m. Flowers June to Oct. See 22(f), 72(j), 112(j), 148(b).
**Hoary Ragwort** *S. erucifolius* L. A native perennial of roadsides, field edges, grassy banks and waste places, particularly on calcareous soil. Common in south east England. Similar to 104(g) but covered in grey down and has pointed leaf tips. Flowers July to Aug.

(h) **Great Willowherb** or **Codlins and Cream** *Epilobium hirsutum* L., family Onagraceae. A native perennial of damp hedgerows, ditches, stream sides and marshes. Common throughout Britain but rare or absent in north Scotland. Height to 1.5m. Distinguished by its hairy texture and large, pink flowers. Flowers July to Aug. See 78(a), 94(h).
**Small-flowered Hairy Willowherb** *E. parviflorum* Schreb. Native perennial of streamsides, fens and marshes. Common in England and Wales. Similar to Great Willowherb, with smaller flowers and leaves and long soft hairs on lower stem. Flowers July to Aug.

(i) **Hoary Plantain** *Plantago media* L., family Plantaginaceae. A native perennial. Most common in southern England on grassland, waste places and roadsides, also as a garden weed; less common in north England and Wales and rare in Scotland and Ireland. Height to 25cm. Leaves may be used in similar ways to *P. major* and *P. lanceolata*. Flowers May to Aug. See 54(k), 70(c), 90(a).

(j) **Wild Basil** *Clinopodium vulgare* L., family Labiatae. Another illustration of the plant described at 102(h).

(k) **Dotted Loosestrife** *Lysimachia punctata* L., family Primulaceae. An introduced perennial. Naturalised in some marshy fields and by rivers. Uncommon and scattered through Britain. Height to 80cm. Flowers July to Oct. See 40(k), 92(m), 140(e).

(l) **Perennial Sow-thistle** *Sonchus arvensis* L., family Compositae. A native perennial of streamsides, marshes, arable land and edges of salt marshes. Common throughout lowland Britain. Height to 1.5m. Flowers July to Oct. See other sowthistles 86(k), 86(l), 146(a).

photograph taken 4 July ◯ represents 1 centimetre

photograph taken 4 July

(**e**) **Stinking Iris** or **Gladdon** *Iris foetidissima* L., family Iridaceae. A native perennial of hedgebanks, damp woods and sea cliffs. Fairly common in south England, introduced in Ireland and Scotland. Height to 70cm. Despite its name, this plant does not stink although it does have a curious smell when leaves are crushed. It was once used as a herbal purgative. Flowers May to July. See Fruit 18(i) and Yellow Flag 76(i).

(**f**) **Meadow Thistle** *Circium dissectum* (L.) Hill, family Compositae. A native perennial found on wet peat at bog and fen edges. Common in Ireland and south England and Wales; absent elsewhere. Height to 60cm. Flowers June to Aug. See 112(e).

(**g**) **Valerian** *Valeriana officinalis* L., family Valerianaceae. A native perennial. Common throughout Britain on rough, damp grassland and scrub. Height to 1.2m. Cats are said to love the smell of the dried root which was placed among clean linen in the 16th century. In Europe, Valerian tea is taken to calm the nerves. Flowers June to Aug. **Marsh Valerian** *V. dioica* L. Native perennial of marshes and fens. Common in England and Wales, but rare in Ireland and Scotland. Height to 30cm. Smaller than Valerian, with oval, undivided leaves at the base of the stem. Flowers May to June.

(**h**) **Marsh Cinquefoil** *Potentilla palustris* (L.) Scop., family Rosaceae. A native perennial, found in fens, marshes, bogs, wet heaths and moors. Fairly common throughout Britain but rarer in south Wales and south England. Height to 40cm. Distinct among cinquefoils and tormentils by its purplish, rather than yellow, flowers. Flowers May to July.

(**i**) **Marsh Dock** *Rumex palustris* Sm., family Polygonaceae. A native annual, biennial or perennial found on bare mud by lakes and reservoirs and on dried-up ponds. Uncommon, mainly in east England. Rare elsewhere and absent in Scotland and Ireland. Height to 1m. Flowers June to Sept. See 64(j), 126(e), 126(i), 126(j), 126(k).

(**j**) **Monkey-flower** *Mimulus guttatus* DC., family Scrophulariaceae. An introduced perennial, naturalised and now common by streams and rivers throughout Britain, though rare in south Ireland. Height to 20cm. The bright yellow flowers have red spots in the throat and often on the lower lip. Flowers July to Sept.

(**k**) **Greater Spearwort** *Ranunculus lingua* L., family Ranunculaceae. A native perennial of fens and marshes. Rather uncommon, but scattered throughout most of Britain. Absent from north west Scotland. Flowers June to Sept. See 74(b).

(**a**) **Spiny Restharrow** *Ononis spinosa* L., family Leguminosae. A native perennial. Common on rough, grassy places in the south and east of England and Midlands. Rare elsewhere. Height to 40cm. Very similar to Restharrow but has hard, sharp prickles. Flowers June to Sept. See Restharrow 92(i).

(**b**) **Lesser Sea Spurrey** *Spergularia marina* (L.) Grisb., family Caryophyllaceae. A native annual drier areas of salt marshes. Fairly common on coasts. More robust than 81(b) and with paler flowers. Flowers June to Sept.
**Sand Spurrey** *S. rubra* (L.) J. & C. Presl. A native annual or biennial. Common on chalky soil, rare in Ireland and north Scotland. Leaves are not fleshy and have a short point at their tips. Flowers May to Sept.

(**c**) **Sea Lavender** *Limonium vulgare* Mill., family Plumbaginaceae. A native perennial found in muddy salt marshes. Common on some English coasts, rare elsewhere and absent in Ireland and north Scotland. Height to 12cm. Flowers July to Oct. See 120(l), 146(c).
**Lax-flowered Sea Lavender** *L. humile* Mill. A native perennial of muddy salt marshes. Fairly common on Irish coasts. Height to 12cm. Similar to 106(c), with narrower leaves and a stem which branches lower. Flowers July to Aug.

(**d**) **Stemless Thistle** or **Dwarf Thistle** *Cirsium acaule* Scop., family Compositae. A native perennial. Common on grazing land, especially on chalk or limestone in the south and east of England; absent elsewhere. Height to 5cm. Flowers July to Sept.

photograph taken 4 July ○ represents 1 centimetre

photograph taken 5 July

(a) **Fen Orchid** *Liparis loeselii* (L.) Rich., family Orchidaceae. A native pseudo-bulb. Very rare, found only in the fen districts of Norfolk and Suffolk and the Welsh coast near the Gower Peninsula and near Barnstaple. Grows in wet fen-peat and dune-slacks. Height to 20cm. Flowers July.

(b) **Bastard Toadflax** *Thesium humifusum* DC., family Santalaceae. A native perennial. Rare, found only in southern England, mainly on Salisbury Plain and near Cambridge. This plant is parasitic on the roots of other chalk and limestone plants. Length of the normally prostrate stems may reach 40cm. Flowers June to Aug.

(c) **Thyme-leaved Sandwort** *Arenaria serpyllifolia* L., family Caryophyllaceae. A native annual to biennial. Fairly common on bare ground, arable land, walls, chalk downs and cliffs, throughout Britain. Rather rare in north west Scotland and Northern Ireland. Height to 15cm. Flowers June to Aug.

(d) **Cornflower** or **Bluebottle** *Centaurea cyanus* L., family Compositae. A native annual, sometimes overwintering. Found over most of the British Isles, most commonly as a corn field weed. Height to 80cm. At one time, Cornflower was common but is now much reduced due to cleaner seed-grain supplies. Flowers June to Aug.

(e) **Slender Thistle** *Carduus tenuiflorus* Curt., family Compositae. A native annual or biennial of waste places, roadsides and fields, especially near the sea. Fairly common on English and Welsh coasts but rather rare in Scotland and Ireland. Height to 1m. Flowers June to Aug.

(f) **Fine-leaved Water Dropwort** *Oenanthe aquatica* (L.) Poir., family Umbelliferae. A native perennial. Rather rare, except in a band from Hull down to Dover. Found in stagnant or slow flowing water. May be as high as 1.5m. The stem is hollow. Flowers June to Sept. See 64(e), 156(f).

(a) **White Climbing Fumitory** *Corydalis claviculata* (L.) DC., family Papaveraceae. A native annual found over most of the British Isles and most common around north Wales. Rare elsewhere. It grows in woods and shady places on acid soils. The stems climb and sprawl to a length of 75cm. Flowers June to Sept. See 48(a).

(b) **Wall Rocket** or **Wall Mustard** *Diplotaxis muralis* (L.) DC., family Cruciferae. An introduced annual or biennial. Quite common in south west England, rare elsewhere. It has become naturalised on walls, wasteland and limestone rocks and is a weed of arable land. Height to 50cm. Flowers June to Sept. See 82(b).

(c) **Fragrant Evening Primrose** *Oenothera stricta* Ledeb. ex Link, family Onagraceae. Introduced from Chile. An annual or biennial, spreading from southern England. Grows on dunes. Height to 85cm. Flowers June to Sept. See 156(b).
**Common Evening Primrose.** *O. biennis* L., Introduced biennial of roadsides, dunes and waste ground. Height to 80cm. Smaller flowers than above and unspotted stems. Flowers June to Sept.

(d) **Small-flowered Catchfly** *Silene gallica* L., family Caryophyllaceae. A native annual. Rare, found in southern England and in a few places in Ireland; not in Scotland. Found on waste land and sandy soil. Height to 40cm. Flowers June to Oct.

(e) **Dwarf Spurge** *Euphorbia exigua* L., family Euphorbiaceae. A native annual. Common weed; on arable land in south and west England. Rare elsewhere. Height to 25cm. Flowers June to Oct. See other spurges.

(f) **Yellow Bartsia** *Parentucellia viscosa* (L.) Caruel, family Scrophulariaceae. A native annual found only in a few places, mainly in the west. Most common in Cork, Kerry and Cornwall. Grows near the coast in damp, grassy places. Height may be to 45cm. Flowers June to Oct. See 58(k), 90(b).

photograph taken 8 July

(e) **Tuberous Thistle** *Cirsium tuberosum* (L.) All., family Compositae. A native perennial. Very rare, found only in south Wales and the Wiltshire area and Cambridge on chalk downs. Height to 60cm. Very similar to *C. dissectum* 106(f) except that it has tuberous roots. Flowers June to Aug.

(f) **Michaelmas Daisy** *Aster novi-belgii* L., family Compositae. A perennial. This is the garden plant often found as an escape sometimes in large patches on roadsides, waste places near habitation. Height to 2m. Flowers Aug. to Oct.

(g) **Corn Marigold** *Chrysanthemum segetum* L., family Compositae. An annual, probably introduced in the neolithic era. Fairly common in arable land throughout the British Isles. Height to 45cm. Flowers June to Aug. See 30(f).

(h) **Duke of Argyll's Tea Plant** *Lycium chinense* Mill., family Solanaceae. An introduced shrub. It is found naturalised in hedges and waste places. Fairly common in East Anglia and southern England; rare in Scotland and Ireland except on the coast near Dublin. Common in gardens. Height to 2.5m. Named because it was sent to the Duke of Argyll in the 18th century mis-named as a tea plant. Flowers June to Aug. Fruits Aug. to Oct.
**Duke of Argyll's Tea Plant** *L. barbarum* L. An introduced shrub. Height to 2.5m. Naturalised in similar habitats to 112(h). More common, except on coastal sites. The leaves are long and thin. Both shrubs bear bright red berries in the autumn. Flowers June to Sept. Fruits Aug. to Oct.

(i) **Yellow Chamomile** *Anthemis tinctoria* L., family Compositae. A biennial and introduced. Found as a garden escape in a few places on roadsides and banks. Height to 50cm. The flowers yield a yellow dye. Flowers July to Aug.

(j) **Broad-leaved Ragwort** *Senecio fluviatilis* Wallr., family Compsitae. An introduced perennial. Very rare. Found near streams and fens in a few places scattered throughout Britain. Height to 1.25m. Flowers July to Oct.

(k) **Scotch Thistle** or **Cotton Thistle** *Onopordum acanthium* L., family Compositae. A biennial, possibly introduced. Fairly common in East Anglia; rare elsewhere especially Scotland. Found on roadsides, waste places and in fields. Height to 1.5m. Although called the Scotch Thistle, this may not be the one depicted on the badge of the Stuart kings which seems more likely to be the Spear Thistle but the argument is academic. Flowers July to Sept. See 112(c).

(l) **Star Thistle** *Centaurea calcitrapa* L., family Compositae. Probably introduced biennial. Rare, only on waste places on chalk in the south of England especially on the Sussex coast. Height to 60cm. Flowers July to Sept.

(a) **Marsh Bedstraw** *Galium palustre* L., family Rubiaceae. A native perennial. Very common throughout the British Isles in wet places, marshes, ditches and on the banks of streams. The sprawling stems can be up to 1m. or even longer when supported by other vegetation. Flowers May to June. See 56(g), 64(a), 78(d), 120(i).
**Fen Bedstraw** *G. uliginosum* L. A perennial native quite common in fens. Similar to 112(a). Flowers July to Aug.

(b) **Blue Sowthistle** *Cicerbita macrophylla* (Willd.) Wallr., family Compositae. Introduced perennial, established in scattered places in England. Height to 1m. Flowers July to Sept. Compare 114(a).

(c) **Spear Thistle** *Cirsium vulgare* (Savi) Ten., family Compositae. A native biennial. Common in waste places, fields, roadsides and gardens throughout the British Isles. Height to 1.25m. Flowers July to Oct. See 112(k).

(d) **Meadowsweet** *Filipendula ulmaria* (L.) Maxim, family Rosaceae. A native perennial. Common all over the British Isles in wet places, meadows, marshes, swamps and river sides. Height to 1m. or more. Medicinally, Meadowsweet has the same properties as aspirin. Steep 45grm. of dried flowers in one litre of near-boiling water for 10 minutes; the dose is three cupfuls a day between meals. Flowers June to Aug. See 100(k).

(**a**) **Chicory** or **Wild Succory** *Cichorium intybus* L., family Compositae. Probably native perennial. Common on roadsides and waste places in southern England; rare elsewhere. Height to 1.2m. The swollen roots, dried and ground, yield chicory which is often added to coffee giving it a bitter flavour. Flowers July to Oct. Photographed July 4.

(**b**) **Yellow Horned Poppy** *Glaucium flavum* Crantz, family Papaveraceae. A native perennial or biennial of the seaside. Absent from the north of Scotland but fairly common on coasts elsewhere. Height to 80cm. Flowers June to Sept. See Red Horned Poppy 82(i). Photographed July 5.

(**c**) **Birthwort** *Aristolochia clematitis* L., family Aristolochiaceae. An introduced perennial, naturalised in some places in south England. Height to 70cm. Once cultivated in herb gardens. Birthwort was used to aid conception and childbirth and to ward off demons. Flowers June to Sept. Photographed June 29.

(**d**) **Henbane** *Hyoscyamus niger* L., family Solanaceae. A native annual or biennial on disturbed ground and sandy places near the sea. Rare in Scotland, Ireland and north England; more frequent in the south. Height to 75cm. Henbane is extremely poisonous. Dr Crippen used it to murder his wife in 1910. Flowers June to Aug. Photographed July 13.

(**e**) **Spiked Speedwell** *Veronica spicata* L., family Scrophulariaceae. A native perennial of limestone rocks and dry grasslands. Very rare but often grown in gardens. Height to 50cm. Spiked Speedwell is protected by law under the Conservation of Wild Creatures and Wild Plants Act 1975, and must not be picked. Flowers July to Sept. See other speedwells. Photographed July 12.

(**f**) **Sea Milkwort** *Glaux maritima* L., family Primulaceae. A native perennial of grassy salt marshes and sea cliffs. Fairly common on all British coasts. Height to 20cm. though the stems tend to creep along the ground. Flowers June to Aug. Photographed July 5.

(a) **St Dabeoc's Heath** *Daboecia cantabrica* (Huds.) C. Koch, family Ericaceae. A native shrub of heaths and rocks only in Mayo and West Galway. Absent from the rest of Britain though often cultivated in gardens. Height to 50cm. Flowers July to Sept. Photographed July 12.

(b) **Field Madder** *Sherardia arvensis* L., family Rubiaceae. A native annual of waste places and arable fields. Fairly common in England and Wales; rare elsewhere. Height to 2.5cm. Flowers May to Oct. Photographed July 23.

(c) **Water Lobelia** *Lobelia dortmanna* L., family Campanulaceae. A native perennial found in shallow water of stony, acid lakes particularly in mountain areas. Common in Scotland, Wales, Lake District and west Ireland. Height to 50cm. Flowers July to Aug. Photographed July 13.

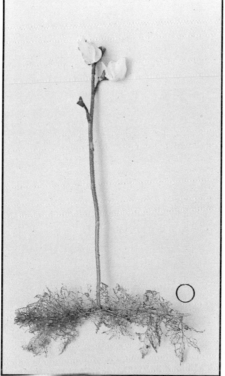

(d) **Lesser Water-plantain** *Baldellia ranunculoides* (L.) Parl., family Alismataceae. A native perennial found on damp ground by streams, lakes and ditches. Scattered throughout Britain, uncommon in most places and rare in Scotland. Height to 20cm. Flowers May to Aug. See 102(d). Photographed July 17.

(e) **Greater Bladderwort** *Utricularia vulgaris* L., family Lentibulariaceae. A native perennial of lakes, ponds and ditches throughout Britain. Rather rare. Height to 40cm. The root-like leaves bear tiny bladders which trap small water animals and so supply the plant with nutrients. Flowers July to Aug. See 46(b), 51(a), 150(i), 150(j), 154(a). Photographed July 24.

(f) **Unbranched Bur-reed** *Sparganium emersum* Rehm., family Sparganiaceae. A native perennial found in shallow water of ponds, rivers and lakes, never in acid water. Fairly common throughout Britain but rarer in Scotland and Ireland. Height to 50cm. Flowers June to July. See Bur-reed 132(g). Photographed July 13.

photograph taken 8 July

**(a) Common Centaury** *Centaurium erythraea* Rafn,
family Gentianaceae. A native annual of dry grassy
places, sand dunes, waste places and roadsides.
Common in England, Wales and Ireland but rather
rare in Scotland. Height to 15cm. Flowers June to
Oct. See 128(b).
**Slender Centaury** *C. pulchellum* (Sw.) Druce.
Native annual of damp grassy places near the sea
but also inland. Common on the south coast of
England, rare elsewhere. Height to 10cm. Similar to
Common Centaury but flowers are stalked, giving a
looser cluster, and usually a darker pink. Flowers
June to Sept.
**Yellow Centaury** *Cicendia filiformis* (L.) Delarbre,
family Gentianaceae. A native annual of damp,
sandy and peaty places near the sea. Rare. Height to
8cm. Similar to Common Centaury but has a yellow
flower with only four petals. Flowers June to Oct.

**(b) Policeman's Helmet** or **Indian Balsam**
*Impatiens glandulifera* Royle, family Balsaminaceae.
An introduced annual naturalised on waste places
and river banks. Fairly common in parts of England
and Wales, elsewhere rare. Height to 1.5m.
Flowers July to Oct. See 120(f), 134(c).

**(c) Wood Vetch** *Vicia sylvatica* L., family
Leguminosae. A native perennial found in rocky
woods and scrub and on shingle and cliffs by the sea.
Uncommon and scattered throughout Britain; rare
in Ireland. Climbing stems reach 1.3m. Flowers
June to Aug. See 32(e), 56(e), 84(i).

**(d) Annual Mercury** *Mercurialis annua* L., family
Euphorbiaceae. An annual, possibly native.
Common as a garden and arable weed and on waste
ground in south England. Rare elsewhere. Height to
35cm. The stems are branched (not shown in
photograph) and the leaves paler than perennial
Dogs Mercury. Flowers July to Oct. See 12(d).

**(e) Dittander** or **Broad-leaved Pepperwort**
*Lepidium latifolium* L., family Cruciferae. Native in
salt marshes. Rather rare, only found in a few places
in England and Wales, most frequently in East
Anglia. Height to 1m. The lower leaves are similar
to the one illustrated but much larger (30cm. long).
Not to be confused with horseradish which has
wavy-edged leaves. Flowers June to July. See
Horseradish 64(g) and other pepperworts 100(b),
118(b).

**(f) Large Dodder** *Cuscuta europaea* L., family
Convolvulaceae. A native annual which grows
parasitically on nettles and hops and sometimes
other plants. Rather rare; found only in south
England. This specimen is growing on a nettle.
Flowers July to Sept. See Common Dodder 156(d).

**(g) Black Nightshade** *Solanum nigrum* L., family
Solanaceae. A native annual of waste places,
roadsides and as a garden weed. Common
throughout England, particularly in the east; rare
in the north and absent from Ireland and north
Scotland. Height to 50cm. In the autumn it bears a
shiny black fruit. Flowers July to Sept. See Fruit
172(g) and other nightshades 48(j), 72(h).

**(h) Good King Henry** or **Mercury** *Chenopodium
bonus-henricus* L., family Chenopodiaceae. An
introduced perennial, naturalised on waste ground,
rich pasture, arable land and roadsides. Fairly
common throughout Britain, except in Scotland
and Ireland where it is rare. Height to 50cm. The
Germans called this plant Good Henry. Tudor
herbalists added the 'King' producing the modern
name. Flowers May to July. See 116(i), 116(k),
142(d), 166(a), 166(c).

**(i) Sowbane** *Chenopodium hybridum* L., family
Chenopodiaceae. Possibly native. Found on waste
places and arable land. Rare; found only in south
east England. Height to 12cm. Flowers July to Oct.
See 116(h), 116(k), 142(d), 166(a), 166(c).

**(j) Mountain Sorrel** *Oxyria digyna* (L.) Hill, family
Polygonaceae. A native perennial found in damp,
rocky places and streamsides on mountains. Fairly
common in north west Scotland; rare elsewhere
though found in the Lake District, north Wales, and
west Ireland. Height to 20cm. Flowers July to Aug.
See 36(h), 36(l).

**(k) Fig-leaved Goosefoot** *Chenopodium ficifolium*
Sm., family Chenopodiaceae. An annual, native, of
waste and arable land, especially near manure
heaps. Rather rare; most frequent in south east
England. Height to 60cm. Flowers July to Sept. See
116(h), 116(i), 142(d), 166(a), 166(c).

photograph taken 9 July ◯ represents 1 centimetre

photograph taken 9 July

(e) **Golden-rod** *Solidago virgaurea* L., family Compositae. A native perennial of dry pasture, heaths, mountain slopes and roadsides. Rare in the south east but common elsewhere in Britain particularly in Scotland. Height to 70cm. Once used in folk medicine to treat both internal and external wounds. Flowers July to Sept. See 122(d).

(f) **Sickle Hare's Ear** *Bupleurum falcatum* L., family Umbelliferae. A native perennial of waste places and hedgebanks. Very rare and may now be extinct. Height to 1m. Flowers July to Oct.

(g) **Longleaf** *Falcaria vulgaris* Bernh., family Umbelliferae. An introduced perennial, naturalised in south east England and East Anglia. Height to 45cm. Flowers July.

(h) **Hog's Fennel** or **Sulphur-weed** *Peucedanum officinale* L., family Umbelliferae. A native perennial which grows on banks by the sea. Rare found only in east Kent and Essex. Height to 1m., ours is a rather tall specimen. Flowers July to Sept. See 144(h).

(i) **Fennel** *Foeniculum vulgare* Mill., family Umbelliferae. Probably native perennial on waste places, roadsides and sea cliffs. Common round English and Welsh coasts and inland on the south east. Rare elsewhere. Height to 1.2m. Fennel has a distinctive smell rather like aniseed and its leaves are used to flavour fish and egg dishes. The stems may be candied though they are very tough to eat. Flowers July to Oct.

(j) **Fool's Parsley** *Aethusa cynapium* L., family Umbelliferae. A native annual. Common as a weed of cultivated ground throughout Britain though rarer in Scotland and Ireland. Height to 1m. Flowers July to Aug.

(k) **Danewort** or **Dwarf Elder** *Sambucus ebulus* L., family Caprifoliaceae. Possibly native perennial which grows on waste places and roadsides. Rather uncommon but scattered throughout Britain. Very rare in north Scotland. Height to 1m. Legend has it that Danewort grew from the blood of Danes but Parkinson, in 1640, wrote that by purging, it produced the 'danes' or diarrhoea. It bears a black berry in autumn. Flowers July to Aug. See Fruit 162(m) and Elder 38(e).

(l) **Burnet Saxifrage** *Pimpinella saxifraga* L., family Umbelliferae. A native perennial of dry grassy places. Common throughout Britain except in north Scotland and north Ireland. Height to 1m. The lower leaves are burnet-like. Burnet Saxifrage was once used by herbalists to treat liver and kidney stones. Flowers July to Aug. See 126(f).

(a) **Strapwort** *Corrigiola litoralis* L., family Caryophyllaceae. A native annual. Rare, found only on sand and gravel banks in south Devon and Cornwall. Introduced in a few other places. Trailing stems may reach 15cm. Flowers July to Aug.

(b) **Smith's Cress** *Lepidium heterophyllum* Benth., family Cruciferae. A native perennial of dry banks, roadsides and arable land. Scattered throughout Britain though rare in north west Scotland, west Ireland and east England. Height to 35cm. Flowers May to Aug. See pepperworts 100(b), 116(e).

(c) **Sharp-leaved Fluellen** *Kickxia elatine* (L.) Dum., family Scrophulariaceae. A native annual of arable land, particularly cornfields. Rather uncommon; mostly frequent in south England and Wales and rarely further north and in Ireland. Trailing stems may reach 40cm. Flowers July to Oct.

**Round-leaved Fluellen** *K. spuria* (L.) Dum. A native annual of cornfields. Less common than 118(c); confined to south England and Wales. The leaves are round and flowers slightly larger. Flowers July to Oct.

(d) **Shrubby Seablite** *Suaeda vera* J. F. Gmelin, family Chenopodiaceae. A native shrub of shingle banks and other well-drained sites near the sea above the high tide mark. Rather rare, only in East Anglia, Kent and south coast. Height to 1m. Distinct from Annual Seablite by having rounded leaf tips. Flowers July to Oct. See 164(c).

e    f    g    h    i    j    k    l

photograph taken 9 July ◯ represents 1 centimetre

photograph taken 12 July

**(e) Large Thyme** *Thymus pulegioides* L., family Labiatae. A native shrub of dry, calcareous grassland. Common only in south and east England. Height to 20cm. Much larger than other thymes and very aromatic. Flowers July to Aug. See 44(c), 124(k).

**(f) Small Balsam** *Impatiens parviflora* DC., family Balsaminaceae. An introduced annual, naturalised in woods and shady waste places. Most common in south east England, scattered elsewhere, rare in Scotland and absent from Ireland. Height to 45cm. Similar to Touch-me-not but with smaller, paler yellow flowers. The ripe seed pods are explosive when touched. Flowers July to Nov. See 116(b), 134(c).

**(g) Saw-wort** *Serratula tinctoria* L., family Compositae. A native perennial of woods, wood edges and clearings and on moist, calcareous grassland. Fairly common throughout England and Wales, rare in Scotland, absent in north Scotland and only one record in Ireland. Height to 80cm. 'Saw-wort' comes from the saw-edged leaves and the plant was used to treat all types of wounds. The leaves, with alum, provide a yellow-green dye for wool. This specimen is of the variety *monticola*. The flower heads of the more common form are stemmed and not bunched together. Flowers July to Sept.

**(h) Wall Germander** *Teucrium chamaedrys* L., family Labiatae. An introduced perennial, naturalised on old walls and commonly grown in gardens. Rather rare in the wild, mainly in England and Wales. Height to 20cm. Flowers July to Sept. See 108(d), 138(j).

**(i) Northern Bedstraw** *Galium boreale* L., family Rubiaceae. A native perennial of scree, streamsides, shingle moraines and sand dunes. Common in Scotland and north England; rare elsewhere and absent from the south and Midlands. Height to 40cm. Flowers July to Aug. See other bedstraws 32(d), 56(g), 78(d), 112(a).

**(j) Small Scabious** *Scabiosa columbaria* L., family Dipsacaceae. A native perennial. Common on dry calcareous pasture in England but absent from Scotland and Ireland. Height to 65cm. Flowers June to Aug. See 84(e), 138(g), 150(e).

**(k) Common Calamint** *Calamintha sylvatica* Bromf. ssp. *ascendens* (Jord.) P. W. Ball syn. *C. ascendens* Jord., family Labiatae. A native perennial on dry, calcareous banks. Fairly common in the south of England and Wales, rare elsewhere and absent from Scotland. Height to 50cm. The pleasant smell of calamint used to be employed to sweeten old meat and as a syrup used to treat coughs and colds. Flowers July to Sept. See 120(c), 124(j).

**(l) Rock Sea Lavender** *Limonium binervosum* (G.E.Sm.) Salmon, family Plumbaginaceae. A native perennial of sea cliffs and rocks. Rather rare, found only on certain English, Welsh and Irish coasts. Height to 30cm. Flowers July to Sept. See 106(c), 146(c).

**(a) Lesser Meadow Rue** *Thalictrum minus* L., family Ranunculaceae. A native perennial of dry limestone slopes, cliffs, sand dunes and on damp ground by streams and lakes. Rare in most areas, but fairly common on northern coasts and Wales. Height to 1.2m. This is an extremely variable plant. The specimen is poor since it has finished flowering. Flowers June to Aug. See Common Meadow Rue 128(g).

**(b) Chamomile** *Chamaemelum nobile* (L.) All., family Compositae. A native perennial of sandy grassland and roadsides. Fairly common in south England and south west Ireland. Rare elsewhere though often grown in gardens. Height to 25cm. Chamomile is still taken as a herbal tea to aid digestion and calm the nerves. Dried flowerheads are infused in boiling water. Flowers June to July. See 36(g), 78(c), 100(e), 124(b).

**(c) Lesser Calamint** *Calamintha nepeta* (L.) Savi, family Labiatae. A native perennial of dry calcareous banks. Rather rare; most common in south east England. Absent from Ireland and Scotland. Height to 45cm. Flowers July to Sept. See 120(k), 124(j).

**(d) Sheep's-bit Scabious** *Jasione montana* L., family Campanulaceae. A native perennial of grassy places and heaths, usually on lime free soil. Common in western parts of Britain but absent from north Scotland. Height to 40cm. Not to be confused with Devils Bit Scabious. Flowers May to Aug. See 150(e).

photograph taken 15 July

**(e) Monkshood** *Aconitum napellus* L., family Ranunculaceae. A native perennial of shady stream banks in south Wales and south west England, although, together with other varieties, it is often grown in gardens. Flowers May to July. See 76(e).

**(f) Soapwort** *Saponaria officinalis* L., family Caryophyllaceae. A native or introduced perennial. Fairly common on roadsides and hedgerows throughout England and Wales. Less common elsewhere and rare in Ireland. Height to 80cm. The leaves and roots, when boiled in water, yield a lather which was used to wash wool. Soapwort was commonly cultivated near woolmills for this purpose. Flowers July to Sept.

**(g) Hoary Alison** *Berteroa incana* (L.) DC., family Cruciferae. An introduced annual, naturalised in waste places and sometimes found in cultivated ground. Rather rare. Height to 50cm. Flowers June to Sept.

**(h) Dwarf Mallow** *Malva neglecta* Wallr., family Malvaceae. A native annual of waste places, roadsides and as a garden weed. Fairly common in south east England the Midlands, rare elsewhere. The trailing or sometimes erect stems may reach 50cm. Distinct from Common Mallow by its much smaller flowers and creeping stems. Flowers June to Sept. See other mallows 74(f), 96(f).

**(i) Berry Catchfly** *Cucubalus baccifer* L., family Caryophyllaceae. An introduced perennial, naturalised in a few places in south east England and frequently grown in gardens. Height to 80cm. In the autumn, Berry Catchfly bears shiny, black berries which are much-loved by birds. Flowers July to Sept.

**(j) Knotted Cranesbill** *Geranium nodosum* L., family Geraniaceae. An introduced perennial, sometimes found as a garden escape but rather rare. Height to 40cm. Similar to French Cranesbill but the stems are swollen at leaf junction and the petals have dark veins. Flowers May to Sept. See 104(a).

**(k) Rape** or **Cole** *Brassica napus* L., family Cruciferae. Probably introduced annual or biennial, cultivated as a fodder crop but frequently naturalised on roadsides and streamsides near arable land throughout Britain. Rare in Ireland. Height to 60cm. There is a huge number of cultivated varieties of Rape which may also be found as escapes. Flowers May to Aug. See 22(h), 51(d).

**(l) Broad-leaved Spurge** *Euphorbia platyphyllos* L., family Euphorbiaceae. A native annual of waste places and arable land. Rather rare, found only in south England. Height to 70cm. Flowers June to Oct. See other spurges.

**(a) Keeled Garlic** *Allium carinatum* L., family Liliaceae. An introduced bulb, naturalised but rare throughout Britain. Height to 30cm. Flowers July to Aug. See 48(k), 130(b).

**(b) Clustered Bellflower** *Campanula glomerata* L., family Campanulaceae. A native perennial of calcareous grassland. Fairly common in the south and east of England, rare in Scotland and absent from Ireland and north Scotland. Height to 15cm. The flowers are grouped together in a distinct cluster at the top of their stem. Flowers May to Sept. See 122(c), 136(b).

**(c) Nettle-leaved Bellflower** or **Bats-in-the-belfry** *Campanula trachelium* L., family Campanulaceae. A native perennial of woods and hedgebanks. Fairly common in south England and Wales, rare in Ireland and absent from Scotland and north England. Height to 80cm. A common country name is Throatwort which indicates its medicinal use in treating sore throats and tonsilitis. Flowers July to Sept. See 122(b), 136(b).

**(d) Canadian Golden-rod** *Solidago canadensis* L., family Compositae. An introduced perennial, commonly grown in gardens and sometimes escaping onto waste ground. Height to 1.5m. Flowers July to Oct. Compare 118(e).

photograph taken 15 July ○ represents 1 centimetre

photograph taken 16 July

(**a**) **Sea Holly** *Eryngium maritimus* L., family Umbelliferae. A native perennial of sand dunes and shingle sea shores. Fairly common on all British coasts except in Scotland. Height to 50cm. The roots of Sea Holly used to be candied with sugar and orange flower water and used as an aphrodisiac, particularly by older men. Falstaff mentions it in 'The Merry Wives of Windsor'. Flowers July to Aug. See 142(h).

(**b**) **Scentless Mayweed** *Matricaria maritima* (L.) Koch, family Compositae. A native annual to perennial. Common throughout Britain as an arable weed on roadsides and by the sea. Height to 50cm. A variable plant which is divided into further subspecies. Flowers July to Sept. See 36(g), 100(e), 120(b).

(**c**) **Sea Spurge** *Euphorbia paralias* L., family Euphorbiaceae. A native perennial of sand dunes. Fairly common on Welsh, west English and Irish coasts. Rare in north and east. Height to 35cm. Flowers July to Oct. See other spurges.

(**d**) **Carline Thistle** *Carlina vulgaris* L., family Compositae. A native biennial of calcareous grassland and sand dunes. Common in England, Wales and central Ireland. Rare elsewhere. Height to 20cm. Flowers July to Oct.

(**e**) **Spiny Cocklebur** *Xanthium spinosum* L., family Compositae. An introduced annual, grown in gardens and now naturalised in scattered localities. Height to 60cm. Flowers July to Oct.

(**f**) **Balm** *Melissa officinalis* L., family Labiatae. An introduced perennial, frequently naturalised in south England and south Wales, rare in Ireland and absent from Scotland. Height to 50cm. Balm used to be cultivated in cottage gardens for its scent and also for its popularity with bees. Flowers July to Sept.

(**g**) **Borage** *Borago officinalis* L., family Boraginaceae. An introduced annual, found as a garden escape on waste ground particularly near houses. Height to 50cm. Commonly grown in gardens as a culinary herb. Borage also has many medicinal uses, since it stimulates sweating and urination. May be eaten as a salad vegetable. Flowers June to Sept.

(**h**) **Creeping Bellflower** *Campanula rapunculoides* L., family Campanulaceae. An introduced perennial now naturalised in fields, open woods and railway banks and as a garden weed. Uncommon and scattered throughout Britain and rare in Ireland. Creeping stems may reach a length of 50cm. Flowers July to Sept. See other bellflowers 122(b), 122(c), 136(b).

(**i**) **Apple-scented Mint** *Mentha rotundifolia* (L.) Huds., family Labiatae. A native perennial of ditches, waste places and roadsides. Uncommon but most frequent in south west England. Wales and Ireland; rare elsewhere. Height to 70cm. Flowers July to Sept. See 134(i), 138(i), 138(l), 140(d), 142(b).

(**j**) **Wood Calamint** *Calamintha sylvatica* Bromf., family Labiatae. A native perennial. Rare, growing only on chalky banks on the Isle of Wight. Height to 50cm. Flowers end of July to Sept. See other calamints 120(c), 120(k).

(**k**) **Wild Thyme** *Thymus serpyllum* L., family Labiatae. A native undershrub of sandy heaths and grassland. Rare, found only in the Breckland of East Anglia. Mat-forming stems to 5cm. Similar to Common Wild Thyme but smaller, with the flowering stems evenly covered with hairs all round, rather than on two sides only. Flowers July to Aug. See 44(c), 120(e).

(**l**) **Alkanet** *Anchusa officinalis* L., family Boraginaceae. An introduced biennial to perennial, naturalised in some waste places. Rather rare. Height to 30cm. Flowers June to Sept. Compare 100(g), 124(g).

photograph taken 16 July

(a) **Square-stemmed St John's Wort** *Hypericum tetrapterum* Fr., family Guttiferae. A native perennial of damp meadows and grassland, marsh and by rivers and ponds. Fairly common throughout Britain except in the north of Scotland. Height to 60cm. Flowers June to Sept. See 98(b), 98(c), 104(e), 104(f), 128(k).
**Slender St John's Wort** *H. pulchrum* L., Native perennial found on hedgerows, rough grassy places and in woods, avoiding calcareous soil. Common throughout Britain. Height to 50cm. Similar to Square-stemmed St John's Wort but rather delicate and with a smooth, round stem. Flowers June to Aug.

(b) **Parsley Water Dropwort** *Oenanthe lachenalii* C.C. Gmel., family Umbelliferae. A native perennial of marshes and fens both brackish and freshwater. Uncommon and scattered near the sea around most British coasts except north and east Scotland. Also occurs inland in England. Height to 80cm. Flowers June to Sept. See 64(e), 110(f), 156(f).

(c) **Brookweed** *Samolus valerandi* L., family Primulaceae. A native perennial of wet places near the sea. Fairly common throughout Britain except in north and east Scotland, and many inland areas. Height to 40cm. Flowers June to Aug.

(d) **Marsh Arrow-grass** *Triglochin palustris* L., family Aponogetonaceae. A native annual or perennial found in marshes. Common throughout Britain but less so in the south of England. Height to 40cm. Flowers June to Aug. See 52(k), 90(a).

(e) **Sharp Dock** *Rumex conglomeratus* Murr., family Polygonaceae. A native biennial to perennial of damp grassy places and sometimes woods. Common throughout England, Wales and Ireland but rather rare in Scotland. Height to 1m. Very similar to Red-veined Dock with which it is often confused. Flowers July to Aug. See 64(j), 106(i), 126(i), 126(j), 126(k).

(f) **Greater Burnet Saxifrage** *Pimpinella major* (L.) Huds., family Umbelliferae. A native perennial of wood edges and hedgebanks. Fairly common in south east England and Midlands and in south west Ireland. Rare or absent elsewhere. Height to 1m. Once used medicinally for colic and indigestion and also to break up kidney and bladder stones. Flowers June to July. See 118(l).

(g) **Water Parsnip** *Sium latifolium* L., family Umbelliferae. A native perennial of marshes and fens. Rather uncommon; found most frequently in south east England. Rare or absent elsewhere. Height to 2m. The seeds of Water Parsnip are recommended by Culpepper in the treatment of many diseases, including tumours in the breast. Flowers July to Aug.

(h) **Pepper Saxifrage** *Silaum silaus* (L.) Schinz & Thell., family Umbelliferae. A native perennial of grassy banks and meadows. Fairly common throughout England but rare or absent elsewhere. Height to 80cm. Flowers June to Aug.

(i) **Red-veined Dock** *Rumex sanguineus* L., family Polygonaceae. A native perennial found on waste ground, grassy places and woods. Common in Wales, England and Ireland but rare in north Scotland. Height to 1m. The large leaves frequently have a red or purple veining (unfortunately not clear in this specimen) which distinguishes it from other docks. The stem is also coloured. Flowers June to Aug. See 64(j), 106(i), 126(e), 126(j), 126(k).

(j) **Great Water Dock** *Rumex hydrolapathum* Huds., family Polygonaceae. A native perennial found in shallow water and wet places. Fairly common in south England and the Midlands but rare elsewhere. Height to 2m. An infusion of the roots was once used as a mouth wash. Flowers July to Sept. See 64(j), 106(i), 126(e), 126(i), 126(k).

(k) **Curled Dock** *Rumex crispus* L., family Polygonaceae. A native perennial of grassy places, cultivated and waste ground. Common throughout Britain, often as a troublesome weed on farmland. Height to 1m. The leaves usually have wavy, crisped edges. Flowers June to Oct. See 64(j), 106(i), 126(e), 126(i), 126(j).

photograph taken 17 July ◯ represents 1 centimetre

photograph taken 17 July

**(e) Lesser Snapdragon** or **Weasel's Snout** *Misopates orontium* (L.) Raf., family Scrophulariaceae. A native annual of cultivated land. Rather uncommon; most frequently found in south west Wales and south England. Rare elsewhere and absent from Scotland. Height to 30cm. Flowers July to Oct.

**(f) Pale Toadflax** *Linaria repens* (L.) Mill., family Scrophulariaceae. A native perennial of waste places and dry fields usually on calcareous soil. Rather uncommon, scattered throughout England and Wales. Rare in Scotland and Ireland. Height to 60cm. Flowers June to Sept. See other toadflaxes 42(b), 86(i), 92(j).

**(g) Common Meadow Rue** or **Yellow Meadow Rue** *Thalictrum flavum* L., family Ranunculaceae. A native perennial found in meadows and fens. Fairly common in south and east England. Rare elsewhere. Height to 80cm. Flowers July to Aug. See Lesser Meadow Rue: 120(a).
**Alpine Meadow Rue** *T. alpinum* L. Native perennial of mountain rocks. Most common in north west Scotland but also found in north England, north Wales and Ireland. Height to 12cm. Similar to other meadow rues but much smaller with few flowers on a single spike. Flowers June to July.

**(h) Catmint** *Nepeta cataria* L., family Labiatae. A native perennial of hedgebanks and roadsides. Fairly common on calcareous soil in south and east England, rare or absent elsewhere. Height to 1m. Highly scented. Flowers July to Sept. See 66(d).
**White Horehound** *Marrubium vulgare* L., family Labiatae. Native perennial of roadsides and waste places. Scattered throughout England and Wales but rare in Scotland and Ireland. Height to 50cm. Smaller than Catmint with clusters of small white flowers up the stems and more rounded leaves. Flowers June to Oct.

**(i) Round-headed Leek** *Allium sphaerocephalon* L., family Liliaceae. A native bulb. Very rare, found only on limestone rock near Bristol and in Jersey. Height to 80cm. Flowers June to Aug. See 80(e), 130(f), 130(g).

**(j) Downy Woundwort** *Stachys germanica* L., family Labiatae. A native perennial or biennial. Very rare; found only in meadows and hedgebanks in Oxfordshire. Height to 60cm. Similar to Field Woundwort but covered in dense, white hairs. Flowers July to Aug. See other woundworts 50(c), 58(l), 96(j), 102(f), 128(f).

**(k) Imperforate St John's Wort** *Hypericum maculatum* Crantz, family Guttiferae. A native perennial of damp wood edges and hedgebanks. Rather uncommon but scattered throughout Britain. Rare in Scotland and north England. Height to 50cm. This St John's Wort has a square but unwinged stem and no black dots on the leaves. Flowers June to Aug. See other St John's Worts 98(b), 98(c), 104(e), 104(f), 126(a).

**(a) Red-rattle** or **Marsh Lousewort** *Pedicularis palustris* L., family Scrophulariaceae. A native annual of wet heaths and meadows. Fairly common throughout Britain except in the south of England and Midlands, where it is rather rare. Height to 50cm. Similar to Lousewort but is usually larger, having a single branching stem rather than several and the whole plant is often coloured reddish purple. Flowers May to Sept. See 56(j).

**(b) Seaside Centaury** *Centaurium littorale* (D. Turner) Gilmour, family Gentianaceae. A native annual of sand dunes. Rather rare found only on coasts of north west Wales, north west England and Scotland. Height to 15cm. Recognisable from Common Centaury by its narrow leaves. Flowers July to Aug. See 116(a).

**(c) Marsh Woundwort** *Stachys palustris* L., family Labiatae. A native perennial, common by streams, ponds and ditches and in marshes and fens throughout Britain. Height to 80cm. Marsh Woundwort was used as a healing agent on cuts and wounds. Flowers July to Sept. See 50(c), 58(l), 96(j), 102(f), 128(j).

**(d) Gromwell** *Lithospermum officinale* L., family Boraginaceae. A native perennial of hedgerows, wood edges and scrub, usually on basic soil. Fairly common in south England, south Wales and the Midlands but rare elsewhere. Height to 60cm. Gromwell produces small grey-white nutlets in the autumn and it is believed that these may contain a contraceptive substance. Flowers June to July. See 44(f).

photograph taken 17 July

**(a) Travellers Joy** or **Old Man's Beard** *Clematis vitalba* L., family Ranunculaceae. A native perennial of hedgerows, wood edges and scrub mainly on calcareous soil. Very common in the south of England and Wales. Introduced and naturalised, though rare, in Ireland and Scotland. Climbing stems may reach as much as 30m. Flowers July to Aug. See Fruits 172(f).

**(b) Crow Garlic** *Allium vineale* L., family Liliaceae. A native bulb of fields and roadsides. Fairly common in England and Wales but rare in Ireland and Scotland. Height to 70cm. A common form has no flowers but only a cluster of bulbils. Flowers June to July. See 80(e), 122(a).

**Field Garlic** *A. oleraceum* L. A native bulb of dry grassy places. Rather rare and scattered through England and south Scotland; rare in Wales and the north. Height to 70cm. Flowers are in a looser bunch and the leaves flatter than on Crow Garlic. Flowers July to Aug.

**(c) Canadian Fleabane** *Conyza canadensis* (L.) Cronq., family Compositae. An introduced annual. Common on waste land and roadsides in south east England. Rare elsewhere and absent from Ireland and Scotland. Height to 1m. Originally from North America, this weed has become well established during the last 200 years and is expected to spread further along the banks of roads and motorways. Flowers end of July to Sept. See 150(a).

**(d) Hawkweed** *Hieraceum umbellatum* L., family Compositae. A native perennial of roadsides, hedgebanks, open woods and heaths. Found throughout Britain, but more common in the lowlands. Absent from Orkney, Shetland, and the Outer Hebrides. Height to 60cm. Variable; the most distinctive feature of these hawkweeds are the numerous leaves covering the stem and numerous flowerheads in groups. Flowers June to Oct. See 54(h), 66(l), 142(f).

**(e) Cabbage Thistle** *Cirsium oleraceum* (L.) Scop., family Compositae. An introduced perennial, established in some marshes, fens, woods and streamsides in Scotland and England. Rather rare. Height to 1m. Flowers July to Sept.

**(f) Babington's Leek** *Allium babingtonii* Borrer, family Liliaceae. A native bulb. Rare, growing only in rock clefts and sandy places on the coast of Cornwall, Dorset and west Ireland. Height to 2m. Flowers July to Aug. See 80(e), 128(i), 130(g).

**(g) Wild Leek** *Allium ampeloprasum* L., family Liliaceae. A native bulb. Very rare, growing only on rocky and waste places on the coast of Cornwall, Somerset, Glamorgan, Pembroke and Guernsey. Height to 2m. Flowers July to Aug. See 80(e), 128(i), 130(f).

**(h) Teasel** *Dipsacus fullonum* L., family Dipsacaceae. A native biennial. Common on roadsides, pasture, wood edges and stream banks in south England and Midlands. Rare elsewhere and absent from north Scotland. Height to 2m. A subspecies of teasel was cultivated and the heads used to tease fabrics, particularly woollens. It is often grown in gardens to encourage goldfinches which love to eat the seeds which appear in autumn. Flowers end of July to Aug. See Small Teasel 144(d).

**(i) Hemp Agrimony** *Eupatorium cannabinum* L., family Compositae. A native perennial of marshes, fens, damp woods, ditches and stream edges. Common throughout England and Wales but rather rare elsewhere and absent from north Scotland. Height to 1m. Once used as a cure for jaundice and to cleanse the kidney and bladder. The leaves resemble those of Hemp, 154(d), hence the common name. Flowers July to Sept.

**(j) Woolly Thistle** *Cirsium eriophorum* (L.) Scop., family Compositae. A native biennial of grassland scrub and roadsides on calcareous soil. Rather uncommon, found only in parts of south England, south Wales and the Midlands. Height to 1.2m. Flowers July to Sept.

photograph taken 17 July ○ represents 1 centimetre

**(a) Marsh Helleborine** *Epipactis palustris* (L.) Crantz, family Orchidaceae. A native rhizome of fens and dune slacks. Rather uncommon and scattered throughout England, Wales and Ireland. Rare in Scotland. Height to 40cm. Flowers June to Aug. See 71(b), 89(c), 94(b), 132(b). Photographed July 16.

**(b) Dune Helleborine** *Epipactis dunensis* (T. & T. A. Steph.) Godf., family Orchidaceae. A native rhizome of moist hollows in sand dunes or beneath pine plantations. Very rare, found only in Lancashire and Anglesey. Height to 40cm. Similar to Narrow-lipped Helleborine but the flowers never quite open. Flowers June to July. See 71(b), 89(c), 94(b), 132(a). Photographed July 16.

**(e) Flowering Rush** *Butomus umbellatus* L., family Butomaceae. A native perennial of ponds, ditches, canals and river edges. Rather uncommon but found throughout England, particularly the south and Midlands. Rare or absent elsewhere. Height to 1.5m. This is a beautiful plant which is popular for gardens. It was introduced to North America for this purpose and has now become established as an escape along the St Lawrence and the Great Lakes. Flowers July to Sept.

**(f) Arrowhead** *Sagittaria sagittifolia* L., family Alismataceae. A native perennial found in shallow water of ponds, canals and slow-moving rivers. Fairly common in England but rare elsewhere and absent from Scotland. Height to 90cm. Named Arrowhead from the shape of the leaves. Flowers July to Aug.

**(g) Bur-reed** *Sparganium erectum* L., family Sparganiaceae. A native perennial in shallow water of ponds, ditches and slow rivers and in marshes. Common throughout Britain but rare in north Scotland. Height to 1.5m. This is the most common of the Bur-reeds and has been divided by botanists into several varieties. There are two types of flowerheads on each plant – male and female. Flowers June to Aug. See 115(f).

**(h) White Water-lily** *Nymphaea alba* L., family Nymphaeceae. A native rhizome. The leaves float in lakes and ponds throughout Britain. Height to 10cm. Seeds of the White Water-lily were eaten in broth in Elizabethan times to cool the passions. Many of the cultivated varieties are descended from this British species crossed with other exotic ones. Flowers July to Aug. See 132(i), 140(c).

**(c) Frog Orchid** *Coeloglossum viride* (L.) Hartm., family Orchidaceae. A native tuber of calcareous pasture and hillsides and also on sand dunes. Rather uncommon but may be found in suitable places throughout Britain, though more often in the north. Height to 20cm. The specimen is rather small. Flowers June to Aug. Photographed July 30.

**(d) Creeping Lady's Tresses** *Goodyera repens* (L.) R. Br., family Orchidaceae. A native rhizome of pine woods and sometimes birchwood and most fixed sand dunes. Most common in north east Scotland. Absent elsewhere except East Anglia, Cumberland, Northumberland and south Scotland. Height to 20cm. Flowers July to Aug. See 156(e). Photographed July 30.

**(i) Yellow Water-lily** or **Brandy Bottle** *Nuphar lutea* (L.) Sm., family Nymphaeceae. A native rhizome of lakes, ponds and streams. Fairly common throughout Britain but rare in north Scotland. Height to 10cm. Rhizomes of this and White water-lilies were mixed with tar and applied to the scalp to cure balding. The name Brandy Bottle comes from the shape of the fruit capsule and also its slightly stale alcoholic smell. Flowers June to Aug. See 132(i), 140(h).

photograph taken 17 July ○ represents 1 centimetre

photograph taken 20 July

**(a) Goosegrass, Cleavers** or **Sticky Willie** *Galium aparine* L., family Rubiaceae. This shows the bristly fruit. Flowers May to Aug. See 64(a) and 32(d), 56(g), 78(d), 112(a), 120(i).

**(b) Hedge Bindweed** or **Bellbine** *Calystegia sepium* (L.) R. Br., family Convolvulaceae. An introduced perennial common on hedges and waste places throughout Britain though rarer in Scotland. The climbing, trailing stems may reach as much as 3m. Flowers July to Sept. See 78(b), 90(c).

**(c) Orange Balsam** *Impatiens capensis* Meerburgh, family Balsaminaceae. An introduced annual, naturalised on river and canal banks, particularly in the south on the Thames and on estuaries. Absent from Scotland, Ireland and north England and most of Wales. Height to 50cm. See 116(b), 120(f).
**Touch-me-not** *I. noli-tangere* L. This is the native

balsam but the most rare. Found in streams and wet ground in the Lake District and north Wales and a few other places. Similar to 134(c) but with larger leaves and yellow flowers. Flowers July to Sept.

**(d) Lords and Ladies** or **Cuckoo Pint** *Arum maculatum* L., family Araceae. Poisonous. Fruits July to Aug. See flowers 40(b) and 76(g).

**(e) Common Hemp Nettle** *Galeopsis tetrahit* L., family Labiatae. A native annual of arable land, damp woods, heaths and waste places. Common throughout Britain. Height to 80cm. Flowers July to Sept. See 138(k), 140(f).
**Red Hemp Nettle** *G. angustifolia* Ehrh. ex Hoffm. A native annual of arable land. Fairly common in south and east England, rare or absent elsewhere. Height to 60cm. The flowers are deep pink with white spots on the lip. Flowers July to Oct.

**(f) Black Bindweed** *Bilderdykia convolvulus* Dumort., syn. *Polygonum convolvulus* L., family Polygonaceae. A native annual of waste places and a weed of arable land and gardens. Common throughout Britain. The scrambling stems may grow to 1.2m in length. The seeds have a high starch content and were used as a food source as long ago as 400AD. Flowers July to Oct.

**(g) Upright Hedge Parsley** *Torilis japonica* (Houtt.) DC., family Umbelliferae. A native annual of hedges, grassy places and roadsides. Common throughout Britain except in north Scotland. Height to 1m. Flowers July to Aug.
**Spreading Hedge Parsley** *T. arvensis* (Huds.) Link. A native annual of arable land. Uncommon but scattered throughout England and Wales. Height to 40cm. Similar to Upright Hedge Parsley but smaller and more spreading. The tiny fruits have two long styles at their tips. Flowers July to Sept.

**(h) Red Shank** or **Persicaria** *Polygonum persicaria* L., family Polygonaceae. A native annual. Very common all over Britain on waste ground, by water and as an arable weed. Height to 70cm. Easily recognised by the dark spot on its leaves which has been attributed in legend to the blood of Christ or to being pinched by the Virgin Mary or the Devil. Flowers June to Oct. See 56(d), 162(c), 170(b), 170(d), 170(e).

**(i) Corn Mint** *Mentha arvensis* L., family Labiatae. A native perennial of arable fields, woods and damp places. Common all over Britain though rarer in Scotland. Height to 50cm. Has been put in haystacks to keep mice out. Flowers May to Oct. See other mints 124(i), 138(i), 138(l), 140(d), 142(b), 150(c).

**(j) Coltsfoot** *Tussilago farfara* L., family Compositae. The leaves only are illustrated here since these appear after flowering. Flowers March to Apr. See Flowers 14(j).

**(k) Gipsywort** *Lycopus europaeus* L., family Labiatae. A native perennial of river and canal banks, ditches, marshes and fens. Common in England and Wales, rarer in Scotland and Ireland. Height to 1m. Named Gipsywort since gipsies were meant to have blackened themselves with it to pass off as Africans while performing their magic and fortune-telling. Flowers June to Sept.

**(l) Knotgrass** *Polygonum aviculare* L., family Polygonaceae. A native annual of waste places, sea shores, arable land and roadsides. Very common throughout Britain. Trailing stems may reach as much as 1.5m. Flowers July to Oct. See 134(h).
**Ray's Knotgrass** *Polygonum oxyspermum* Meyer & Bunge *P. raii* Bab. A native annual of Atlantic shores above high spring water mark. Rather rare. Straggling stems to 1m.

**(m) Large Birdsfoot-trefoil** *Lotus pedunculatus* Cav., family Leguminosae. A native perennial of damp, grassy places. Common throughout Britain but rare in Scottish and Irish Highlands. Climbing stems may reach 1m. Differs from Common Birdsfoot-trefoil by being larger and having hollow stems. Flowers June to Aug. See 38(a).

photograph taken 20 July ◯ represents 1 centimetre

**(a) Ivy-leaved Bellflower** *Wahlenbergia hederacea* (L.) Rchb., family Campanulaceae. A native perennial. Fairly common in Wales, Cornwall and Devon but rare elsewhere. Grows in damp, peaty moors, heaths and by streams. The creeping stems may reach 30cm. Flowers July to Aug.

**(b) Giant Bellflower** *Campanula latifolia* L., family Campanulaceae. A native perennial of woods and hedgebanks. Rare in north west Scotland and southern England and absent from Ireland. Fairly common elsewhere. Height to 1m. The lower leaves are nettle-shaped and stalked. Young shoots may be cooked and eaten as a green vegetable. Flowers July to Aug. See 122(b), 122(c).

**(c) Round-headed Rampion** *Phyteuma tenerum* R. Schulz, family Campanulaceae. A native perennial. Rare, found only from Dorset and Wiltshire to Kent where it can be locally abundant. Grows in woods and thickets. Height to 75cm. Flowers July to Aug.

**(d) Deptford Pink** *Dianthus armeria* L., family Caryophyllaceae. A native biennial. Rare, found in the south of England and occasionally as an introduction as far north as southern Scotland. Grows on roadsides, hedgebanks and dry pastures, especially on sandy soil. Height to 50cm. Flowers July to Aug. See 80(a), 80(b).

**(e) Toothed Wintergreen** *Orthilia secunda* (L.) House, family Pyrolaceae. A native rhizome. Rare, found mainly in the Highlands of Scotland, the Lake District and one or two other sites. Height to 10cm. Flowers July to Aug.

**(f) Cowbane** *Cicuta virosa* L., family Umbelliferae. A native perennial. Rare in England and Scotland, a little more common in northern Ireland. Found in marshes, dykes and ditches in shallow water. Height to 1.2m. Flowers July to Aug.

(a) **Cudweed** *Filago vulgaris* Lam., family Compositae. A native annual found scattered all over the British Isles. Uncommon in Wales, Ireland and Scotland; more common on the east side of England. Grows on roadsides, fields, heaths and dry pastures, mainly on acid, sandy soils. Height to 30cm. Flowers July to Aug. See 137(f).

(b) **Night-flowering Campion** *Silene noctiflora* L., family Caryophyllaceae. A native annual with scattered distribution over south west England. Rare elsewhere. Found especially on sandy soils as a weed of arable fields. Height to 50cm. The petals roll inwards during the day and at night spread open giving off a scent. Flowers July to Sept.

(c) **Saltwort** *Salsola kali* L., family Chenopodiaceae. A native annual. Sparsely distributed on the coasts of the British Isles on sandy shores. The prostrate, or often erect stems, may be up to 60cm. long. Flowers July to Sept.

(d) **Great Burdock** *Arctium lappa* L., family Compositae. A native biennial of waste places and roadsides. Common in south east England, absent from Scotland and northern England. Height to 1m. Similar to the Lesser Burdock but the lower leaves do not have hollow stems and the coloured part of the flowerhead is shorter than the lower part. Flowers July to Sept. See 98(m).

(e) **Autumn Hawkbit** *Leontondon autumnalis* L., family Compositae. A native perennial. Very common all over the British Isles, on roadsides, meadows and screes. Height to 50cm. Flowers June to Oct. See 60(l).

(f) **Small Cudweed** *Logfia minima* Sm. (Dumort) syn. *Filago minima* (Sm.) Pers., family Compositae. A native annual. Fairly rare, found scattered over mainland Britain. Rare in Ireland. Found in fields and sandy heaths, it avoids calcareous soils. Height to 15cm. Flowers June to Oct. See 137(a).

photograph taken 24 July

**(e) Dragon's Teeth** *Tetragonolobus maritimus* (L.) Roth, family Leguminosae. An introduced perennial, naturalised on rough calcareous grassland. Rather rare, found only in south England. Height to 20cm. Flowers June to Sept.

**(f) Corn Cockle** *Agrostemma githago* L., family Caryophyllaceae. An introduced annual, once widely established in cornfields, now rather rare. Scattered throughout England and Wales, rare elsewhere. Height to 1m. Flowers June to Aug.

**(g) Devil's Bit Scabious** *Succisa pratensis* Moench, family Dipsacaceae. A native perennial. Common in marshes, meadows, fens, roadsides and damp woods throughout Britain. Height to 80cm. The Devil was said to have bitten off the root in anger against the Virgin Mary, hence Devil's Bit(e). The flowers are usually a lilac blue, see 150(e), this specimen is a less common pinky-white. Flowers June to Oct. See 68(g), 84(e), 120(d).

**(h) Narrow-leaved Everlasting Pea** *Lathyrus sylvestris* L., family Leguminosae. A native perennial. Rather rare in southern England, very rare in the north, unknown in Ireland. It is found in woods and hedges, normally near habitation. Scrambling stems as long as 1.75m. Flowers June to Aug. See 82(d), 102(k).

**(i) Peppermint** *Mentha × piperita* L., family Labiatae. A cultivated perennial, possibly a native hybrid between Spearmint and Watermint. Found on roadsides and ditches throughout Great Britain; not common. Height to 60cm. It was at one time grown commercially around Mitcham in Surrey for the oil extracted from it, which is strong in menthol, and was used medicinally for toothache and respiratory difficulties. Flowers July to Sept. See 125(i), 134(i), 138(l), 140(d), 142(b), 150(c).

**(j) Water Germander** *Teucrium scordium* L., family Labiatae. A native perennial. Common along the River Shannon but elsewhere very rare. Height to 60cm. Flowers July to Oct. See 108(d), 120(h).

**(k) Downy Hemp Nettle** *Galeopsis segetum* Neck, family Labiatae. A native annual. Very rare, found in agricultural land; almost extinct. Height to 70cm. Flowers July to Oct. See 134(e), 140(f).

**(l) Horse Mint** *Mentha longifolia* (L.) Huds., family Labiatae. A possibly native perennial. Fairly rare but can be found all over the British Isles on damp roadsides and waste places. Height to 75cm. Flowers July to Sept. See 124(i), 134(i), 138(i), 140(d), 142(b), 150(c).

**(a) Savory** *Satureja montana* L., family Labiatae. An introduction undershrub, cultivated and sometimes naturalised on old walls. Height to 40cm. Used as a culinary herb, particularly with beans. It is also an intestine antiseptic and has been attributed aphrodisiac qualities. An infusion is recommended for stomach pains and indigestion. Flowers July to Oct.

**(b) Small Toadflax** *Chaenorhinum minus* (L.) Large, family Scrophulariaceae. A native annual of waste places, arable land and railway banks. Fairly common in England and Wales; less common in Ireland and rare in Scotland. Height to 20cm. Flowers May to Oct.

**(c) Red Deadnettle** *Lamium purpureum* L., family Labiatae. This is a rather untypical specimen. Compare with the earlier flowering specimen: 14(f).

**(d) Ground Pine** *Ajuga chamaepitys* (L.) Schreb., family Labiatae. A native annual. Rare, found only on chalk grassland in south east England. Height to 15cm. When crushed, this plant gives off a distinct smell of pine, hence the common name. Flowers May to Sept. See 28(d), 52(b).

photograph taken 24 July ◯ represents 1 centimetre

photograph taken 24 July

(**a**) **Frog-bit** *Hydrocharis morsus-ranae* L., family Hydrocharitaceae. A native perennial. Rather uncommon but scattered through England in ponds and ditches in calcareous areas. Rare in Wales and Ireland, absent from Scotland. Height to about 10cm above water. In dry years it may be found growing on land rather than water. Flowers July to Aug.

(**b**) **Canadian Pondweed** *Elodea canadensis* Michx., family Hydrocharitaceae. An introduced perennial naturalised and common in slow-moving water throughout Britain, though rare in north Scotland. The stems are always submerged and may grow to 3m in length. Introduced from North America in the 19th century, Canadian Pondweed spreads rapidly and has actually blocked many waterways. There are separate male and female

plants, the male being very rare in Britain, the female sometimes producing tiny, floating green-purple flowers on long thin stems. Flowers May to Oct.

(**c**) **Fringed Water-lily** *Nymphoides peltata* (S.G. Gmel.) O. Kuntze, family Menyanthaceae. A native rhizome of ponds, slow-moving rivers and ditches. Rather rare, found in south and east central England and introduced in scattered places elsewhere. Absent in Ireland and Scotland. Floating stems may reach 1.5m. Much smaller than the Yellow Water-lily and with distinctive fringed petals. Flowers July to Aug. See 132(h), 132(i).

(**d**) **Water Mint** *Mentha aquatica* L., family Labiatae. A native perennial of marshes, fens, river and streamsides and damp woods. Common throughout Britain, except in the Highlands. Height to 80cm. Water Mint is highly aromatic producing a beautiful, minty scent when crushed. Flowers July to Oct. See 124(i), 134(i), 138(i), 138(j), 140(d), 150(c).

(**e**) **Yellow Loosestrife** *Lysimachia vulgaris* L., family Primulaceae. A native perennial of river and lake sides, and fens. Fairly common throughout England and Wales. Scattered elsewhere and rare in north Scotland. Height to 1m. The Greeks believed Loosestrife to end strife between oxen and horses when harnessed to the same plough. Flowers July to Aug. See 104(k).

(**f**) **Large-flowered Hemp Nettle** *Galeopsis speciosa* Mill., family Labiatae. A native annual of arable land, particularly on peaty soil. Rather uncommon throughout Britain, rare in the south and west of England and south Ireland. Height to 80cm. Flowers July to Sept. See 134(e), 138(k).

(**g**) **Lesser Reedmace** or **Lesser Bulrush** *Typha angustifolia* L., family Typhaceae. A native perennial of reed swamps and at the edges of lakes, ponds, canals and slow-moving rivers. Rather uncommon and scattered through England and parts of Wales. Rare in Scotland and Ireland. Height to 2m. Distinct difference from the Bulrush is that the male and female parts of the flower head are separate from each other. This specimen has finished flowering and only the female part is left but there is about 4–5cm of green stem above this and below where the male part has been. Flowers June to July. See 102(c), 140(h).

(**h**) **Bulrush, Cat's-tail** or **Great Reedmace** *Typha latifolia* L., family Typhaceae. This specimen may be compared with the Lesser Reedmace. It has finished flowering and only the female part remains. For further text and flowering specimen, see 102(c), 140(g).

(**i**) **Yellow Flag** *Iris pseudacorus* L., family Iridaceae. The fruit of the Yellow Flag is illustrated. It was once recommended that the seeds be roasted and made into a hot drink like coffee. The fruits appear during July and August. For further text and Flowers see 76(i) and also 18(i), 106(e).

photograph taken 25 July ◯ represents 1 centimetre

photograph taken 25 July

**(e) Brown Knapweed** *Centaurea jacea* L., family Compositae. An introduced perennial. Rare, established on waste ground in south England. Height to 50cm. Similar to *C. nigra* but the lower part of the flowerhead is brown rather than black. Flowers end of July to Sept. See 84(h), 100(h).

**(f) Hoary Cinquefoil** *Potentilla argentea* L., family Rosaceae. A native perennial of dry, sandy grassland. Rather rare but most frequent in south east England. Absent from Ireland and north Scotland. Height to 35cm. Flowers June to Sept. See 42(c), 56(i), 60(k), 104(d), 142(g).

**(g) Sulphur Cinquefoil** or **Upright Cinquefoil** *Potentilla recta* L., family Rosaceae. An introduced perennial, cultivated in gardens, sometimes escaping and becoming naturalised on grassy waste places. Rather rare but scattered in south England and the Midlands. Absent elsewhere, except for one record in Scotland. Height to 50cm. Flowers June to July. See 42(c), 56(i), 60(k), 104(d), 142(f).

**(h) Field Eryngo** *Eryngium campestre* L., family Umbelliferae. A native perennial of dry, grassy places. Rare, found only in south England. Height to 50cm. Flowers July to Aug. See 124(a).

**(i) Wild Madder** *Rubia peregrina* L., family Rubiaceae. A native perennial found in hedges, scrub, thickets and stony ground, usually near the sea. Rather uncommon, found only in south and south west England and on Welsh and Irish coasts. Height to 1m. The roots provide a pink dye. Another related plant supplies the crimson madder known to artists. Flowers June to Aug.

**(j) Hawkweed** *Hieraceum vagum* Jord., family Compositae. Native perennial of wood edges and hedgerows. Most common in England and Wales, rarer elsewhere and absent from north Scotland and Ireland. Height to 60cm. Flowers July to Nov. See 54(h), 66(l), 130(d).

**(k) Wormwood** *Artemisia absinthium* L., family Compositae. A native perennial of waste places and roadsides. Fairly common in England and Wales, rare elsewhere. Height to 80cm. Wormwood is highly aromatic and in the past was used on floors to banish fleas. Medicinally, it was used to stimulate digestion. Flowers July to Aug. See 142(a), 146(d), 162(a).

**(a) Mugwort** *Artemisia vulgaris* L., family Compositae. A native perennial, common in waste places, hedgerows and roadsides throughout Britain though rare in Scotland and north England. Height to 1m. Mugwort has long been associated with magic and was used to ward off evil spirits, particularly on St John's Eve. Flowers July to Sept. See 142(k), 146(d), 162(a).

**(b) Spearmint** *Mentha spicata* L., family Labiatae. An introduced perennial, commonly cultivated but also naturalised on roadsides and waste places. Rather uncommon in the wild but scattered throughout Britain. Height to 60cm. This is one of the most popular pot herbs grown in gardens. Flowers end of July to Sept. See 124(i), 134(i), 138(i), 138(l), 140(d), 150(c).

**(c) Prickly Lettuce** or **Compass Plant** *Lactuca serriola* L., family Compositae. An introduced biennial of waste places, walls and roadsides. Common in south east England, scattered and rare elsewhere and absent from north Scotland and Ireland. Height to 1.5m. The upper leaves are held vertically; in full sun they point north and south, a phenomenon which gives it the name Compass Plant. Flowers July to Sept.

**(d) Many-seeded Goosefoot** *Chenopodium polyspermum* L., family Chenopodiaceae. A native annual of waste places, roadsides and as a cultivated weed. Fairly common in south England and the Midlands. Very rare or absent in Scotland and Ireland. Height to 70cm. Flowers July to Oct. See 116(h), 116(i), 116(k), 166(c).

photograph taken 27 July

(**a**) **Crested Cow-wheat** *Melampyrum cristatum* L., family Scrophulariaceae. A native of wood edges and hedgerows. Rare, found only in south east England. Height to 30cm. Our specimen is rather poor since it is usually more highly-coloured, the tops being bright purple with yellow and purple flowers. Flowers June to Aug. See 84(a).
**Field Cow-wheat** *M. arvense* L., A native annual of corn fields. Rare, found only in south east England. Height to 40cm. Similar to Crested Cow-wheat but with looser flowerheads with short, toothed 'crests'. Flowers June to Sept.

(**b**) **Red Bartsia** *Odontites verna* (Bell.) Dum., family Scrophulariaceae. A native annual, common in fields, grassy waste places and roadsides throughout Britain, except in the Highlands. Height to 30cm. Flowers June to Aug.

(**c**) **Fleabane** *Pulicaria dysenterica* (L.) Bernh., family Compositae. A native perennial of marshes, wet meadows, ditches and hedgerows. Common throughout Britain, except in Scotland and north England. Height to 40cm. Fleabane was used to banish fleas. Medicinally, it was used against dysentery. Flowers end of July to Sept.

(**d**) **Small Teasel** *Dipsacus pillosus* L., family Dipsacaceae. A native biennial of damp woods, ditches and hedgebanks. Rather uncommon, scattered in England and Wales. Absent from Scotland and Ireland. Flowers end of July to Aug. See 130(h).

(**e**) **Cone Flower** *Rudbeckia laciniata* L., family Compositae. An introduced perennial, commonly grown in gardens but sometimes escaping and now naturalised in many areas. Height to 2m. Flowers July to Oct.

(**f**) **Marsh Mallow** *Althaea officinalis* L., family Malvaceae. A native perennial of the upper edges of salt marshes and in ditches near the sea. Rather uncommon, but found in south and east England, south Wales and parts of Ireland. Rare elsewhere. Height to 1m. The sweets known as marshmallows were once made from the roots of this wild plant. It also had many medicinal uses for the stomach, kidneys, lungs and skin. Flowers end of July to Sept. See 74(f), 96(f), 157(f).

(**g**) **Ploughman's Spikenard** *Inula conyza* DC., family Compositae. A native biennial to perennial of dry, rocky slopes, cliffs and open woods, preferably on calcareous ground. Fairly common in England and Wales, rarer in the north and absent from Scotland and Ireland. Height to 1m. Spikenard is the name of an Indian plant whose roots were used in perfume making. Ploughman's Spikenard also has fragrant roots but these are only enjoyed by ploughmen, hence the name. Flowers July to Sept.

(**h**) **Milk Parsley** *Peucedanum palustre* (L.) Moench, family Umbelliferae. A native biennial of fens and marshes. Rather rare, found only in south east England and also in Somerset. Height to 1m. Flowers July to Sept. See 118(h).

(**i**) **Thorn-apple** *Datura stramonium* L., family Solanaceae. An introduced annual, naturalised on waste and cultivated ground. Uncommon but throughout England and Wales. Absent from Ireland and north Scotland. Height to 1m. The whole plant is extremely poisonous, containing several narcotic substances which have been put to use in the drug industry. The flower is normally open in a trumpet shape, soon wilting and closing when picked (as illustrated). Flowers July to Oct. See Fruit 164(h).

(**j**) **Hawkweed Ox-tongue** *Picris hieracioides* L., family Compositae. A native biennial to perennial of grassland, hedgebanks and roadside particularly on calcareous soil. Common in south Wales and south England, rare or absent elswhere and introduced in Ireland. Height to 60cm. Flowers July to Sept. See 94(i).

photograph taken 27 July ◯ represents 1 centimetre

(a) **Marsh Sowthistle** *Sonchus palustris* L., family Compositae. A native perennial of marshes, fens and stream sides. Rare, occuring only in south east England. Height to 3m. Similar to other Sowthistles but is larger and the base of the leaf, clasping the stem, is pointed rather than round. Flowers July to Sept. See 86(k), 86(l), 104(l). Photographed July 25.

(b) **Flixweed** *Descurainia sophia* (L.) Webb ex Prantl., family Cruciferae. A possibly native annual of roadsides and waste places. Found throughout Britain but rather uncommon. Rare in north Scotland and Ireland. Height to 60cm. Flixweed used to be taken to cure dysentery which was also known as the 'flux' or 'flix'. Flowers June to Aug. Photographed July 25.

(c) **Matted Sea Lavender** *Limonium bellidifolium* (Gouan) Dum., family Plumbaginaceae. A native perennial of dry, sandy parts of salt marshes. Rare, found only on coasts of Norfolk and Lincolnshire. Height to 20cm. Flowers July to Aug. See 106(c), 120(l). Photographed Aug. 2.

(d) **Sea Wormwood** *Artemisia maritima* L., Compositae. A native perennial of sea walls and dry parts of salt marshes. Common on most British coasts but absent from the north and rare on Irish and Welsh coasts. Height to 40cm. Highly aromatic, the leaves giving off a pleasant scent when crushed. Flowers Aug. to Sept. See 142(a), 142(k), 162(a). Photographed Aug. 5.

(e) **Allseed** *Radiola linoides* Roth, family Linaceae. A native annual of damp grassland, heath and bare ground, usually near the sea. Found throughout Britain but is common nowhere. Rare in the Midlands and east Ireland. Height to 2cm. Allseed is one of the tiniest of British wild flowers. Flowers July to Aug. Photographed Aug. 2.

(f) **Marsh Gentian** *Gentiana pneumonanthe* L., family Gentianaceae. A native perennial of wet heaths. Rather rare, found only in south and east England, Anglesey, Cumbria and Carmarthen. Height to 30cm. The Marsh Gentian usually has more than one flower per stem, may also be distinguished by its narrow leaves. Flowers Aug. to Sept. See 47(a), 157(a), 157(b), 157(c). Photographed Aug. 5.

(a) **Japanese Knotweed** *Polygonum cuspidatum* Sieb. & Zucc., family Polygonaceae. An introduced perennial grown in gardens and now naturalised in many places throughout Britain. Height to 2m. This native of Japan has become a much-hated weed, being very difficult to uproot and destroy once established. Flowers Aug. to Oct. See 86(d), 134(f). Photographed Aug. 5.

(b) **Fuchsia** *Fuchsia magellanica* Lam., family Onagraceae. An introduced shrub, very variable and cultivated in hedges and gardens, but now established in some localities. Common in west Ireland but rather rare on the mainland, occuring on western coasts. Height to 3m. Flowers June to Sept. Photographed July 27.

(c) **Hop** *Humulus lupulus* L., family Cannabiaceae. A native perennial of hedges and thickets. Common in England and Wales rare in Scotland and Ireland. The climbing stems may reach 6m. Hops are cultivated in south England; the female flowers are an essential ingredient of bitter. Both sexes of flower are illustrated, female above, males below. Flowers July to Aug. See Fruit 172(e). Photographed July 27.

(d) **Dewberry** *Rubus caesius* L., family Rosaceae. The fruit and flowers are illustrated. The berry is the most distinctive feature of the Dewberry since it has fewer segments than a bramble and is covered with a blue bloom. Dewberry may be used in the same way as brambles. Fruits Aug. to Oct. For further text see Flowers 62(a) and compare Bramble 108(o), 162(n). Photographed Aug. 5.

(e) **Bird Cherry** *Prunus padus* L., family Rosaceae. The fruit and leaves are illustrated. Although an extremely attractive tree, its fruits have no uses, being rather bitter, but they are much loved by birds. Fruits July to Sept. For further text see Flowers 34(i). Photographed July 25.

(f) **Dorset Heath** *Erica ciliaris* L., family Ericaceae. A native shrub of heaths in Dorset, south Devon, west Cornwall and west of Ireland. Absent elsewhere. Height to 50cm. Differs from Bell Heather and Cross-leaved Heath by having the flowers in a spike, not clustered together. Commonly grown in rock gardens. Flowers June to Sept. See 154(m), 154(n). Photographed July 27.

photograph taken 31 July

(a) **Upright Hedge Parsley** *Torilis japonica*
(Houtt.) DC., family Umbelliferae. A native annual
of hedges, grassy places and roadsides. Common
throughout Britain except in north Scotland.
Height to 1m. Flowers July to Aug. See 134(g).
**Knotted Hedge Parsley** *T. nodosa* (L.) Gaertn. A
native annual of dry grassy places. Common in
south east England. Stems to 25cm. Differs from
Upright Hedge Parsley by creeping along the
ground; smaller with few flowers in each cluster.
Flowers May to July.

(b) **Marsh Ragwort** *Senecio aquaticus* Hill, family
Compositae. A native biennial of marshes, ditches
and wet meadows. Common throughout Britain.
Height to 60cm. Distinct among ragworts due to its
leaves with rounded ends and loose groups of
flowers. Flowers July to Aug. See 22(f), 72(j),
104(g).

(c) **Wild Angelica** *Angelica sylvestris* L., family
Umbelliferae. A native perennial of fens, damp
woods, hedgerows and meadows. Common
throughout Britain. Height to 1.5m. Flowers July to
Sept. See 62(g).

(d) **Montbretia** *Crocosmia × crocosmiiflora*
(Lemoine) N.E.Br., family Iridaceae. An
introduced perennial, commonly cultivated and
now naturalised by lakes, rivers, streams and
ditches. Fairly common in all western parts,
particularly in Ireland. Height to 70cm. The flowers
may be picked in summer and pressed in newspaper
under a carpet or in a flower press. The colour lasts
well and makes a pretty winter bouquet. Flowers
July to Aug.

(e) **Starry Saxifrage** *Saxifraga stellaris* L., family
Saxifragaceae. A native perennial. Fairly common
in north Scotland, rare in other areas, unknown in
the Midlands and southern England. Found by
mountain streams and on wet rocks. Height to
25cm. Flowers June to Aug.

(f) **Mountain Avens** *Dryas octopetala* L., family
Rosaceae. This specimen shows the ripe fruits after
flowering. For main text and flowers see 52(c).

(g) **Alpine Saussurea** *Saussurea alpina* (L.) DC.,
family Compositae. A native perennial. Found on
mountains. Fairly common in the Scottish
Highlands, otherwise very rare. Height to 40cm.
Flowers Aug. to Sept.

(h) **Yellow Mountain Saxifrage** *Saxifraga aizoides*
L., family Saxifragaceae. A native perennial.
Common in the Scottish Highlands, otherwise
found only in Yorkshire, northern Ireland and
Westmorland, on mountains in stony places and by
streams. Height to 20cm. Flowers June to Sept.

(i) **Alpine Scurvy-grass** *Cochlearia alpina* (Bab.)
H. C. Watson, family Cruciferae. A native
biennial or perennial. Found in wet places on
mountains in Wales, north England and Scotland.
Stems often horizontal to a length of 45cm. The
leaves are less fleshy than those of the seaside species.
Flowers May to Aug. See 26(b), 52(j), 158(b).

(j) **Moss Campion** *Silene acaulis* (L.) Jacq., family
Caryophyllaceae. A native perennial. Found fairly
commonly in the Scottish Highlands otherwise only
in the Lake District and north Wales. Grows on
mountains, cliffs, screes and stony ledges. Height to
8cm. Flowers July to Aug.

(k) **Purple Saxifrage** *Saxifraga oppositifolia* L.,
family Saxifragaceae. A native perennial. Common
in the Scottish Highlands, rare in Wales, Ireland
and north England. Found on mountains, stony
ground and damp rocks. Height to 15cm. Flowers
March to May and then sometimes again July to Aug.

photograph taken 1 August ◯ represents 1 centimetre

**(a) Blue Fleabane** *Erigeron acer* L., family Compositae. A native annual or biennial. Fairly common in southern England, rare in northern England and Ireland and very rare in Scotland. It grows on dry grassland, banks, dunes, and walls mainly in calcareous areas. Height to 35cm. Flowers July to Aug. See 130(c). Photographed Aug. 1.

**(b) Cornish Moneywort** *Sibthorpia europaea* L., family Scrophulariaceae. A native perennial of damp, shady places. Rather uncommon, growing only in Sussex, Somerset, Devon, Cornwall and south Wales. Also recorded in Co. Kerry and once in Lewis. The trailing stems root at the nodes and may reach 30cm. Flowers July to Oct. Photographed Aug. 2.

**(e) Devil's Bit Scabious** *Succisa pratensis* Moench, family Dipsacaeae. Usually lilac blue, as shown, the flower colour may also be pale, pinkish-white. See main text 138(g). Flowers June to Oct. See also 68(g), 84(e), 120(d).

**(f) Harebell** or **Scottish Bluebell** *Campanula rotundifolia* L., family Campanulaceae. A native perennial of dry, grassy places, fixed dunes, hedgebanks and roadsides, often on poor soils. Common throughout Britain, though rare in south and east Ireland, Cornwall and Devon. Height to 25cm. Although the stem leaves are long and thin, there are small, round long-stalked lower leaves which are a distinctive feature. Flowers July to Sept.

**(g) Bog Asphodel** *Narthecium ossifragum* (L.) Huds., family Liliaceae. A native rhizome of bogs, wet heath, moorland and acid places on mountains. Common throughout Britain except in south east England and the Midlands. Height to 30cm. In the Shetlands, Bog Asphodel has been used in place of saffron for both medicine and dyeing. The flowerheads turn a deep saffron colour after flowering. Flowers July to Sept.

**(h) Grass of Parnassus** *Parnassia palustris* L., family Parnassiaceae. A native perennial of marshes, wet moors and mountains. Common in north England, Scotland and Ireland but rare in south and west of England and Wales. Height to 25cm. A stunningly beautiful flower, which smells faintly of honey. It was used for complaints of the liver and an infusion of the leaves aids digestion. Flowers July to Oct.

**(i) Sundew** *Drosera rotundifolia* L., family Droseraceae. A native perennial of bogs, wet moors and heaths. Common throughout Britain except in the Midlands and southern England. Height to 15cm. The leaves are covered in red sticky hairs which are used to catch insects as they settle. They are digested and absorbed through the leaves, and in this way, the Sundew obtains nutrients unavailable to them from the poor, waterlogged soils in which they grow. On this specimen, only the uppermost flower is left. They rarely open and are most usually found in this bud-like form. Flowers June to Aug. See other sundews 150(j), 145(e) and other insectivorous plants 46(b), 51(a), 115(e).

**(j) Great Sundew** *Drosera anglica* Huds., family Droseraceae. A native perennial of the wetter parts of bogs. Rarer than the Sundew but fairly common in north west Scotland and west Ireland. Height to 25cm. The Great Sundew catches and digests insects in a similar way to the Sundew. This specimen has finished flowering and only the fruits remain. It has small, white flowers which rarely open fully. Flowers July to Aug. See other sundews 150(i), 154(e) and also 46(b), 51(a), 115(e).

**(c) Pennyroyal** *Mentha pulegium* L., family Labiatae. A native perennial of wet places on sandy soil. Rather uncommon but scattered throughout England and Wales, rare in the north and Ireland and absent from Scotland. Height to 20cm. Pennyroyal is still grown in many gardens. Flowers Aug. to Oct. Photographed Aug. 5.

**(d) Hairy Stonecrop** *Sedum villosum* L., family Crassulaceae. A native perennial of wet, stony ground and streamsides on mountains. Rather uncommon, confined to the mountains of north England, south and central Scotland and the Grampians. Height to 8cm. Our specimen is rather small but shows essential details. Flowers June to July. Photographed July 31.

photograph taken 1 August ◯ represents 1 centimetre

photograph taken 6 August

(**e**) **Lovage** *Ligusticum scoticum* L., family Umbelliferae. A native perennial of rocky places near the sea. Fairly common on all Scottish coasts and north Ireland but absent elsewhere. Height to 60cm. Lovage was eaten by the Scots to prevent scurvy. Flowers July to Aug.

(**f**) **Marsh Ragwort** *Senecio aquaticus* Hill, family Compositae. A native biennial of marshes, ditches and wet meadows. Common throughout Britain. Height to 60cm. This specimen has unusual flowers since they are usually much looser in appearance and in a looser group. The leaves, however, are typical, the lower ones being undivided and all with rounded tips. Flowers July to Aug. See 22(f), 72(j), 104(g), 148(b).

(**g**) **Wood Cudweed** *Omalothcea sylvatica* (L.) Shultz Bip. & F. W. Shultz, syn. *Gnaphalium sylvaticum* L., family Compositae. A native perennial of open wood, heaths and pastures. Height to 50cm. Flowers July to Sept. See 108(a).

(**h**) **Wood Groundsel** *Senecio sylvaticus* L., family Compositae. A native annual, found in open habitats, waste ground and roadsides, avoiding calcareous soils. Fairly common throughout Britain but rare in Ireland and north west Scotland. Height to 50cm. Flowers July to Sept. See other groundsels 14(e), 100(l).

(**i**) **Marsh Speedwell** *Veronica scutellata* L., family Scrophulariaceae. A native perennial of bogs, wet meadows, and pond sides, often on acid soil. Fairly common throughout Britain. The stems are often creeping but may be erect and reach 25cm in length. The pale pink flowers are in distinctive loose groups, alternating up the stem. Flowers June to Aug. See 74(a), 90(i).

(**j**) **Sea Aster** *Aster tripolium* L., family Compositae. A native perennial found in salt marshes and on sea cliffs. Common on all British coasts though rare in east Scotland. Height to 50cm. In Elizabethan times, Sea Aster was a popular garden plant but it has now been superseded by the introduced Michaelmas Daisy. The roots were once used in folk medicine to heal wounds. Flowers July to Oct. See 112(f).

(**a**) **Western Gorse** *Ulex gallii* Planch., family Leguminosae. A native shrub of heaths and hilly grassland, always avoiding calcareous soil. Common in Wales, western parts of England and in southern and west Ireland. Rare elsewhere. Height to 1.5m. Similar to Dwarf Gorse but the upper petals (or wings) are longer than the lower (or keel). Flowers July to Sept. See 20(c), 154(h).

(**b**) **Asparagus** *Asparagus officinalis* L., ssp. *prostratus* (Dum.) E. F. Warb., family Liliaceae. A native rhizome of grassy places and sea cliffs. Rare, confined to Dorset, Cornwall, Gloucester, Wales and south east Ireland. Height to 30cm. Another subspecies *officinalis* has been introduced and cultivated. Flowers June to Aug.

(**c**) **Orpine** or **Livelong** *Sedum telephium* L., family Crassulaceae. A native perennial of woods and hedgebanks. Fairly common in most parts of Britain but rare in north Scotland, east England and Ireland. Height to 30cm. When picked, Orpine stays alive for a long time due to its fleshy leaves. This property earned it the name 'Livelong'. Flowers July to Sept.

(**d**) **Orange Hawkweed** *Hieracium brunneocroceum* Pugsl., family Compositae. Introduced perennial. Grown in gardens and commonly escaping and becoming established on roadsides, hedgebanks, waste ground and as a garden weed. Fairly common in England and Wales, rarer elsewhere. Height to 20cm. Flowers June to July.

photograph taken 6 August ◯ represents 1 centimetre

**(a) Larger Wintergreen** *Pyrola rotundifolia* L., family Pyrolaceae. A native perennial of bogs, fens, woods and rock ledges. Rather rare but may be found in suitable habitats throughout Britain. Height to 30cm. Flowers June to Sept. See 88(e), 154(b). Photographed Aug. 2.

**(b) Intermediate Wintergreen** *Pyrola media* Sw., family Pyrolaceae. A native perennial of moors and woods, especially pine. Rather uncommon but most often found in north Scotland. Height to 25cm. Similar to Common Wintergreen but has leaves more rounded and a style protruding from the flower. This specimen has few flowers. Flowers June to Aug. See 88(e), 154(a). Photographed Aug. 5.

**(e) Long-leaved Sundew** *Drosera intermedia* Hayne, family Droseraceae. A native perennial of damp peaty moors and heaths. Rather uncommon but mostly in western parts of the British Isles. Height to 10cm. This specimen has finished flowering and has the fruiting heads. Flowers June to Aug. See sundews 150(i), 150(j) and other insectivorous plants 46(b), 51(a), 115(e).

**(f) Cranberry** *Vaccinium oxycoccus* L., family Ericaceae. The photograph shows the berries. Fruits Aug. to Oct. For further text see Flowers 80(f).

**(g) Bilberry, Blaeberry** or **Whortleberry** *Vaccinium myrtilis* L., family Ericaceae. The photograph shows the berries which are good to eat raw but also tasty stewed, in pies and as jam. Fruits July to Sept. For further text see Flowers 66(i).

**(h) Dwarf Gorse** or **Dwarf Furze** *Ulex minor* Roth., family Leguminosae. A native shrub of heaths. Fairly common in south east England, rare elsewhere and absent from Scotland and Ireland. Height to 80cm. Similar to Western Gorse but usually smaller with shorter spines and upper petals (wing) equalling the lower ones (keel). Flowers July to Sept. See 20(c), 152(a).

**(i) Crowberry** *Empetrum nigrum* L., family Empetraceae. Native shrub, common on moors and mountains in Scotland, north England and Wales. Height to 40cm. Flowers are small, 1–2mm., pink and 6 petalled. Flowers April to June. Fruits July to Sept.

**(j) Bearberry** *Arctostaphylos ura-ursi* (L.) Spreng., family Ericaceae. The photograph shows berries which are rather unpleasant due to many seeds. Fruits July to Sept. For further text see Flowers 40(e).

**(k) Cowberry** or **Red Whortleberry** *Vaccinium vitis-idaea* L., family Ericaceae. The photograph shows the red berries which have a high vitamin C content. They make delicious jelly and are good raw, for stimulating the appetite. Fruits Aug. to Oct. For further text see Flowers 40(g).

**(l) Heather** or **Ling** *Calluna vulgaris* (L.) Hull, family Ericaceae. A native shrub of heaths, moors, bogs and open wood on acid soil. Very common throughout Britain. It has had many uses through the centuries, including bedding, fuel, thatching and basketry. It also yields an orange dye and has been used to flavour beer. White flowers are also shown. Flowers July to Sept.

**(m) Bell Heather** *Erica cinerea* L., family Ericaceae. A native shrub of the drier parts of heaths and moors. Common throughout Britain except in the Midlands and central Ireland. Height to 40cm. Flowers July to Sept. See 147(f), 154(n).

**(n) Cross-leaved Heath** or **Bog Heather** *Erica tetralix* L., family Ericaceae. A native shrub of bogs and heaths. Common throughout Britain except in the Midlands. Height to 40cm. Differs from Bell Heather by having larger, pale pink flowers and whorls of four leaves up the stems. The two species are often found together, the Bell Heather on dry tussocks and the Cross-leaved Heath in the wet hollows between. Flowers July to Sept. See 147(f), 154(m).

**(c) Arctic Mouse-ear Chickweed** *Cerastium arcticum* Lange., family Caryophyllaceae. A native perennial of mountain rock ledges in north Wales and Scotland. Flowering shoots may reach 15cm. Flowers June to Aug. See 52(a), 90(g). Photographed Aug. 5.

**(d) Hemp** *Cannabis sativa* L., family Cannabiaceae. An introduced annual, cultivated and sometimes becoming established on waste ground. Height to 3m. Hemp has provided fibre for rope-making since 2800 BC. In Britain, it is illegal to grow it without licence. Male and female flowers occur on different plants. Both are shown, the male on the right. Flowers Aug. to Sept. Photographed Aug. 10.

photograph taken 16 August ◯ represents 1 centimetre

**(a) Violet Helleborine** *Epipactis purpurata* Sm., family Orchidaceae. A native rhizome, only found in southern England as far west as the Welsh border, Somerset, and as far north as the Wash. Grows in woods on calcareous soils. Height to 60cm. Flowers Aug. to Sept. See 71(b), 89(c), 94(b), 132(a), 132(b).

**(b) Large-flowered Evening Primrose** *Oenothera erythrosepala* Borbas, family Onagraceae. Introduced from America; normally biennial. Rare, but spreading and it has become naturalised in southern England and Wales and occasionally in the Midlands. Grows in waste places, roadsides, railway embankments and dunes. Height to 1m. Flowers June to Sept. See 111(c).

**(c) Blinks** *Montia fontana* L., family Portulacaceae. A native annual to perennial. Common in Scotland and Wales, scattered elsewhere. It grows in wet places near streams, and in meadows. A tiny plant with tiny flowers but the stems may be up to 40cm long. Flowers May to Oct. See 32(a).

**(d) Common Dodder** *Cuscuta epithymum* (L.) L., family Convolvulaceae. A native annual found normally on Heather or Gorse in the south of England and one or two places elsewhere. The leaves are reduced to tiny scales. Flowers July to Sept. See 116(f).

**(e) Autumn Lady's Tresses** *Spiranthes spiralis* (L.) Chevall., family Orchidaceae. A native tuberous root. Found quite commonly near the south coast of England and Wales, otherwise rare. Absent from Scotland. Grows on downs, moist meadows and grassy dunes. Height to 20cm. Flowers Aug. to Sept. See 132(d).

**(f) Water Dropwort** *Oenanthe fistulosa* L., family Umbelliferae. A native perennial. Fairly common in central and southern England but rare in Cornwall, west Wales, northern England and Ireland. Found in marshes and shallow water. Height to 60cm. Flowers July to Sept. See 64(e), 110(f).

(a) **Small Gentian** or **Snow Gentian** *Gentiana nivalis* L., family Gentianaceae. A native annual found only on rock ledges in Perth and Angus. Height to 12cm. Flowers July to Sept. See 47(a), 146(f), 157(b), 157(c).

(b) **Felwort** *Gentianella amarella* (L.) Borner, family Gentianaceae. A native biennial. The most common of the gentians except in Scotland. It is found on calcareous grassland and dunes. Height can be up to 25cm. This gentian has been divided into many subspecies. Flowers late July to Sept. See 47(a), 146(f), 157(a), 157(c).

(c) **Field Gentian** or **Field Felwort** *Gentianella campestris* (L.) Borner, family Gentianaceae. A native annual or biennial. Rare in England and Ireland. Quite common in northern Scotland, more so than Felwort. Grows on pastures, grassland and dunes often on acid soil. Height to 25cm. Flowers July to Oct. See 47(a), 146(f), 157(a), 157(b).

(d) **Tree Mallow** *Lavatera arborea* L., family Malvaceae. A native biennial. Rare, found only on the west coast – mainly Wales and Cornwall. Usually grows on rocks or waste ground near the sea. Height to as much as 3m. Called a Tree Mallow as, in size, it generally resembles a bush or small tree. Flowers July to Oct. See 74(f), 96(f), 144(f).

(e) **Martagon Lily** *Lilium martagon* L., family Liliaceae. A bulb, probably introduced. It is commonly grown in gardens but is also found naturalised in woods in a few scattered places in England and Wales. Height to 1m. Flowers Aug. to Sept. See 50(e).

(f) **Cloudberry** *Rubus chamaemorus* L., family Rosaceae. Fruit. The fruit can be eaten as you would eat brambles, in a pie or in jam. To gather sufficient quantity you would need to be in the Highlands of Scotland or possibly the Pennines. The fruits are red, then orange when ripe. Fruits Aug. to Oct. See 88(c).

photograph taken 16 August

(**e**) **Beech** *Fagus sylvatica* L., tamily Fagaceae. The photograph shows the nuts and leaves. The nuts are known as beechmast and may be gathered and pressed to give an excellent vegetable oil. In America, the oil is sometimes used to make beechnut butter. Nuts ripen end Aug. to Oct. For main text see 24(f).

(**f**) **Copper Beech** *Fagus sylvatica* L., family Fagaceae. Copper leaved variety of 24(f). The photograph shows the nuts and leaves. The nuts may be used in the same way as ordinary Beech. For main text see 24(g).

(**g**) **English Elm** *Ulmus procera* Salisb., family Ulmaceae. The photograph shows the leaves. Note the size difference between this and Wych Elm 158(h). The main text is with the Flowers 12(l), Fruit 24(i).

(**h**) **Wych Elm** *Ulmus glabra* Huds., family Ulmaceae. The photograph shows the leaves. Note how much larger they are than the English Elm 158(g). The main text is with the Flowers 12(k) and Fruit 24(h).

(**i**) **Raoul** or **Southern Beech** *Nothofagus procera* (Poepp. and Endl.) Oerst., family Fagaceae. An introduced tree, native of Chile and becoming popular in forestry due to its fast growth. Height to 25m. The leaves and fruit are illustrated. Fruits Aug. to Oct. Compare with Beech 158(e), Hornbeam 108(h) and Roble Beech 158(j).

(**j**) **Roble Beech** *Nothofagus obliqua* (Mirb.) Bl., family Fagaceae. An introduced tree. Height to 30m. Similar to Raoul and also increasingly popular in forestry. Has been known to grow 1.5m. in a year. The leaves are darker and more toothed. Note the similarity of the fruit to the Beech. Fruits Aug. to Oct. Compare with Beech 158(e) and Raoul 158(i),

(**k**) **Common Lime** or **Linden** *Tilia* × *vulgaris* Hayne, family Tiliaceae. The photograph shows the fruit and leaves. For main text see Flowers 108(p).

(**l**) **Small-leaved Lime** *Tilia cordata* Mill., family Tiliaceae. The photograph shows the fruit and leaves. A native tree, fairly common in England, particularly on limestone but rare in Scotland and Ireland. Height to 25m. Easily distinguished from the other two British limes by its much smaller leaves which are hairless except for little rust coloured tufts in the axils of the veins on the lower side. Flowers are rather similar to Common Lime. Flowers July. Fruits Aug. to Sept. See 108(p).

(**m**) **Box** *Buxus sempervirens* L., family Buxaceae. The leaves and fruit are illustrated. These dry, brown capsules contain shiny, black seeds. For main text see Flowers 18(b).

(**n**) **Large-leaved Lime** *Tilia platyphyllos* Scop., family Tiliaceae. A possible native tree, rather uncommon, preferring base rich or calcareous soils. Height to 30m. A distinctive feature is the large leaves. **Flowers and fruit are similar to other** limes. Flowers late June. Fruits July to Sept. See 108(p).

(**o**) **Alder** *Alnus glutinosa* (L.) Gaertn., family Betulaceae. The photograph shows the fruit and leaves. The fruits look like tiny cones. For main text see Flowers 12(n).

(**p**) **Grey Alder** *Alnus incana* (L.) Moench, family Betulaceae. The photograph shows the fruit and leaves. For main text see Flowers 20(f).

(**a**) **Common Orache** or **Iron Root** *Atriplex patula* L., family Chenopodiaceae. A native annual. Rather common except in northern Ireland and Scotland. Grows in waste places, roadsides and cultivated ground. Height to 1m. It can be eaten boiled as greens. Flowers July to Sept. See 164(b), 166(b), 166(d).

(**b**) **Scurvy-grass** *Cochlearia officinalis* L.ssp. *officinalis,* family Cruciferae. A native biennial to perennial. Common on drier salt and brackish marshes and sea cliffs on all British coasts except the south of England. Height to 30cm. Sailors found it an excellent preventative of scurvy. Similar to Alpine Scurvy-grass but with fleshier leaves. Flowers May to Aug. See 26(b), 52(j), 148(i).

(**c**) **Rock Samphire** *Crithmum maritimum* L., family Umbelliferae. A native perennial. Fairly common on the coast of Cornwall, the south coast, the coast of Wales and the coast of southern Ireland; otherwise rare. Found on rocks, cliffs, shingle and sometimes, sand by the sea. Height to 30cm. Once a favourite vegetable, the leaves and stalks are cooked and eaten like asparagus. Flowers June to Aug.

(**d**) **Golden Samphire** *Inula crithmoides* L., family Compositae. A native perennial. Found on salt marshes and sea cliffs and rocks. Rare, except in the Thames Estuary, Essex, around Portsmouth, south Wales, Anglesey and around Dublin. Height to 80cm. Flowers July to Aug.

photograph taken 25 August

(**d**) **Balsam Poplar** *Populus gileadensis* Rouleau, family Salicaceae. The photograph shows the leaves which are sticky and have a strong smell of balsam. For main text see Flowers 12(j).

(**e**) **Lombardy Poplar** *Populus nigra* L., var. *italica* Duroi, family Salicaceae. The photograph shows the leaves. For main text see Flowers 12(i).

(**f**) **White Poplar** *Populus alba* L., family Salicaceae. The photograph shows the leaves which have distinctive white hairs on the undersides. For main text see Flowers 12(h).

(**g**) **Aspen** *Populus tremula* L., family Salicaceae. The photograph shows the leaves. For main text see Flowers 12(f).

(**h**) **Hybrid Black Poplar** *Populus × euramericana* (Dode) Guinier, family Salicaceae. The photograph shows leaves. For further text see Flowers 12(g) and compare 160(i).

(**i**) **Black Poplar** *Populus nigra* L., family Salicaceae. Possibly native tree of wet woods and streamsides. Fairly common in east and central England. Height to 35m. The catkins are not shown but are similar to the Lombardy Poplar. The trunk usually has large gnarled bosses which are very distinctive. Flowers April. See 12(g), 160(e), 160(i).

(**j**) **London Plane** *Platanus × hybridus* Brot., family Platanaceae. The photograph shows the leaves and fruit. For main text see Flowers 24(p).

(**k**) **Yew** *Taxus baccata* L., family Taxaceae. The photograph shows the leaves and fruit. These beautiful red berries are actually very poisonous and should not be eaten. Fruits Aug. to Sept. For main text see Flowers 18(d).

(**l**) **Grey Poplar** *Populus canescens* (Ait.) Sm., family Salicaceae. The photograph shows the leaves only. Grey Poplar is a cross between White Poplar and Aspen. Compare the leaves and note the combination of characteristics. See 160(f), 160(g). See Flowers 12(e).

(**a**) **Alpine Forget-me-not** *Myosotis alpestris* Schmidt, family Boraginaceae. A native perennial of basic mountain rock. Rare, growing only in certain mountains in Westmorland and Perthshire. Height to 15cm. The flowers are usually much larger than in the photographed specimen. Flowers July to Sept. See 30(b), 30(e), 90(h).

(**b**) **Corn Spurrey** *Spergula arvensis* L., family Caryophyllaceae. A native annual, common on non-calcareous arable land throughout Britain. Height to 30cm. Spurrey is derived from the Dutch name for this plant. It has been grown as a fodder crop in Britain and there is evidence of its use as human food during Roman times. The seeds were used as oats. Flowers June to Aug.

**Knotted Pearlwort** *Sagina nodosa* (L.) Fenzl., family Caryophyllaceae. A native perennial found in damp sandy or peaty places. Fairly common throughout Britain. Height to 15cm. Smaller than Corn Spurrey with pairs of needle like leaves up the stems. There are normally several stems with solitary white flowers. Flowers July to Sept.

(**c**) **Sea Heath** *Frankenia laevis* L., family Frankeniaceae. A native perennial of the upper margins of salt marshes on sandy or gravelly soil. Rather rare, found only on the south and east coasts of England. The stems trail along the ground and may be as long as 15cm. Flowers July to Aug.

photograph taken 26 August ○ represents 1 centimetre

photograph taken 26 August

(e) **Elder** *Sambucus nigra* L., family Caprifoliaceae. The photograph shows the berries which are popular in home-made wine and jam. They are also much loved by starlings and blackbirds. Fruits Aug. to Nov. For main text see Flowers 38(e).

(f) **Mountain Ash** or **Rowan** *Sorbus aucuparia* L., family Rosaceae. The photograph shows the orange-red berries which are mixed with crab apples to make a jelly. Fruits Aug. to Sept. For main text see Flowers 34(d).

(g) **Guelder Rose** *Viburnum opulus* L., family Caprifoliaceae. The photograph shows the red berries which are not edible raw and need to be cooked. The American name is European Cranberry as the berries are used there as a substitute for Cranberries. Fruits Aug. to Nov. For main text see Flowers 58(b).

(h) **Tutsan** *Hypericum androsaemum* L., family Guttiferae. The photograph shows the fruit which turns from red to black when ripe. In the Hebrides, it was believed that these produced madness and were given the name Devil's Berries. Fruits Aug. to Sept. For main text see Flowers 76(c).

(i) **Hawthorn, May Tree** or **Whitethorn** *Crataegus monogyna* Jacq., family Rosaceae. The photograph shows the red berries. Fruits Aug. to Nov. For main text see Flowers 38(g).

(j) **Wayfaring Tree** *Viburnum lantana* L., family Caprifoliaceae. When ripe and black, the fruits are edible but not particularly pleasant. They have been used with the leaves as a gargle to settle the stomach. Fruits July to Sept. For main text see Flowers 34(b).

(k) **Honeysuckle** *Lonicera periclymenum* L., family Caprifoliaceae. The bright red fruit enhances the beauty of the hedgerows in autumn. Fruits Aug. to Sept. For main text see Flowers 86(b).

(l) **Deadly Nightshade** *Atropa bella-donna* L., family Solanaceae. The black berries are extremely poisonous as is the whole plant. Fruits Aug. to Nov. For main text see Flowers 72(h).

(m) **Danewort** or **Dwarf Elder** *Sambucus ebulus* L., family Caprifoliaceae. These black berries are poisonous and should not be confused with elderberries. Fruits Aug. to Sept. For main text see Flowers 118(k).

(n) **Bramble** or **Blackberry** *Rubus fruticosus* agg., family Rosaceae. The familiar bramble has probably been eaten by man for thousands of years. It is popular in pies and jellies and for eating straight from the bush. In Scotland, it is said that, before the end of Sept. the fruit will have the spit of the Devil but in England, the Devil is said to have spat or urinated on them at Michaelmas and therefore, it is unwise to eat them after this date. See Flowers 108(o).

(a) **Field Wormwood** *Artemisia campestris* L., family Compositae. A native perennial of heaths. Rare, found only in the Breckland of Suffolk, Norfolk and Cambridge; recorded only as a casual elsewhere. Height to 40cm. Unlike most of the other wormwoods, this one has no scent. Flowers Aug. to Sept. See 142(a), 142(k), 146(d).

(b) **Spanish Catchfly** *Silene otites* (L.) Wibel, family Caryophyllaceae. A native perennial. Rare, found only on Breckland heaths of Norfolk, Suffolk and Cambridge. Height to 60cm. Flowers June to Aug.

(c) **Pale Persicaria** *Polygonum lapathifolium* L., family Polygonaceae. A native annual of waste places, roadsides and as a garden and arable weed. Fairly common in England and Wales but rare in Scotland and Ireland. Similar to Red Shank but with greenish-white flowers and without the dark mark on the leaves. Height to 70cm. Flowers June to Oct. See Red Shank 134(h) and 56(d), 170(b), 170(e).

(d) **Balm-leaved Figwort** *Scrophularia scorodonia* L., family Scrophulariaceae. A native perennial of hedgebanks. Rare, found only in cornwall, Devon and on Lundy Is. Height to 80cm. Flowers June to Aug. See 74(k), 98(h).

photograph taken 26 August ○ represents 1 centimetre

photograph taken 27 August

**(e) Hazel** or **Cob-nut** *Corylus avellana* L., family Corylaceae. The leaves and nuts are shown. These are much loved by squirrels as well as people. They are a rich food source, containing more protein, weight for weight, than hen's eggs. Fruits Aug. to Oct. See Flowers 12(m).

**(f) Sloe** or **Blackthorn** *Prunus spinosa* L., family Rosaceae. These luscious-looking blue berries are extremely acid or astringent to taste but are used to make a pleasant jelly. Sloe gin is made by soaking the berries in gin which turns bright pink. Fruits Aug. to Oct. See Flowers 16(a).

**(g) Snowberry** *Symphoricarpos rivularis* Suksdorf, family Caprifoliaceae. The English name of this shrub is taken from the soft white berries which often persist through winter. They are edible but relatively tasteless and rarely used. Fruits Sept. to Nov. See Flowers 81(d).

**(h) Thorn-apple** *Datura stramonium* L., family Solanaceae. The photograph shows the prickly fruits which dry out as they ripen, splitting to release the black seeds. All parts of the Thorn-apple are extremely poisonous. Fruits Aug. to Oct. For main text see Flowers 144(i).

**(i) Dogwood** *Cornus sanguinea* L., family Cornaceae. The photograph shows the fruit. These ripen from green to black at the beginning of Sept. and have a high oil content, once used for lighting lamps. Fruits Sept. See Flowers 58(c).

**(j) Sea Buckthorn** *Hippophae rhamnoides* L., family Elaeagnaceae. The berries are shown. Fruits Sept. See Flowers 34(g).

**(k) Burnet Rose** *Rosa pimpinellifolia* L., family Rosaceae. A native shrub of sand dunes, sandy heaths and on limestone, especially near the sea. Fairly common around most British coasts but rare in south east England. Height to 40cm. Differs from other roses by being much shorter and having smaller leaflets. The dark black hips are also distinctive. Fruits Aug. to Sept. See Flowers 50(d).

**(l) Buckthorn** *Rhamnus catharticus* L., family Rhamnaceae. The photograph shows the fruit and leaves. The berries can be used as a dye, unripe for yellow and ripe for green, both with an alum mordant. Fruits Sept. to Oct. For main text see Flowers 60(c).

**(m) Alder Buckthorn** or **Black Dogwood** *Frangula alnus* Mill., family Rhamnaceae. The photograph shows the leaves and the berries. These ripen from red to black and although sweet to the taste, have a strong laxative effect. Fruits Aug. to Nov. For main text see Flowers 76(a).

**(a) Glasswort** or **Marsh Samphire** *Salicornia europaea* L., family Chenopodiaceae. A native annual, found on bare mud in salt marshes. Found only in south and east England. Height to 20cm. Ashes of Glasswort were once used in glassmaking as a source of carbonate of soda. A strange looking plant, more like a cactus than a herb. The flowers are insignificant, the tiny stamens being the most noticeable part. Flowers Aug.

**(b) Frosted Orache** *Atriplex laciniata* L., family Chenopodiaceae. A native annual of shores at the high-tide mark. Fairly common on most British coasts but rather rare in Ireland and north Scotland. Height to 25cm. Has a distinct mealy or 'frosted' appearance. Flowers Aug. to Sept. See 158(a), 166(b), 166(d).

**(c) Annual Seablite** *Suaeda maritima* (L.) Dum., family Chenopodiaceae. A native annual of sea shores and salt marshes, usually below the high water mark of spring tides. Common on all British coasts, though rare in north Scotland. Height to 25cm. Similar to Shrubby Seablite. Flowers July to Oct. See 118(d).

**(d) Sea Purslane** *Halimione portulacoides* (L.) Aell., family Chenopodiaceae. A native shrub of salt marshes, especially around pools. Common on English and Welsh coasts, absent from Scotland except in Ayrshire and Wigtownshire and only on eastern Irish coasts. Height to 80cm. Flowers July to Sept.

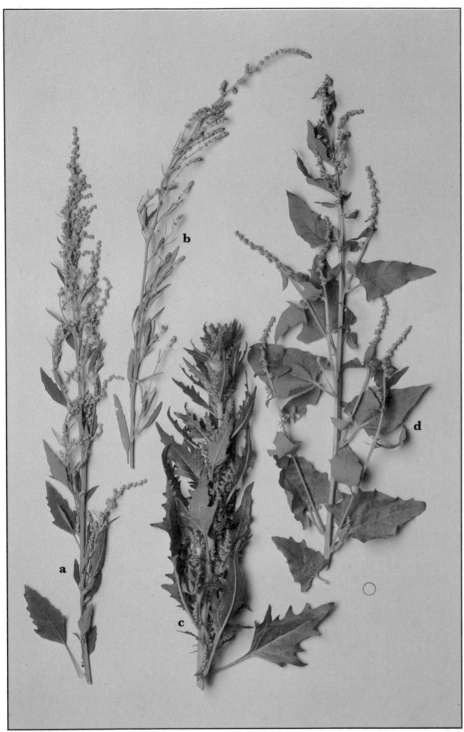

photograph taken 1 September

(**a**) **Fat Hen** *Chenopodium album* L., family Chenopodiaceae. A native annual of waste places and cultivated ground. Common throughout Britain except in mountain areas. Height to 1m. Fat Hen has had many uses. The fatty seeds were eaten in ancient times, the leaves used as a vegetable and to provide an orange dye. Flowers July to Oct. See 116(h), 116(i), 116(k), 142(d), 166(c).

(**b**) **Shore Orache** *Atriplex littoralis* L., family Chenopodiaceae. A native annual, found on mud by the sea. Most common on east coasts. Rare in Ireland and west Scotland. Recognisable by its habitat and long, thin leaves. Height to 70cm. Flowers Aug. to Sept. 158(a), 164(b), 166(d).

(**c**) **Red Goosefoot** *Chenopodium rubrum* L., family Chenopodiaceae. A native annual of waste places and cultivated ground, often near the sea. Fairly common in south east England and the Midlands but rare elsewhere. Height to 60cm. Flowers July to Sept. See 116(h), 116(i), 116(k), 142(d), 166(a).

(**d**) **Spear-leaved Orache** *Atriplex hastata* L., family Chenopodiaceae. A native annual of waste ground, roadsides and disturbed ground. Common in south east England and the Midlands and near the sea elsewhere. Height to 70cm. Recognised by its leaves which are shaped like a spear head. Flowers July to Sept. See 158(a), 164(b), 166(b).

(**e**) **Crack Willow** *Salix fragilis* L., family Salicaceae. A native tree, growing by rivers, streams, marshes and fens. Common in England and Wales. Less common in Ireland and north Scotland. Height to 20m. Often pollarded and may be confused with White Willow but has longer leaves and a more open appearance to the whole tree. Flowers May to June. Fruits June to July.

(**f**) **Weeping Willow** *Salix babylonica* L., family Salicaceae. An introduced tree, commonly planted by rivers and lakes and in gardens in south England. Height to 20m. A well-known tree, particularly near the Thames. It is thought to be a native of China. Female flowers are rare. Flowers April to May.

(**g**) **Common Osier** *Salix viminalis* L., family Salicaceae. A native shrub found by rivers and streams throughout Britain and commonly planted. Height to 4m. Osier has been widely used in basket-making. The trees would be cut back severely each year to encourage a mass of thin branches. Flowers April to May. Fruits May.

(**h**) **White Willow** *Salix alba* L., family Salicaceae. A native tree by rivers and streams and wet woods, particularly on base rich soils. Rare in north west Scotland and Wales. Height to 20m. The bark has been used in tanning leather. Flowers April to May. Fruits June.

(**i**) **Purple Willow** *Salix purpurea* L., family Salicaceae. A native shrub of fens and marshes. Rather uncommon but found throughout Britain. Height to 3m. Has been planted and used as an osier in basket-making. Flowers March to April. Fruits May.

(**j**) **Sallow** *Salix atrocinerea* Brot., syn. *S. oleifolia* Sm. family Salicaceae. A native shrub of woods and heaths, marshes, fens and by ponds and rivers. Fairly common throughout Britain. Height to 3m. The undersides of the leaves usually have rusty coloured hairs on the veins. Flowers March to April. Fruits May to June.

(**k**) **Hybrid Sallow** *Salix caprea* L. × *S. aurita* L., family Salicaceae. A hybrid, native shrub or small tree. Fairly common throughout Britain. Height to 5m. Eared Willow *S. aurita* has two little 'ears' at the base of the leaves. These do not appear on this hybrid which looks more like the Goat Willow. Flowers March to April. Fruits May.

(**l**) **Pussy Willow, Goat Willow** or **Great Sallow** *Salix caprea* L., family Salicaceae. The photograph shows the leaves only. Flowers March to April. Fruits May. For full text see Flowers 12(o).

(**m**) **Creeping Willow** *Salix repens* L., family Salicaceae. A native shrub of heaths, throughout Britain though more common in north Scotland. Rare in the Midlands and central Ireland. The stems creep along the ground and may reach 1.5m. Flowers April to May. Fruits June to July.

photograph taken 2 September ○ represents 1 centimetre

photograph taken 4 September

(**a**) **Meadow Saffron** or **Autumn Crocus**
*Colchicum autumnale* L., family Liliaceae. The photograph shows the flower which appears without the leaves. Flowers Aug. to Oct. For full text see Fruit and Leaves 36(a).
**Autumnal Crocus** *Crocus nudiflorus* Sm., family Iridaceae. An introduced corm. Rare but naturalised in meadows and grown in gardens. Similar to Meadow Saffron in that the leaves appear in spring and solitary flowers in autumn but the leaves are small and narrow and the flower has three stamens rather than six. Flowers Sept. to Oct.

(**b**) **Autumn Squill** *Scilla autumnalis* L., family Liliaceae. A native bulb of dry grassland near the sea. Rather uncommon, found on south English coasts. Height to 15cm. Flowers July to Sept. See 26(f), 28(b).

(**c**) **Lily-of-the-valley** *Convallaria majalis* L., family Liliaceae. The ripe berries are shown. These are not always produced and although they are very attractive, are extremely poisonous, containing a substance which has dangerous effects on the heart. Fruits Aug. to Sept. For full text see Flowers 30(k).

(**d**) **Cyclamen** or **Sowbread** *Cyclamen hederifolium* Ait., family Primulaceae. An introduced corm. Rarely naturalised in woods and hedgerows in England and Wales. Height to 15cm. Note that the leaf does not normally occur with the flowers but appears when flowering has finished. The flowers may be pink or white. Flowers Aug. to Sept.

(**e**) **Douglas Fir** *Pseudotsuga menziesii* (Mirb.) Franco, family Pinaceae. An introduced tree; coniferous. Commonly planted in forestry and as ornament. Height to 50m. a fast growing tree which has a spectacular appearance. The cones have distinctive three-pronged bracts which point upwards, giving them a feathery appearance. Flowers May.

(**f**) **Scots Pine** *Pinus sylvestris* L., family Pinaceae. The photograph shows the unripe cones on a branch. These take two years, after flowering, to come to maturity, finally falling from the tree, drying out and releasing their seeds. A mature cone is also shown. For full text see Flowers 62(d).

(**g**) **Lodge Pole Pine** *Pinus contorta* Dougl. ex Loud., family Pinaceae. An introduced tree; coniferous. Fairly widely used in forestry, particularly in experimental work. Height to 20m. The leaves are in pairs and are slightly twisted, hence the Latin name '*contorta*'. Flowers May. See 170(f), 170(g).

(**h**) **Japanese Larch** *Larix kaempferi* (Lamb.) Carr., syn. *L. leptolepis* (Sieb. et Zucc.) Gord., L., family Pineaceae. The photograph shows cones and foliage. The bracts on the cones turn back giving the appearance of small roses. The needles have two white lines on the underside distinguishing this from European Larch. Further text see Flowers 24(n) and compare 168(i).

(**i**) **European Larch** *Larix decidua* Mill., family Pinaceae. An introduced tree, coniferous. Commonly planted and often naturalised. It is a popular tree for forestry since it has a high growth rate, sometimes reaching 1.5m in the first 2 years. Height to 45m. Flowers March to April. Compare 168(h).

(**j**) **Sitka Spruce** *Picea sitchensis* (Borg.) Carr., family Pinaceae. An introduced tree; coniferous. Planted throughout Britain as one of the main forestry trees, particularly in the west. Height to 50cm. Once three years old, Sitka Spruce has a rapid growth rate and may grow 1.5m. in a year. Differs from Norway Spruce by its hard, pointed needles, bluish colour and smaller cones. Fruits Oct. Flowers May. See 168(l).

(**k**) **Western Hemlock** *Tsuga heterophylla* (Raf.) Sarg., family Pinaceae. An introduced tree; coniferous. Commonly planted in Scotland often under broadleaved trees. Height to 50m. The leaves are soft, rounded and with two white bands beneath and the cones rather smaller than other conifers. Flowers April to May.

(**l**) **Norway Spruce** *Picea abies* (L.) Kart., family Pinaceae. An introduced tree; coniferous. Commonly planted throughout Britain. Height to 40m. Norway Spruce is planted to provide timber and cover for pheasants and other game, shelter belts and Christmas trees. It has a fast growth rate when young. Compared to Sitka Spruce it has softer, greener foliage and larger cones. Flowers May to June. Fruits Oct. See 168(j).

photograph taken 4 September ○ represents 1 centimetre

photograph taken 8 September

(**f**) **Black Pine** *Pinus nigra* Arnold, family Pinaceae. The photographs shows an open cone. For full text see Flowers 60(d) and also 62(d), 168(f), 168(g), 170(g).

(**g**) **Monterey Pine** *Pinus radiata* D. Don, family Pinaceae. An introduced tree; coniferous. Common in south west England, Irish coasts and in north west Scotland. Height to 40m. The needles are a brighter, more yellow-green than the other pines and the cones much larger and distinctively assymetric at the base. Flowers March to April. See 60(d). 62(d), 168(f), 168(g), 170(f).

(**h**) **Noble Fir** *Abies procera* Rehd., family Pinaceae. An introduced tree; coniferous. Common for ornament in Scottish gardens and sometimes planted for forestry. Height to 45m. Has a distinctive, blue bloom and large cones which have long bracts pointing downwards. An unripe cone is illustrated. It will turn a purplish-brown at maturity. Flowers April to May.

(**i**) **Redwood** *Sequoia sempervirens* (Lamb.) Endl., family Taxodiaceae. An introduced tree; coniferous. Planted in parks and gardens. It grows, normally, to about 35m. in Britain but in its native America, one has reached 112.4m. They also have unusually long life-spans, averaging between 700 and 1,000 years. Flowers Dec. to Feb.

(**j**) **Wellingtonia** *Sequoiadendron giganteum* Bucholz, family Taxodiaceae. An introduced tree. Coniferous. Commonly planted in parks, avenues churchyards and gardens. Height in Britain is to 45m. but in west America it can reach 80m. It has been known to live for 3,400 years. Flowers Feb. to April.

(**k**) **Lawson's Cypress** *Chamaecyparis lawsonii* (A. Murr.) Parl., family Cupressaceae. An introduced tree; coniferous. Common in parks, gardens, cities and suburbs. Height to 40m. in Britain. Lawson's Cypress is popular for ornament and hedging. The 'leading' shoot is distinctively drooping. Flowers Feb. to April.

(**l**) **Leyland Cypress** × *Cupressocyparis leylandii* (Jacks. Dallim.) Dallim., family Cupressaceae. Raised in Britain in 1888, a hybrid between a false cypress, the Nootka Cypress, *Chamaecyparis nootkatensis* (Lamb.) Spach and the Monterey Cypress, *Cupressus macrocarpa* Hartw. Planted in gardens, especially as a fast growing hedge, and also as a forestry tree. Height to about 30m. in Britain. Flowers Feb. to April.

(**m**) **Cedar of Lebanon** *Cedrus libani* A. Rich., family Pinaceae. An introduced tree; coniferous. Common in parks, large gardens and churchyards. Height to 40m. in Britain. Cedar of Lebanon grows slowly in height but fairly rapidly in girth. The unripe cone is illustrated and ripens to purplish brown in two to three years after flowering. Flowers Oct. to Feb.

(**a**) **Nodding Bur Marigold** *Bidens cernua* L., family Compositae. A native annual. Scattered over southern England, rare elsewhere. Grows on the edges of ponds, and streams. Height to 60cm. The seeds have little hooks by which they stick to the hair of passing animals so distributing themselves. Flowers July to Oct. See 170(c).

(**b**) **Water Pepper** *Polygonum hydropiper* L., family Polygonaceae. A native annual. Common, except in northern Scotland. It grows in wet places, by streams, ponds, ditches. Height to 65cm. Distinguished by the hot peppery taste of the leaves. Flowers July to Oct. See 56(d), 134(l), 162(c), 170(d), 170(e).

(**c**) **Trifid Bur Marigold** *Bidens tripartita* L., family Compositae. A native annual. Scattered over

southern England, rare elsewhere. Grows on the edges of ponds, streams and ditches. Height to 80cm. The seeds have little hooks by which they stick to the hair of passing animals ensuring distribution. Flowers July to Oct. See 170(a).

(**d**) **Red Shank** or **Persicaria** *Polygonum persicaria* L., family Polygonaceae. This specimen is shown for comparison. See 134(h).

(**e**) **Amphibious Bistort** *Polygonum amphibium* L., family Polygonaceae. A native perennial. Common in southern and central England. Grows by or in canals, slow-moving rivers. The upper specimen is the land form and the lower is the water form. Height on land to 50cm. In water, the stems can reach 1m. Flowers July to Sept. See 56(d), 134(l), 162(c), 170(b), 170(d).

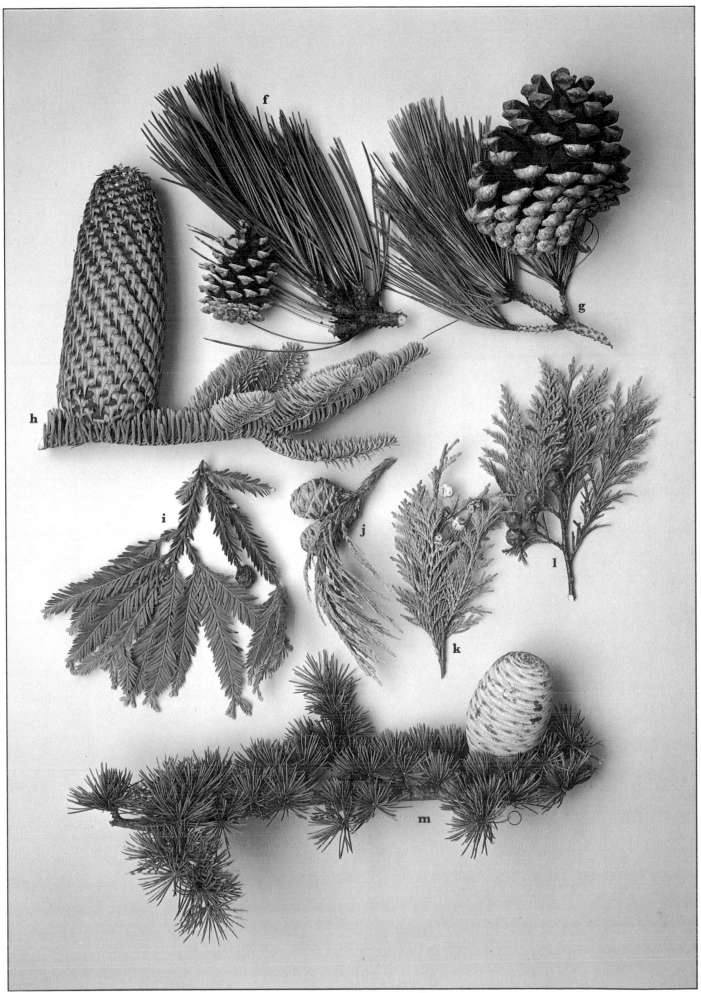

photograph taken 20 September ◯ represents 1 centimetre

photograph taken 24 September

(**e**) **Hop** *Humulus lupulus* L., family Cannabiaceae. The photograph shows the ripe fruit which forms an essential ingredient of ales and beer. Fruits Sept. to Oct. See Flowers 147(c).

(**f**) **Traveller's Joy** or **Old Man's Beard** *Clematis vitalba* L., family Ranunculaceae. The ripe fruits with their long silvery awns are shown. This fluffy appearance gives it the name of Old Man's Beard. Fruits Sept. to Oct. See Flowers 130(a).

(**g**) **Black Nightshade** *Solanum nigrum* L., family Solanaceae. The photograph shows the ripe, black berries. These are poisonous, particularly after a very sunny season. Fruits Sept. to Oct. See Flowers 116(g).

(**h**) **Bittersweet** or **Woody Nightshade** *Solanum dulcamara* L., family Solanaceae. The photograph shows the berries and the typical leaf. The berries start green and ripen through yellow to red. They have a bittersweet taste but do contain traces of poison so are not recommended for consumption. Fruits Sept. to Oct. See Flowers 48(j).

(**i**) **Black Bryony** *Tamus communis* L., family Dioscoreaceae. The ripe, red berries are shown. These are poisonous and may cause sickness and paralysis in children. The leaves usually turn yellow and wither away as the fruits ripen leaving the berries exposed like a necklace of beads. Fruits Aug. to Oct. See Flowers 82(f).

(**j**) **White Bryony** or **Red Bryony** *Bryonia cretica* L., ssp. *dioica* (Jacq.) Tutin, syn. *Bryonia dioica* Jacq., family Cucurbitaceae. The photographs shows the fruit which are extremely poisonous, only fifteen being fatal to a child. They differ from Black Bryony fruit by being spherical and a duller red. Fruits Aug. to Oct. See Flowers 82(a).

(**k**) **Dog Rose** *Rosa canina* L., family Rosaceae. The photograph shows the ripe fruit, or hips. These may be collected and made into jelly or syrup, providing a valuable source of vitamin C. Later in the season, frosts make the hips go soft and at this stage they may be used in home-made wine. Note that unlike Sweet Briar the fruits do not retain their sepals. Fruits Aug. to Nov. See Flowers 76(b).

(**l**) **Ivy** *Hedera helix* L., family Araliaceae. A native, perennial climber. Common in woods, on hedges, walls and rocks, both climbing and creeping. Stems may reach 30m. in length. The flowering shoots have different shaped leaves from the non-flowering, climbing stems which have the typical ivy-shaped leaf. At flowering, Ivy is usually covered in insects since it is one of the few plants providing abundant honey at this time of year. Flowers Sept. to Nov. See Fruit 18(c).

(**a**) **Wild Crab Apple** *Malus sylvestris* Mill. ssp. *sylvestris,* family Rosaceae. A native tree of hedgerows, scrub and woods. Height to 10m. The photograph shows the fruit. These are usually rather sour but may be used in cooking and are popularly made into a jelly, often mixed with other fruit. The tree is usually thorny. Flowers May. Fruits Sept. to Oct. See 24(m), 172(b).

(**b**) **Crab Apple** *Malus sylvestris* Mill. ssp. *mitis* (Wallr.) Mansf., family Rosaceae. The photograph shows the fruit which are larger than the Wild Crab Apple and are not in bunches. Fruits Sept. to Oct. For further text see Flowers 24(m) and compare 172(a).

(**c**) **Spindle-tree** *Euonymus europaeus* L., family Celastraceae. The photograph shows the fruit which are very striking in appearance. The brilliant orange seeds are poisonous and a violent purgative. However, they are harmless to birds and a favourite of blackbirds. Fruits Sept. to Oct. For further text see Flowers 58(a).

(**d**) **Common Privet** *Ligustrum vulgare* L., family Oleaceae. The photograph shows the ripe, black berries. These are poisonous, containing a substance which can be fatal if taken by children. However, they do provide a useful crimson dye. Fruits Sept. to Oct. For further text see Flowers 86(c).

photograph taken 24 September ◯ represents 1 centimetre

**(e) White Beam** *Sorbus aria* agg., family Rosaceae. The photograph shows the leaves and fruit. The berries are usually longer rather than broad. They rarely last on the tree as they are quickly taken by birds. They are edible but not very pleasant. Fruits Sept. to Oct. See Flowers 58(d).

**(f) Ash** *Fraxinus excelsior* L., family Oleaceae. The photograph shows leaves and fruit, or keys. Ash was believed to guard against evil and the keys would be carried as protection from witchcraft. Fruits Oct. to Nov. See Flowers 26(d).

**(g) Sweet Chestnut** or **Spanish Chestnut** *Castanea sativa* Mill., family Fagaceae. The photograph shows the leaves and fruit. The shiny, brown nut is good to eat roasted and chestnut sellers are a popular feature of wintry, London streets. Fruits Oct. See Flowers 108(e) also horse chestnuts 174(l), 174(m).

**(h) Holm Oak** or **Evergreen Oak** *Quercus ilex* L., family Fagaceae. The fruit, or acorns, and the evergreen leaves are shown. Fruits Sept. to Oct. See Flowers 76(d) also 174(i), 174(j).

**(i) Sessile Oak** or **Durmast Oak** *Quercus petraea* (Mattuschka) Liebl., family Fagaceae. The photograph shows acorns and mature leaves. Note the stalked leaves and unstalked fruit. Fruits Sept. to Oct. See Flowers 34(e).

**(j) English Oak** or **Pedunculate Oak** *Quercus robur* L., family Fagaceae. The photograph shows the acorns and mature leaves. Note the unstalked leaves and stalked fruits and compare with the Sessile Oak. Acorns may be roasted and ground to produce an acceptable coffee substitute which lacks the caffeine of real coffee. Fruits Sept. to Oct. See Flowers 34(f).

**(k) Walnut** *Juglans regia* L., family Juglandaceae. The photograph shows the fruit and leaves which appear after flowering. The nut within the fruit is well-known. It is extremely high in calories and very good to eat raw and also popular pickled. The unripe fruit should be pricked and soaked in brine for about a week till they turn black, then drained, dried for two days and then bottled. Fruits Sept. to Oct. See Flowers 24(j).

**(l) Horse Chestnut** or **Conker Tree** *Aesculus hippocastaneum* L., family Hippocastanaceae. The fruits are illustrated with an autumn leaf. Horse chestnuts are usually the first trees to turn golden in the autumn. The fruit is most commonly covered in prickles and yields the shiny, brown conkers much-loved by children who play 'conquer' when the nuts are threaded on to a string and contested with each other. The conker which splits all others is the champion. They are not poisonous but rather unpalatable. Fruits Aug. to Oct. See Flowers 38(h).

**(m) Red Horse Chestnut** *Aesculus carnea* Hayne, family Hippocastanaceae. The photograph shows the fruit only. These are similar to Horse Chestnut but are usually smaller, rounder and rarely prickly. Fruits Aug. to Oct. See Flowers 38(i).

**(a) Butcher's Broom** *Ruscus aculeatus* L., family Liliaceae. The ripe fruit is illustrated. These berry-bearing twigs were used as Christmas decorations in homes and churches. Fruits Oct. to May. See Flowers 18(a). Photographed Dec. 10.

**(b) Juniper** *Juniperus communis* L., family Cupressaceae. A native shrub of heaths, moors, chalk downs, birch and pinewoods. Common in Scotland, Lake District, south east England and north west Ireland. Rare elsewhere. height to 5m. The flowers are tiny cones (May to June) which ripen in their second or third years, from green to blue black. Fruits Sept. to Oct. Photographed Sept. 24.

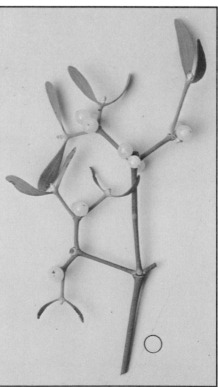

**(c) Holly** *Ilex aquifolium* L., family Aquifoliaceae. The photograph shows the fruit which persists all winter and makes a popular Christmas decoration. Even before Christian times, it was believed that sprays of holly berries warded off evil spirits. Fruits Sept. to March. See Flowers 38(f). Photographed Sept. 24.

**(d) Mistletoe** *Viscum album* L., family Loranthaceae. The photograph shows the fruit. These are rather poisonous but are eaten by the Mistle Thrush who then carries seeds to a new host. Mistletoe bearing berries is another Christmas decoration for homes and it is traditional for ladies to be kissed under it. Fruits Nov. to Dec. See Flowers 24(o). Photographed Dec. 10.

photograph taken 2 October ○ represents 1 centimetre

# Further reading

# Index of plants by family

## Standard academic works

*Atlas of the British Flora,* edited by F. H. Perring and S. M. Walters for the Botanical Society of the British Isles (E. P. Publishing, 2nd Edition, 1976). Dot maps showing the distributions of the British Flora.

*Flora Europaea,* Vols I–IV, edited by T. G. Tutin *et al.* (Cambridge University Press, 1966, 1968, 1972, 1976). Standard modern European Flora—a fifth volume to be published.

*Flora of the British Isles,* by A. R. Clapham, T. G. Tutin, and E. F. Warburg. (Cambridge University Press, 2nd edition, 1962). The standard British Flora.

*Flora of the British Isles*—Illustrations, Vols I–IV, by A. R. Clapham, T. G. Tutin, and E. F. Warburg. Drawn by Sybil J. Roles. (Cambridge University Press, 1957, 1960, 1963, 1965). Line drawings of the species mentioned in *Flora of the British Isles.*

## Other books of interest

*A Field Guide to the Trees of Britain and Northern Europe,* by Alan Mitchell (Collins 1974).

*Food for Free,* by Richard Mabey (Collins, 1971).

*The Concise British Flora in Colour,* by W. Keble Martin (Michael Joseph, 3rd edition, 1974).

*The Englishman's Flora,* by Geoffrey Grigson (Paladin, 1975). Compilation of English names and derivations.

*The Oxford Book of Wild Flowers,* by B. E. Nicholson, S. Ary and M. Gregory (Oxford University Press, 1960).

*The Wild Flowers of Britain and Northern Europe,* by Richard Fitter, Alistair Fitter and Marjorie Blamey (Collins, 1974).

*Wild Orchids of Britain,* by V. S. Summerhayes (Collins, 2nd edition, 1968).

This index has been provided to show the groupings of plants into families, since this is not reflected by their arrangement in the photographs.

Scientific classification works by dividing plants into groups of those having certain chacteristics in common. There are 5 major divisions: 1) Fungi; 2) Algae; 3) Mosses and Liverworts; 4) Ferns, Horsetails and Clubmosses; 5) Conifers and Flowering Plants.

Within these, plants are grouped into families which have a name usually ending in **-aceae** eg **Caryophyllaceae**. These contain closely related plants in smaller groups or genera (singular-genus) within which plants have even more characteristics in common. The name of the genus forms the first part of the botanical name eg *Stellaria* and *Cerastium* are 2 genera of the family **Caryophyllaceae.**

The genera are further divided into species. The name of the species is indicated by the second part of the Latin name eg *Stellaria media* and *S.holostea* are 2 species of the same genus.

Species remain distinct because pollen from one cannot usually fertilise an individual from another. However, two plants of the same genus will sometimes produce seed which grows to become what is known as a hybrid. This is usually denoted thus: *Salix capraea* × *S.aurita.* These hybrids are usually sterile, being unable to reproduce themselves, but there are inevitable exceptions, notably *Primula veris* × *P.vulgaris.*

Species may be further divided into subspecies which display some minute difference, usually morphological. They will usually interbreed and so are not classed as separate species. A subspecies is denoted by a third part to the botanical name e.g. *Raphanus raphanistrum* ssp. *maritima* and *R. raphanistrum* ssp. *raphanistrum* are two subspecies of the same species.

It should be noted that the system of naming is artificial by nature, being imposed by man on the plants. For this reason certain plants may be placed in different groups by different people and have even been given more than one name, or have their name and/or grouping changed according to prevailing botanical opinion.

The Conifers and Flowering Plants form the largest group of plants and differ from each other in their general mode of reproduction. Conifers, or Gymnosperms, bear cones, containing seeds which are not surrounded by an ovary. These are represented in this book by the Families: **Cupressaceae, Pinaceae, Taxaceae, Taxodiaceae.** The Flowering Plants, or Angiosperms, have their seeds surrounded by an ovary and these plants provide the main content of this book.

Ferns, Horsetails and Clubmosses do not reproduce by seed but by spore, and have a rather complicated life-cycle. These are not wild flowers but are represented in this book by the Families: **Equisetaceae, Hippuridaceae, Ophioglossaceae.**

The families are presented here alphabetically so that they may be easily located. The genera are also in alphabetical order within the families. Synonyms have not been included in this index. Main characteristics of the major families are briefly described, but any reader wishing to find out more about classification should consult one of the standard works mentioned in Further Reading, p. 177.

**Aceraceae Maple Family**
Trees or shrubs. Leaves palmately
lobed, long-stalked. Male and female
flowers on same tree, small, 5-petalled,
greenish-yellow. Fruit, a pair of keys
with long wings.
Acer campestre 34(l), 108(g)
  platanoides 34(k), 108(f)
  pseudoplatanus 34(j), 108(l)

**Adoxaceae Moschatel Family**
Adoxa moschatellina 22(e)

**Alismataceae
Water-plantain Family**
Aquatic plants. Leaves all coming
from roots. Flowers, 3-petalled. Fruit
forms a rounded nutlet.
Alisma plantago-aquatica 102(d)
Baldellia ranunculoides 115(d)
Sagittaria sagittifolia 132(f)

**Amaryllidaceae Daffodil Family**
Bulbous herbs. Leaves from roots,
linear with parallel veins. Flower buds
are enclosed by a papery sheath.
Flowers usually have parts in two
rings of 3 petals or petal-like sepals
each.
Galanthus nivalis 12(b)
Leucojum aestivum 20(n)
  vernum 12(c)
Narcissus pseudonarcissus 18(h)

**Apocynaceae Periwinkle Family**
Vinca major 24(e)
  minor 16(f)

**Aquifoliaceae Holly Family**
Ilex aquifolium 38(f), 171(c)

**Araceae Arum Family**
Arum italicum 76(g)
  maculatum 40(b), 134(d)

**Araliaceae Ivy Family**
Hedera helix 18(c), 172(l)

**Aristolochiaceae
Birthwort Family**
Aristolochia clematitis 114(c)
Asarum europaeum 20(e)

**Balsaminaceae Balsam Family**
Impatiens capensis 134(c)
  glandulifera 116(b)
  noli-tangere 134(c)*
  parviflora 120(f)

**Berberidaceae Barberry Family**
Berberis vulgaris 60(h)

**Betulaceae Birch Family**
Trees or shrubs. Leaves alternate.
Male and female flowers on same
tree. Females in spikes and males in
catkins.
Alnus glutinosa 12(n), 158(o)
  incana 20(f), 158(p)
Betula pendula 20(d)
  pubescens 108(i)

**Boraginaceae Borage Family**
Herbs, nearly all with stiff hairs on

stems and leaves. Leaves undivided
and alternate. Flowers with 5 sepals,
petals and stamens, petals joined.
Flowerspikes usually one-sided and
tightly coiled, unfurling as flowers
open. Fruit consists of four nutlets.
Anchusa officinalis 124(l)
Borago officinalis 124(g)
Buglossoides purpurocoerulea 44(f)
Cynoglossum officinale 89(a)
Echium vulgare 84(k)
Lithospermum officinale 128(d)
Lycopus arvensis 100(g)
Mertensia maritima 71(f)
Myosotis alpestris 160(a)
  arvensis 30(e)
  caespitosa 90(h)*
  discolor 30(b)*
  ramosissima 30(e)*
  scorpioides 90(h)
  secunda 90(h)*
  sylvatica 30(b)
Omphalodes verna 18(e)
Pentaglottis sempervirens 24(b)
Pulmonaria angustifolia 16(i)
  longifolia 16(i)*
  officinalis 16(j)
Symphytum officinale 40(c), 58(i)
  orientale 22(n)
  tuberosum 42(l)

**Buddlejaceae Buddleja Family**
Buddleja davidii 108(n)

**Butomaceae
Flowering Rush Family**
Butomus umbellatus 132(e)

**Buxaceae Box Family**
Buxus sempervirens 18(b), 158(m)

**Callitrichaceae
Water Starwort Family**
Callitriche stagnalis 47(d)

**Campanulaceae
Bellflower Family**
Herbs. Leaves, alternate, undivided
without stipules. Petals joined to form
5-lobed tube. Flowers may be
bunched into a head. Fruit, a capsule.
Campanula glomerata 122(b)
  latifolia 136(b)
  rapunculoides 124(h)
  rotundifolia 150(f)
  trachelium 122(c)
Jasione montana 120(d)
Legousia hybrida 70(b)
Lobelia dortmanna 115(c)
Phyteuma tenerum 136(c)
Wahlenbergia hederacea 136(a)

**Cannabaceae Hemp Family**
Cannabis sativa 154(d)
Humulus lupulus 147(c), 172(e)

**Caprifoliaceae
Honeysuckle Family**
Shrubs or shrubby herbs. Leaves
opposite. Five joined petals, usually
equal. Fruit may be an achene, a stone
with fleshy covering or a berry.

Linnaea borealis 88(a)
Lonicera periclymenum 86(b), 162(k)
Sambucus ebulus 118(k), 162(m)
  nigra 38(e), 162(e)
Symphoricarpos rivularis 81(d),
  164(g)
Viburnum lantana 34(b), 162(j)
  opulus 58(b), 162(g)

**Caryophyllaceae Pink Family**
Herbs. Leaves paired, stalkless,
opposite. Usually 5 sepals, 5 petals, 10
stamens. Petals often deeply notched,
sepals sometimes joined to form a
tube. Flower stems usually branched.
Ovary superior.
Agrostemma githago 138(f)
Arenaria serpyllifolia 110(c)
Cerastium arcticum 154(c)
  arvense 52(a)
  diffusum 90(g)*
  fontanum 90(g)
  glomeratum 90(g)*
  semidecandrum 52(a)*
Corrigiola litoralis 118(a)
Cucubalus baccifer 122(i)
Dianthus armeria 136(d)
  deltoides 80(a)
  gratianopolitus 80(b)
Honkenya peploides 52(g)
Illecebrum verticillatum 46(a)
Lychnis flos-cuculi 90(f)
  viscaria 48(d)
Minuartia verna 47(b)
Moehringia trinervia 54(m)
Myosoton aquaticum 78(a)
Sagina nodosa 160(b)*
  procumbens 47(f)
Saponaria officinalis 122(f)
Scleranthus annuus 81(a)*
  perennis 81(a)
Silene acaulis 148(j)
  alba 48(f)
  armeria 96(i)
  conica 72(c)
  dioica 30(h)
  gallica 111(d)
  noctiflora 137(b)
  nutans 78(f)
  otites 162(b)
  vulgaris 66(b)
  vulgaris ssp. maritima 44(d)
Spergula arvensis 160(b)
Spergularia marina 106(b)
  rubra 106(b)*
  rupicola 81(b)
Stellaria alsine 14(a)*
  graminea 22(m)*
  holostea 22(m)
  media 14(a)
  nemorum 14(a)*
  palustris 22(m)*

**Celastraceae Spindle-tree Family**
Euonymus europaeus 58(a), 172(c)

**Chenopodiaceae
Goosefoot Family**
Annual herbs or shrubs often mealy in
appearance. Leaves alternate,

toothed. Flowers in spikes, greenish
and insignificant. Male and female
flowers often on separate plants
(Atriplex). Minute detail of seeds
gives the main diagnostic features.
Atriplex hastata 166(d)
  laciniata 164(b)
  littoralis 166(b)
  patula 150(a)
Beta vulgaris ssp. maritima 86(f)
Chenopodium album 166(a)
  bonus-henricus 116(h)
  ficifolium 116(k)
  hybridum 116(i)
  polyspermum 142(d)
  rubrum 166(c)
Halimione portulacoides 164(d)
Salicornia europaea 164(a)
Salsola kali 137(c)
Suaeda maritima 164(c)
  vera 118(d)

**Cistaceae Rockrose Family**
Helianthemum apenninum 42(d)
  nummularium 47(c)

**Compositae Daisy Family**
The largest family of flowering plants.
Flowers are tiny and closely bunched
into a 'composite' head surrounded by
sepal-like bracts. Petals form a tube of
two types, ray florets with the tube
ending in a petal-like strap, or disc
florets with the tube ending in five
short teeth. Flowerheads may have
all ray florets (as in dandelions), all
discs (as in thistles) or a combination
with discs in the centre (as in daisy).
Fruit is tiny, often carried on the wind
by a 'parachute of hairs' or pappus.
Stems often contain milky juice.
Achillea millefolium 66(e)
  ptarmica 98(i)
Antennaria dioica 68(d)
Anthemis arvensis 100(e)
  cotula 100(c)*
  tinctoria 112(i)
Arctium lappa 137(d)
  minus 98(m)
Artemisia absinthum 142(k)
  campestris 162(a)
  maritima 146(d)
  vulgaris 142(a)
Aster novi-belgii 112(f)
  tripolium 152(j)
Bellis perennis 14(i)
Bidens cernua 170(a)
  tripartita 170(c)
Carduus acanthoides 76(j)
  nutans 94(m)
  tenuiflorus 110(e)
Carlina vulgaris 124(d)
Centaurea calcitrapa 112(l)
  cyanus 110(d)
  jacea 142(e)
  montana 48(i)
  nigra 84(h)
  scabiosa 100(h)
Chamaemelum nobile 120(b)

Chamomilla recutita 36(g)
 suaveolens 78(c)
Chrysanthemum segetum 112(g)
Cicerbita macrophylla 112(b)
Cichorium intybus 114(a)
Cirsium acaule 106(d)
 arvense 86(j)
 dissectum 106(f)
 eriophorum 130(j)
 helenioides 78(j)
 oleraceum 130(e)
 palustre 98(j)
 tuberosum 112(e)
 vulgare 112(c)
Conyza canadensis 130(c)
Crepis biennis 54(l)*
 capillaris 68(c)
 paludosa 82(g)
 vesicaria 54(l)
Doronicum pardalianches 30(i)
Erigeron acer 150(a)
Eupatorium cannabinum 130(i)
Filaginella uliginosum 108(a)
Filago vulgaris 137(a)
Galinsoga ciliata 108(c)
 parviflora 108(c)*
Hieracium brittanicum 66(l)
 brunneocroceum 152(d)
 pilosella 54(h)
 umbellatum 130(d)
 vagum 142(j)
Hypochoeris maculata 68(l)
 radicata 74(g)
Inula conyza 144(g)
 crithmoides 158(d)
Lactuca serriola 142(c)
Lapsana communis 86(h)
Leontodon autumnalis 137(e)
 hispidus 60(l)
 taraxacoides 60(l)*
Leucanthemum vulgare 30(f)
Logfia minima 137(f)
Matricaria maritima 124(b)
Mycelis muralis 94(e)
Omalotheca sylvaticum 152(g)
Onopordum acanthium 112(k)
Petasites fragrans 26(a)
 hybridus 14(l)
Picris echioides 94(i)
 hieracioides 144(j)
Pulicaria dysenterica 144(c)
Rudbeckia laciniata 144(e)
Saussurea alpina 148(g)
Senecio aquaticus 148(b), 152(f)
 erucifolius 104(g)*
 fluviatilis 112(j)
 integrifolius 72(j)
 jacobea 104(g)
 squalidus 22(f)
 sylvaticus 152(h)
 viscosus 100(l)
 vulgaris 14(e)
Serratula tinctoria 120(g)
Silybum marianum 76(h)
Solidago canadensis 122(d)
 virgaurea 118(e)
Sonchus arvensis 104(l)
 asper 86(k)
 oleraceus 86(l)
 palustris 146(a)
Tanacetum parthenium 100(j)
 vulgare 98(k)
Taraxacum officinale 20(i)
 spectabile 20(i)*
Tragopogon pratensis 81(e)
Tussilago farfara 14(j), 134(j)
Xanthium spinosum 124(e)

**Convolvulaceae**
**Bindweed Family**
Climbing plants. Leaves alternate
without stipules. Flower, trumpet-
shaped with 5 lobes, 5 stamens arising
between lobes. Fruit is a capsule.
Cuscuta europaea 116(f)
 epithymum 156(d)
Convolvulus arvensis 78(b)
Calystegia soldanella 90(c)
 sepium 134(b)

**Cornaceae Dogwood Family**
Cornus mas 16(c)
 sanguinea 58(c), 164(i)

**Corylaceae Hazel Family**
Carpinus betulus 20(a), 108(h)
Corylus avellana 12(m), 164(e)

**Crassulaceae Stonecrop Family**
Hairless perennial. Fleshy leaves with
small or no stalks. Usually 5 petals and
sepals. Carpels always equal the
petals in number, stamens may be the
same or twice as many.
Sedum acre 84(c)
 album 90(d)
 anglicum 89(f)
 reflexum 100(a)
 telephium 152(c)
 villosum 150(d)
Rhodiola rosea 51(e)
Umbilicus rupestris 72(k)

**Cruciferae Cabbage Family**
Four, usually separate, petals forming
a cross. Four sepals, six stamens.
Flowers usually in spikes. The fruit is a
seed pod which varies greatly in
appearance and often used as a
diagnostic feature.
Alliaria petiolata 22(l)
Arabidopsis thaliana 14(c), 78(h)
Arabis glabra 72(i)
 hirsuta 66(f)
Armoracia rusticana 64(g)
Barbarea vulgaris 36(c)
Berteroa incana 122(g)
Brassica napus 22(h), 122(k)
 nigra 51(d)*
 rapa 51(d)
Cakile maritima 100(d)
Capsella bursa-pastoris 14(b), 54(i)
Cardamine amara 40(a)
 flexuosa 14(d)
 hirsuta 26(c)
 impatiens 82(h)
 pratensis 18(f)
Cardaria draba 40(d)
Cheiranthus cheiri 48(h)
Cochlearia alpina 148(i)
 anglica 52(j)
 danica 26(b)
 officinalis ssp. officinalis 158(b)
Coronopus didymus 92(e)
 squamatus 72(l)
Crambe maritima 54(d)
Descurainia sophia 146(b)
Diplotaxis muralis 111(b)
 tenuifolia 82(b)
Draba aizoides 20(b)
 incana 71(c)
Erophila verna 40(h)
Erysimum cheiranthoides 94(l)
Hesperis matronalis 78(e)
Iberis amara 100(c)
Isatis tinctoria 42(k)
Lepidium campestre 100(b)
 heterophyllum 118(b)

latifolium 116(e)
 ruderale 100(b)*
Lobularia maritima 47(e)
Lunaria annua 58(f)
Nasturtium officinale 90(l)
Raphanus raphanistrum 86(e)
 raphanistrum ssp. maritimus 86(e)*
Rorippa amphibia 74(j)
 islandica 74(j)*
 sylvestris 74(j)*
Sinapis arvensis 22(g)
Sisymbrium altissimum 94(j)
 officinale 36(b)
 orientale 54(j)
Teesdalia nudicaulis 14(b)*
Thlaspi arvense 58(f)

**Cucurbitaceae Gourd Family**
Bryonia cretica ssp. dioica 82(a),
 172(j)

**Cupressaceae Cypress Family**
Trees or shrubs. Mature leaves,
evergreen, scale-like, pressed closely
to the stems, sometimes needle-like.
Male and female flowers on same
plant. Ripe cones small, usually
woody but fleshy in *Juniperus*.
Chamaecyparis lawsonii 170(k)
 × Cupressocyparis leylandii 170(l)
Juniperus communis 174(b)

**Cyperaceae Sedge Family**
Eriophorum angustifolium 66(h)*
 vaginatum 66(h)

**Dioscoreaceae Yam Family**
Tamus communis 82(f), 172(i)

**Dipsacaceae Teasel Family**
Herbs. Numerous small 4–5 petalled
flowers bunched together in a head,
four stamens projecting from each
one. An individual flower has an
extra calyx at the base of the ovary.
Flowerheads cupped by sepal-like
bracts.
Dipsacus fullonum 130(h)
 pillosus 144(d)
Knautia arvensis 84(e)
Scabiosa columbaria 68(g), 120(j)
Succisa pratensis 138(g), 150(e)

**Droseraceae Sundew Family**
Drosera anglica 150(j)
 intermedia 154(e)
 rotundifolia 150(i)

**Eleagnaceae Oleaster Family**
Hippophae rhamnoides 34(g), 164(j)

**Empetraceae Crowberry Family**
Empetrum nigrum 154(i)

**Equisetaceae Horsetail Family**
Equisetum palustre 64(d)

**Ericaceae Heath Family**
Subshrubs or small trees. Leaves
undivided, untoothed, evergreen.
Usually alternate, margins inrolled in
many species. Flowers usually
globular, bellshaped or flaskshaped
with the petals joined with four or
five lobes.
Andromeda polifolia 40(f)
Arctostaphylos uva-ursi 40(e), 154(j)
Calluna vulgaris 154(l)
Daboecia cantabrica 115(a)
Erica ciliaris 147(f)
 cinerea 154(m)
 tetralix 154(n)

Rhododendron luteum 38(k)
 ponticum 62(c)
Vaccinium myrtilis 66(i), 154(g)
 oxycoccus 80(f), 154(f)
 vitis-idea 40(g), 154(k)

**Euphorbiaceae Spurge Family**
Herbs. Leaves usually undivided,
alternate and untoothed. Flowers in
clusters, yellowish-green insignificant
with no petals and sometimes no
sepals. Male and female parts are in
separate flowers. Female is divided
into three parts and usually
surrounded by males with one anther
and the whole surrounded by a cup-
like bract with two to three leaflike
bracts at its base. Stems usually
contain a milky juice or latex.
Euphorbia amygdaloides 24(a)
 cyparissias 56(a)
 exigua 111(e)
 helioscopia 22(k)
 hyberna 56(b)
 lathyrus 42(j)
 paralias 124(c)
 peplus 14(l)
 platyphyllos 122(l)
 portlandica 70(a)
Mercurialis annua 116(d)
 perennis 12(d)

**Fagaceae Beech Family**
Trees and shrubs. Usually deciduous
but some evergreen. Leaves alternate,
stalked. Male and female on same
tree. Males in catkins, females usually
solitary, sometimes in spikes. Fruit a
nut enclosed by an involucre or
cupule.
Castanea sativa 108(e), 174(g)
Fagus sylvatica 24(f), 24(g), 158(e),
 158(f)
Nothofagus obliqua 158(j)
 procera 158(i)
Quercus ilex 76(d), 174(h)
 petraea 34(e), 174(i)
 robur 34(f), 174(j)

**Frankeniaceae Sea Heath Family**
Frankenia laevis 160(c)

**Geraniaceae Cranesbill Family**
Herbs, usually hairy or downy. Leaves
deeply, palmately lobed with stipules.
Five petals and sepals alternately
arranged. Ten stamens, prominent.
Fruit is a capsule with a long beak
formed by the style, seeds at its base.
Geranium columbinum 68(i)
 dissectum 48(g)
 endressii 104(a)
 lucidum 38(c)
 macrorrhizum 44(l)
 molle 52(h)
 nodosum 122(j)
 phaeum 44(g)
 pratense 66(a)
 pusillum 44(j)
 pyrenaicum 36(i)
 robertianum 32(h), 44(i)
 rotundifolium 44(k)
 sanguineum 44(h)
 sylvaticum 44(e)
Erodium cicutarium 28(i)
 maritimum 28(i)*

**Gentianaceae Gentian Family**
Non-woody herbs. Leaves opposite,

undivided, untoothed without stipules. Petals usually five, sometimes four joined to form a tube to which the five or four stamens are attached between the lobes. The fruit is distinctive, having a single cavity with two rows of seed attached to the inside.
Blackstonia perfoliata 92(f)
Centaurium erythraea 116(a)
  littorale 128(b)
  pulchellum 116(a)*
Cicendia filiformis 116(a)*
Gentiana nivalis 157(a)
  pneumonanthe 146(f)
  verna 47(a)
Gentianella amarella 157(b)
  campestris 157(c)

## St John's Wort Family
Herbs or shrubs. Leaves untoothed, opposite with transparent veins and often transparent dots. Never any stipules. Five sepals and petals, numerous stamens in three or five bunches.
Hypericum androsaemum 76(c), 162(h)
  calycinum 108(k)
  elodes 98(b)
  hirsutum 104(f)
  humifusum 98(c)
  maculatum 128(k)
  montanum 104(f)*
  perforatum 104(e)
  pulchrum 126(a)*
  tetrapterum 126(a)

## Hippocastanaceae Horse Chestnut Family
Aesculus carnea 38(i), 174(m)
  hippocastaneum 38(h), 174(l)

## Hippuridaceae Marestail Family
Hippuris vulgaris 102(a)

## Hydrocharitaceae Frog-bit Family
Elodea canadensis 140(b)
Hydrocharis morsus-ranae 140(a)
Stratiotes aloides 71(e)

## Iridaceae Iris Family
Herbs. Leaves usually flat and sword-shaped with parallel veins mostly from the roots. Flowers usually conspicuous. Perianth in two rings of three, both coloured with petals and joined at base. Buds enclosed by a sheath. Style 3-lobed and sometimes petal-like. Differs from Liliaceae and Amaryllidaceae by having three stamens. Fruit a three-sided capsule.
Crocosmia × crocosmiiflora 148(d)
Crocus nudiflorus 168(a)*
  purpureus 18(k)
Iris foetidissima 18(i), 106(e)
  pseudacorus 76(i), 140(i)
Sisyrinchium bermudiana 78(l)

## Juglandaceae Walnut Family
Juglans regia 24(j), 174(k)

## Juncaginaceae Arrow-grass Family
Triglochin maritima 52(k)
  palustris 126(d)

## Labiatae Deadnettle Family
Herbs with square stems and leaves in opposite pairs. Five petals joined to form a tube with two lips, the upper or hood formed from two petals, the lower from three. The upper lip may sometimes be absent or very short, then the lower is made up of five or three petals. Four stamens, five sepals joined to form a tube. Often aromatic.
Acinos arvensis 46(c)
Ajuga chamaepitys 138(d)
  pyramidalis 52(b)
  reptans 28(d)
Ballota nigra 84(l)
Calamintha nepeta 120(c)
  sylvatica 124(j)
  sylvatica ssp. ascendens 120(k)
Clinopodium vulgare 102(h), 104(j)
Galeopsis angustifolia 134(e)*
  segetum 138(k)
  speciosa 140(f)
  tetrahit 134(e)
Glechoma hederacea 22(a)
Lamiastrum galeobdolon 58(k)
Lamium album 14(g)
  amplexicaule 50(a)
  hybridum 14(f)*
  maculatum 18(g)
  purpureum 14(f), 138(c)
Lycopus europaeus 134(k)
Marrubium vulgare 128(h)*
Melissa officinalis 124(f)
Mentha aquatica 140(d)
  arvensis 134(i)
  longifolia 138(l)
  × piperita 138(i)
  pulegium 150(c)
  rotundifolia 124(i)
  spicata 142(b)
Nepeta cataria 128(h)
  × faassenii 66(d)
Origanum vulgare 108(b)
Prunella vulgaris 84(f)
Salvia pratensis 68(h)
  verbenaca 68(e)
Satureja montana 138(a)
Scutellaria galericulata 84(g)
  minor 84(g)*
Stachys alpina 96(j)
  arvensis 50(c)
  germanica 128(j)
  officinalis 102(f)
  palustris 128(c)
  sylvatica 58(l)
Teucrium chamaedrys 120(h)
  scordium 138(j)
  scorodonia 108(d)
Thymus praecox ssp. arcticus 44(c)
  pulegioides 120(e)
  serpyllum 124(k)

## Leguminosae Pea Family
Herbs or shrubs with distinctive flower shape. Five petals, upper one, usually broad, is the 'standard', the two side ones the 'wings' and the two lower ones often joined, form the 'keel' which encloses the stamens and style. There are ten stamens joined in a tube enclosing the carpel and later becoming the seedpod. Leaves have stipules, usually compound, sometimes forming tendrils.
Anthyllis vulneraria 44(a)
Astragalus danicus 68(b)
  glycophyllos 98(g)
Coronilla varia 100(j)
Cytisus scoparius 34(c)
Galega officinalis 84(j)
Genista anglica 56(k)
  tinctoria 102(i)

Hippocrepis comosa 38(d)
Laburnum anagyroides 34(a)
Lathyrus aphaca 48(b)
  japonicus 54(e)
  latifolius 82(d)
  montanus 56(h)
  niger 102(g)
  nissola 102(e)
  palustris 74(c)
  pratensis 84(b)
  sylvestris 138(h)
  tuberosus 102(k)
Lotus corniculatus 38(a)
  pedunculatus 100(f), 134(m)
  tenuis 38(a)*
Lupinus arboreus 76(f)
Medicago arabica 52(f)
  lupulina 38(b), 52(e)
  polymorpha 60(g)
  sativa 84(d)
Melilotus alba 54(g)
  altissima 72(f)*
  indica 72(f)*
  officinalis 72(f)
Onobrychis viciifolia 54(a)
Ononis repens 92(i)
  spinosa 106(a)
Ornithopus perpusillus 51(f)
Oxytropis campestris 102(l)
  halleri 81(f)
Tetragonolobus maritimus 138(e)
Trifolium arvense 78(k)
  campestre 46(c)
  fragiferum 104(c)
  hybridum 54(f)*
  medium 80(d)
  pratense 52(i)
  repens 54(f)
  striatum 50(f)
Ulex europaeus 20(c)
  gallii 152(a)
  minor 154(h)
Vicia cracca 84(i)
  hirsuta 36(f)
  lathyroides 56(e)*
  sativa 56(c)
  sepium 32(e)
  sylvatica 116(c)
  tetraspermum 81(c)

## Lentibulariaceae Butterwort Family
Pinguicula grandiflora 46(b)
  lusitanica 46(b)*
  vulgaris 51(a)
Utricularia vulgaris 115(e)

## Liliaceae Lily Family
Herbs. Leaves undivided with parallel veins. Flowers with three sepals and petals often the same colour giving the appearance of six petals. Ovary has three compartments. Fruit a capsule.
Allium ampeloprasum 130(g)
  babingtonii 130(f)
  carinatum 122(a)
  oleraceum 130(b)*
  roseum 48(k)
  schoenoprasum 80(e)
  sphaerocephalon 128(i)
  ursinum 24(c)
  vineale 130(b)
Asparagus officinalis ssp. prostratus 152(b)
Colchicum autumnale 36(a), 168(a)
Convallaria majalis 30(k), 168(a)
Endymion non-scriptus 28(b)
Fritillaria meleagris 20(m)

Gagea lutea 18(l)
Lilium martagon 157(e)
  pyrenaicum 50(e)
Lloydia serotina 51(b)
Narthecium ossifragum 150(g)
Ornithogalum umbellatum 64(c)
Polygonatum multiflorum 42(e)
  odoratum 42(c)*
Ruscus aculeatus 18(a), 174(a)
Scilla autumnalis 168(b)
  verna 26(f)

## Linaceae Flax Family
Linum bienne 68(j)*
  catharticum 68(f)
  perenne 68(j)
Radiola linoides 146(e)

## Loranthaceae Mistletoe Family
Viscum album 24(o), 174(d)

## Lythraceae Loosestrife Family
Lythrum hyssopifolia 80(c)
  salicaria 96(g)

## Malvaceae Mallow Family
Herbs or shrubs, downy or softly hairy. Leaves palmately lobed, alternate, stalked and with stipules. Stamens numerous, bunched together in a prominent tuft projecting from the centre of the flower. Five sepals usually with additional three forming an outer calyx. Five petals usually notched.
Althaea officinalis 144(f)
Malva moschata 96(f)
  neglecta 122(h)
  sylvestris 74(f)
Lavatera arborea 157(d)

## Menyanthaceae Bogbean Family
Menyanthes trifoliata 30(d)
Nymphoides peltata 140(c)

## Myricaceae Bog Myrtle Family
Myrica gale 60(a)

## Nymphaeaceae Water-lily Family
Nuphar lutea 132(i)
Nymphaea alba 132(h)

## Oleaceae Olive Family
Fraxinus excelsior 26(d), 174(f)
Ligustrum vulgare 86(c), 172(d)
Syringa vulgaris 38(j)

## Onagraceae Willowherb Family
Herbs, non-woody. Usually four petals and sepals, eight stamens with ovary below.
Circaea alpina 90(e)*
  lutetiana 90(e)
Epilobium angustifolium 94(h)
  hirsutum 104(h)
  montanum 78(g)
  obscurum 78(g)*
  palustre 78(g)*
  parviflorum 104(h)*
  tetragonum 78(g)*
Fuchsia magellanica 147(b)
Oenothera biennis 111(c)*
  erythrosepala 156(b)
  stricta 111(c)

## Ophioglossaceae
Ophioglossum vulgatum 46(f)

## Orchidaceae Orchid Family
Herbs. Large family of complex flowers. Leaves undivided, untoothed,

often linear-lanceolate and keeled. Perianth in six parts. Two rings of three, all coloured. Appearance varies greatly but always two-lipped. The lowest petal often highly developed, prominent and spurred. Flowers usually in a spike with leaf-like bracts at the base of each one.
Aceras anthropophorum 94(c)
Anacamptis pyramidalis 92(d)
Cephalanthera damasonium 96(a)
  longifolia 27(e)
  rubra 96(a)*
Coeloglossum viride 132(c)
Corallorhiza trifida 51(c)
Cypripedium calceolus 27(a)
Dactylorhiza fuchsii 92(a)
  incarnata 27(f)
  maculata 96(d)
  pratermissa 89(b)
  purpurella 71(d)
Epipactis atrorubens 71(b)
  dunensis 132(b)
  helleborine 94(b)
  leptochila 89(c)
  palustris 132(a)
  purpurata 156(a)
Goodyera repens 132(d)
Gymnadenia conopsea 92(b)
Herminium monorchis 70(e)
Liparis loeselii 110(a)
Listera cordata 92(c)*
  ovata 92(c)
Neottia nidus-avis 96(c)
Ophrys apifera 94(d)
  insectifera 27(d)
Orchis mascula 28(c)
  morio 27(b)
Platanthera bifolia 27(c)
  chlorantha 96(b)
Spiranthes spiralis 156(e)

**Orobanchaceae**
**Broomrape Family**
Parasites on roots of other plants. No green leaves, but oval pointed scales, on stems. Flowers two-lipped in spikes usually the same colour as the rest of the plant. Four stamens, one style. Fruit a capsule.
Orobanche elatior 70(f)
  minor 94(a)
  rapum-genistae 94(a)*

**Oxalidaceae Wood-sorrel Family**
Oxalis acetosella 18(m)
  corniculata 60(e)
  europaea 60(f)

**Papaveraceae Poppy Family**
Previously divided into two families. Some have spikes of tubular, two-lipped, spurred flowers with many times lobed or divided leaves. Others have solitary four-petaled flowers with two sepals and many stamens, a milky juice appearing when the stem is broken.
Chelidonium majus 42(f)
Corydalis claviculata 111(a)
  lutea 48(a)
Fumaria capreolata 78(i)
  muralis 52(l)*
  officinalis 52(l)
  parviflora 104(b)
Glaucium corniculatum 82(i)
  flavum 114(b)
Meconopsis cambrica 72(g)
Papaver argemone 71(a)*

dubium 71(a)
rhoeas 64(b)
somniferum 82(c)

**Parnassiaceae**
**Grass of Parnassus Family**
Parnassia palustris 150(h)

**Pinaceae Pine Family**
Trees. Leaves spirally arranged, linear, flat or needle-like. Usually evergreen. Male and female flowers on same tree. Mature cones, woody, usually containing winged seeds.
Abies procera 170(h)
Cedrus libani 170(m)
Larix decidua 168(i)
  kaempferi 24(n), 168(h)
Picea abies 168(l)
  sitchensis 168(j)
Pinus contorta 168(g)
  nigra 60(d), 170(f)
  radiata 170(g)
  sylvestris 62(d), 168(f)
Pseudotsuga menziesii 168(e)
Tsuga heterophylla 168(k)

**Plantaginaceae Plantain Family**
Herbs. Leaves usually growing from base and strongly ribbed. Flowers, four-petalled and tiny in a long, dense spike at the top of a long, leafless stem. Four long stamens, the most prominent feature of the flowers. Fruit a capsule.
Plantago coronopus 54(b)
  lanceolata 54(k)
  major 70(c)
  maritima 90(a)
  media 68(k), 104(i)

**Platanaceae Plane Family**
Platanus hybrida 24(p), 160(j)

**Plumbaginaceae**
**Sea Lavender Family**
Armeria maritima 66(c)
Limonium bellidifolium 146(c)
  binervosum 120(l)
  humile 106(c)*
  vulgare 106(c)

**Polemoniaceae Phlox Family**
Polemonium caeruleum 56(c)

**Polygalaceae Milkwort Family**
Polygala calcarea 28(k)
  serpyllifolia 56(l)
  vulgaris 56(f)

**Polygonaceae Dock Family**
Herbs, shrubs, climbers. Leaves alternate with stipules formed into a sheath around the stem. Flower characteristics vary between genera.
Bilderdykia aubertii 86(d)
  baldschuanica 86(d)*
  convolvulus 134(f)
Oxyria digyna 116(j)
Polygonum amphibium 170(e)
  aviculare 134(l)
  bistorta 56(d)
  cuspidatum 147(a)
  hydropiper 170(b)
  lapathifolium 162(c)
  persicaria 134(h), 170(d)
  raii 134(l)*
Rumex acetosa 36(l)
  acetosella 36(h)
  conglomeratus 126(e)
  crispus 126(k)
  hydrolapathum 126(j)

longifolius 64(j)*
maritimus 64(j)*
obtusifolius 64(j)
palustris 106(i)
sanguineus 126(i)

**Portulacaceae**
Montia fontana 156(c)
  perfoliata 40(l)
  sibirica 32(a)

**Potamogetonaceae**
Potamogeton natans 102(b)

**Primulaceae Primrose Family**
Non-woody herbs. Leaves without stipules. Flowers symmetrical. Five petals joined at base, five stamens opposite petals.
Anagallis arvensis 46(d)
  minima 98(a)*
  tenella 98(a)
Cyclamen hederifolium 168(d)
Glaux maritima 114(f)
Hottonia palustris 74(d)
Lysimachia nemorum 40(k)
  nummularia 92(m)
  punctata 104(k)
  vulgaris 140(e)
Primula elatior 24(d)
  farinosa 20(j)
  scotica 88(b)
  veris 20(h)
  veris × vulgaris 32(b)
  vulgaris 16(h)
Samolus valerandi 126(c)
Trientalis europaea 40(j)

**Pyrolaceae Wintergreen Family**
Evergreen herbs. Creeping. Five petals, leaves usually simple, toothed. Fruit forms a dry capsule.
Moneses uniflora 88(f)
Orthilia secunda 136(e)
Pyrola media 154(b)
  minor 88(e)
  rotundifolia 154(a)
Monotropa hypopitys 89(d)

**Ranunculaceae**
**Buttercup Family**
Herbs or woody plants. A large, varied family. Usually numerous stamens and carpels which are not joined together. Most have five conspicuous petals or petal-like sepals. Many contain nectaries, secreting nectar, and most are poisonous.
Aconitum napellus 76(e), 122(e)
Adonis annua 52(d)
Anemone nemorosa 18(n)
Aquilegia vulgaris 72(a)
Caltha palustris 30(j)
Clematis vitalba 130(a), 172(f)
Delphinium ambiguum 98(f)
Eranthis hyemalis 12(a)
Helleborus foetidus 16(k)
  viridis 36(d)
Myosurus minimus 30(a)
Pulsatilla vulgaris 20(k)
Ranunculus acris 20(g)
  aquatilis 46(e)
  arvensis 72(d)
  auricomus 22(d)
  bulbosus 58(h)
  ficaria 16(e)
  flammula 74(b)
  lingua 106(k)
  parviflorus 72(d)*
  repens 100(i)

sardous 58(h)*
sceleratus 74(e)
Thalictrum alpinum 128(g)*
  flavum 128(g)
  minus 120(a)
Trollius europaeus 88(d)

**Resedaceae**
Reseda alba 96(e)
  lutea 36(k)
  luteola 74(i)

**Rhamnaceae Buckthorn Family**
Frangula alnus 76(a), 164(m)
Rhamnus catharticus 60(c), 164(l)

**Rosaceae Rose Family**
Shrubs, trees and herbs. Leaves alternate, usually pinnate with stipules. Sepals and petals usually five arranged alternately. Other features between genera.
Agrimonia eupatoria 98(e)
Alchemilla alpina 92(k)
  filicaulis ssp. vestita 32(j)
  glabra 60(j)
  xanthochlora 60(i)
Aphanes arvensis 50(b)
Cotoneaster intergerrimus 34(h)
Crataegus laevigata 38(g)*
  monogyna 38(g), 162(l)
Dryas octopetala 52(c), 148(f)
Filipendula ulmaria 112(d)
  vulgaris 100(k)
Fragraria vesca 32(g), 92(h)
Geum × intermedium 32(l)
  rivale 32(k)
  urbanum 36(j)
Malus sylvestris ssp. mitis 24(m), 172(b)
  sylvestris ssp. sylvestris 172(a)
Potentilla anglica 56(i)*
  anserina 48(c)
  argentea 142(f)
  erecta 56(i)
  fruticosa 60(k)
  palustris 106(h)
  recta 142(g)
  reptans 104(d)
  rupestris 72(e)
  sterilis 22(c)
  tabernaemontani 42(c)
Prunus avium 24(k)
  cerasifera 16(d)
  padus 34(i), 147(e)
  spinosa 16(a), 164(f)
Rosa arvensis 70(d)
  canina 76(b), 172(k)
  pimpinellifolia 50(d), 164(k)
  rubiginosa 86(a)
Rubus arcticus 40(i)
  caesius 62(a), 147(d)
  chamaemorus 88(c), 157(f)
  fruticosus 108(o), 162(n)
  idaeus 62(b), 108(j)
  saxatilis 108(o)*
Sanguisorba minor 32(f)
  officinalis 96(h)
Sorbus aria 58(d), 174(e)
  aucuparia 34(d), 162(f)
  torminalis 58(d)*
Spiraea salicifolia 108(m)

**Rubiaceae Bedstraw Family**
Herbs. Leaves usually elliptical or lanceolate, unstalked, in whorls, often with leaflike stipules. Flowers have petals joined in a 4-lobed cross shape with 4 stamens alternating with the petals. Fruit usually a 4-lobed nutlet.

Asperula cynanchica 92(l)
Cruciata laevipes 58(j)
Galium aparine 64(a), 134(a)
  boreale 120(i)
  mollugo 78(d)
  odoratum 32(d)
  palustre 112(a)
  saxatile 56(g)
  uliginosum 112(a)*
  verum 86(g)
Rubia peregrina 142(i)
Sherardia arvensis 115(b)

**Salicaceae Willow Family**
Deciduous trees or shrubs. Male and female flowers catkins, on separate plants, opening before the leaves. Male usually yellow, female green. Seeds have long silky hairs. Leaves usually alternate, finely toothed.
Populus alba 12(h), 160(f)
  canescens 12(e), 160(l)
  × euramericana 12(g), 160(h)
  gileadensis 12(j), 160(d)
  nigra 160(i)
  nigra var. italica 12(i), 160(e)
  tremula 12(f), 160(g)
Salix alba 166(h)
  atrocinerea 166(j)
  babylonica 166(f)
  caprea 12(o), 166(l)
  caprea × S.aurita 166(k)
  fragilis 166(e)
  purpurea 166(i)
  repens 166(m)
  viminalis 166(g)

**Santalacaceae
Sandalwood Family**
Thesium humifusum 110(b)

**Saxifragaceae Saxifrage Family**
Herbs, usually perennial. Leaves usually alternate. 5 petals, sepals and styles and 10 stamens. Fruit is formed by 2 capsules joined at the base, and free above. This distinguishes them from the family Crassulaceae.
Chrysosplenium alternifolium 30(c)*
  oppositifolium 30(c)
Saxifraga aizoides 148(h)
  granulata 30(l)
  hypnoides 44(b)
  oppositifolia 148(k)
  spathularis × umbrosa 66(j)
  stellaris 148(e)
  tridactylites 30(l)*

**Scrophulariaceae
Figwort Family**
Herbs. Flower with 4 or 5 joined petals and 2 or 5 stamens respectively; or 2-lipped (similar to Labiatae). Fruit is a capsule.
Chaenorhinum minus 138(b)
Cymbalaria muralis 42(b)
Digitalis purpurea 94(f)
Erinus alpinus 42(a)
Euphrasia officinalis 92(g)
Kickxia elatine 118(c)
  spuria 118(c)*
Lathraea squamaria 32(i)
Linaria purpurea 92(j)
  repens 128(f)
  vulgaris 86(i)
Melampyrum arvense 144(a)*
  cristatum 144(a)
  pratense 84(a)
  sylvaticum 84(a)*

Mimulus guttatus 106(b)
Misopates orontium 128(e)
Odontites verna 144(b)
Parentucellia viscosa 111(f)
Pedicularis palustris 128(a)
  sylvatica 56(j)
Rhinanthus minor 90(b)
Scrophularia auriculata 74(k)
  nodosa 98(h)
  scorodonia 162(d)
Sibthorpia europaea 150(b)
Verbascum nigrum 98(l)
  thapsus 94(k)
Veronica agrestis 28(g)
  anagallis-aquatica 90(i)
  arvensis 28(f)
  beccabunga 74(a)
  chamaedrys 28(j)
  filiformis 14(k)
  hederifolia 28(e)
  montana 28(a)
  officinalis 68(a)
  persica 28(l)
  scutellata 152(i)
  serpyllifolia 28(h)
  spicata 114(e)

**Solanaceae Nightshade Family**
Herbs or shrubs. Leaves alternate, usually stalked. Flowers with five petals joined at base forming equal lobes between which the five stamens are inserted. Often poisonous.
Atropa bella-donna 72(h), 162(l)
Datura stramonium 144(l), 164(h)
Hyoscyamus niger 114(d)
Lycium barbarum 112(h)*
  chinense 112(h)
Solanum dulcamara 48(j), 172(h)
  nigrum 116(g), 172(g)

**Sparganiaceae Bur-reed Family**
Sparganium emersum 115(f)
  erectum 132(g)

**Taxaceae Yew Family**
Taxus baccata 18(d), 160(k)

**Taxodiaceae Redwood Family**
Sequoia sempervirens 170(i)
Sequoiadendron giganteum 170(j)

**Thymelacaceae Daphne Family**
Daphne laureola 24(l)
  mezereum 16(b)

**Tiliaceae Lime Family**
Tilia cordata 158(l)
  platyphyllos 158(n)
  × vulgaris 108(p), 158(k)

**Trilliaceae Trillium Family**
Paris quadrifolia 32(c)

**Typhaceae Reed-mace Family**
Typha angustifolia 140(g)
  latifolia 102(c), 140(h)

**Ulmaceae Elm Family**
Ulmus glabra 12(k), 24(h), 158(h)
  procera 12(l), 24(i), 158(g)

**Umbelliferae
Parsley or Carrot Family**
Five sepals, petals and stamens. The flowers are grouped to form a shape resembling a flat-topped umbrella known as an umbel. Leaves usually divided and alternate without stipules.
Aegopodium podagraria 64(f)
Aethusa cynapium 118(j)

Angelica archangelica 62(g)
  sylvestris 148(c)
Anthriscus caucalis 22(j)*
  sylvestris 22(j)
Apium graveolens 90(j)*
  inundatum 89(e)
  nodiflorum 90(j)
Astrantia major 72(b)
Berula erecta 90(k)
Bupleurum falcatum 118(f)
Carum carvi 42(h)
Chaerophyllum temulentum 64(i)
Cicuta virosa 136(f)
Conium maculatum 64(h)
Conopodium majus 36(e)
Crithmum maritimum 158(c)
Daucus carota 74(h)
Eryngium campestre 142(h)
  maritimum 124(a)
Falcaria vulgaris 118(g)
Foeniculum vulgare 118(i)
Heracleum mantegazzianum 62(e)
  sphondylium 62(f)
Hydrocotyle vulgaris 98(d)
Ligusticum scoticum 152(e)
Meum athamanticum 82(j)
Myrrhis odorata 22(i)
Oenanthe aquatica 110(f)
  crocata 64(c)
  fistulosa 156(f)
  lachenalii 126(b)
Pastinaca sativa 94(g)
Peucedanum officinale 118(h)
  palustre 144(h)
Pimpinella major 126(f)
  saxifraga 118(l)
Sanicula europaea 30(g)
Scandix pecten-veneris 82(e)
Silaum silaus 126(h)
Sium latifolium 126(g)
Smyrnium olusatrum 42(g)
Torilis arvensis 134(g)*
  japonica 134(g), 148(a)
  nodosa 148(a)*

**Urticaceae Nettle Family**
Parietaria diffusa 66(k)
Urtica dioica 58(m)
  urens 58(m)*

**Valerianaceae Valerian Family**
Centranthus ruber 42(i), 54(c)
Valeriana dioica 106(g)*
  officinalis 106(g)
Valerianella locusta 58(g)

**Verbenaceae Verbena Family**
Verbena officinalis 96(k)

**Violaceae Violet Family**
Ovary has a single cavity with three rows of ovules inside. British subspecies are all in genus Viola and have five unequal petals, the lowest with a spur. Fruit forms a capsule which splits into three when ripe. Leaves are simple and usually have stipules.
Viola arvensis 20(l)
  canina 22(h)*
  hirta 16(g)*
  lutea 66(g)
  odorata 16(g)
  palustris 26(e)
  reichenbachiana 18(g)
  riviniana 22(b)
  tricolor 60(h)

# Index of English names

# Index of botanical names